One Man's Mountain

One Man's Mountain

Published by The Conrad Press in the United Kingdom 2021

Tel: +44(0)1227 472 874
www.theconradpress.com
info@theconradpress.com

ISBN 978-1-914913-37-2

Photographs are author's own and by kind permission of Mortons Archive. Special thanks to Victor Blackman for the cover photograph

Typesetting and Cover Design by: Charlotte Mouncey, www.bookstyle.co.uk
The Conrad Press logo was designed by Maria Priestley.

Printed and bound in Great Britain by Clays Ltd, Elcograf S.p.A.

One Man's Mountain

Graham Bailey

Photograph used in cover design and on the previous page:
'Ago's Leap' 1973 Senior TT taken by Victor Blackman
later gifted to the author, Graham Bailey, with the comment,
'It's OK, there's no negative. It's yours.'
What a privilege!

Lovingly dedicated to Rosemary, my beloved wife;
Mary and Clare, our dear daughters and
their dear husbands, James and Pieter-Bas;
and also to our precious grandchildren: Ruby, Naomi,
Evie and Amy, Jesse, Lizzie, definitely
mountain climbers of the future.

Contents

1   Unusual aromas, things that go bump in the night,
Doodlebugs and V2s   9

2   The bug bites   21

3   No more school books, now work for your living!   31

4   Wheels set in motion   37

5   'Tricks of the trade'   45

6   Getting down to 'the job' proper!   52

7   Those boots are made for walking   58

8   Is this lift-off time?   70

9   Approaching the start line   82

10 Shift work plus   97

11 At last, a real Trafpol   109

12 A new season-a new experience   114

13 A new chapter   126

14 Scandinavian adventure   142

15 Sheep on the mountain   145

16 Don't come back if you break it!   149

17 Just give me the facts   182

18 Candle at both ends   186

19 It's the spark that counts   206

20 1970: a very short season   222

21 Crooks Suzuki   232

22 The still small voice   242

23 A tale of two trophies   246

24 The eye of the storm   270

25 Surely you deserve a medal!   276

26 Just one more lap?   280

27 A case of 'guts for garters'   294

28 The spirit moves   312

29 The final lap   319

30 The end of one mountain trail   325

31 TT Race Mission   346

Postscript, 12th of June 2020   351

Slavery   351

Those involved in Bailey's mountain climbing   355

Road racing and cross-country trials results   359

1

Unusual aromas, things that go bump in the night, Doodlebugs and V2s

I t was the distant sound that got to me.

Having recently moved from our war-time and immediate post-war homes south of London in Bromley, Kent, the family was now settling into our new abode above Dad's office. It was nearer to London in Upper Norwood S.E.19. Crystal Palace, and the now-empty site of the glass and wrought iron building, which had moved from Hyde Park following the Great Exhibition of 1851, was a mile or so down the road. This mysterious noise, rising and falling on the wind, seemed to emanate from that direction. One moment the sound was low pitched, a muted roar, which then developed into an angry staccato rising rhythm. Minutes later the air was filled by a higher note; what sounded like a swarm of equally angry bees travelling at high speed.

Some time later, during an exploratory walk down Church Road towards 'the palace,' one's senses were assailed by a smell difficult to describe but strangely pleasant, and to my youthful senses, a little intoxicating. This aroma, carried on the breeze, came from over the boundary wall of the palace grounds and seemingly accompanied those strange yet wonderful sounds. You've got it. I had discovered that Crystal Palace had its own motorcycle and car road racing track, and it was just a ten-minute walk from home. Your scribe, almost unwittingly, had become well and truly hooked on a sport about which he had heard not very much.

Once, soon after the war, when messing about with my pal Kenny Drew on the Sundridge Park Golf Club in Bromley, he had motioned towards a distant place over the hill and talked about his older brother who had gone to watch the racing at a place called Brands Hatch. That was the limit of my knowledge of things motor racing!

Throughout the war years, the family lived in a rented semi-detached house at 7 New Farm Avenue, which was in the south of Bromley. I recall watching from the front window as men of the local Home Guard, exercising along our road, would duck into our front gate, crouching with their rifles at the ready to gain protection and shield us from *the enemy*!

It is impossible to know exactly when a small child's memory 'kicks off' but I can recall one night quite clearly. There was an air raid going on and the family, plus several neighbours, were gathered in the darkened back room overlooking the garden. The little lad was snuggled up well away from the glazed French doors and was aware that the sky was lit by many different flashing colours. The air was filled by the sounds of what I now know to be enemy aircraft, with anti-aircraft guns trying to knock them out of the sky.

The sound of the engines was strangely off-beat, and in later years, one learned that a 'frightener' tactic of the German Luftwaffe was to run multi-engine aircraft with the motors set slightly out of sync. Thus, a strong unnerving off-beat rhythm was set up to frighten those below. Even today, if a large multi-engine piston engine aircraft passes overhead in dead of night and the atmospheric conditions, cloud and wind, cause an offbeat engine note, one can get the *willies*, as the long-remembered sound pushes through the clouds.

At the end of our road, you could turn right along Cameron Road, climb the steep slope, and enter Stone Road. This road was where the 'posh' houses were and the road surface comprised flints, stones, and earth packed down; not tarmac finished as we understand roads nowadays. Behind Stone Road, farmland stretched towards Hayes, bounded by Pickhurst Lane, Hayes Lane, and Mead Way. Crossing Mead Way, the open land stretched even further southwards, almost to the village of Hayes.

As little children, the farmland was one of our many play-grounds. On occasion, it would have been 1944, we were able to make use of a trench dug across a field which the Home Guards had probably constructed ('there's a war on you know!'), and watching from its protection, were able to observe the odd V1 'Doodlebug' flying bomb, as it approached the end of its destructive journey towards London.

Dad worked on the buses, having joined the LGOC London General Omnibus Company in the 1930s. He was what we kids proudly termed, a gold badge inspector; the real title was Chief Depot Inspector. He, like most of the other folks in what had become London Transport, did what was known as 'shift work.' One of his duties was to ride on buses, check running times, and keep an eye on things. I recall that because he was a *people person,* he seemed to get on alright with the crews. I remember that on the way home from an evening outing by bus, the driver would sometimes draw to a standstill at the end of our road, nowhere near the official bus stop, and allow Mum, Dad and the two children to get off, with a friendly farewell from the Conductor, 'OK, Mr Bailey, this should do you.'

On Sunday19th November 1944, Dad set off for 'late turn' and apparently his duty was to ride on a double-decker along the regular route 94, which ran between Grove Park and Southborough near Petts Wood, where the route would terminate at the Crooked Billet Public House in Southborough Lane. The bus would be parked up at the stop by the pub, allowing the crew their break before its return run towards Bromley and back to Grove Park. This long-established and historic public house was popular and well frequented. As it was a good evening weather-wise, Dad decided to hop off at the earlier fare stage, which was at the Chequers Public House in Southborough Lane, stretch his legs, and take a bit of a walk to re-join the bus at The Crooked Billet in time for its return trip.

Sadly, at approximately 9:12 p.m. from The Hook of Holland, Herr Hitler had launched one of his Vergeltungswaffe-zwei/ Vengeance Weapon 2, the rocket propelled V2 flying bombs which would travel at over three thousand miles per hour. At about 9:18 p.m., as Dad approached the Crooked Billet on foot, this bomb impacted with devastating effect on the forecourt of the public house. Dad arrived upon the scene of the tragedy quickly, to find that an alphabetical list of casualties was being prepared and that his name was on the top of the list of dead and injured. Twenty-seven people, including a sailor who was home on leave from fighting at sea, and three soldiers, based at Thornet Wood Camp, lost their lives. Many more were injured, yet Dad was spared.

I was unaware of Dad's delivery from this tragedy for many years but was blessed by his love and fatherly care throughout my childhood and teenage years. It was an early, but as then unrecognised, lesson in my experience of God's love and hand on my life. (It should be added that it was reported that Adolf Hitler *took* his own life on 30th April 1945, five months and twelve days after the lives so cruelly taken on the borders of Bickley and Southborough).

Historians in the twenty-first century are very keen to describe just what this country was like during and just after the war years. It is claimed by them that it was drab and grey, without any colour at all. Perhaps their research had been somewhat selective and was certainly not experiential, because, although certainly many young children would not have appreciated the situation that the grown-ups faced daily; for us children, being around in those years was quite full of colour and fun!

Sadly, however, as soon as peace returned to little old England, the owners of number seven, who had been *down in the West Country for a short break,* decided that they wanted their house back! ('Was it really six years, dear? You said it would be just a short holiday!')

I believe that in those days, so soon after the time of war, the law allowed that the family resident at number 7 would have been fully entitled to sit tight. Dear Dad, who was such a peaceful guy, not wanting to make a fuss, decided graciously that we would move out. I was later to learn that Ronald Arthur Bailey, with his quiet and friendly manner, was a man of strong principle who could and would stand firm when necessary. Another lesson to be learned by his son. So, there you go!

We were on the move. Thus, in 1946, we arrived at our

new home on the 'other side of town', at 64 Park Road. From my bed, through the ceiling and gaps in the roof, I could see the sky. And we didn't even have a bathroom. This little lad, in his seven long years, had become so used to such a luxury. Apparently, a kind builder, putting to rights the bomb damage, somehow managed to fit us up with a lovely bathroom in what had been one of the bedrooms.

The Bromley playground for a lad after the war; there were places to go, apart from adventures on the farm and common land. As well as exploring around the edges of the local Sundridge Park Golf Club, we found various bombed-out buildings, whose skeletal stairs were possible to climb.

We could watch the world from high above the ground through holes in the roofs and walls. From one house in Ravensbourne Road, we could look down on the trains entering and leaving Bromley South Station. Being fairly close to Biggin Hill, the wartime fighter airbase, Bromley had endured its fair share of bombs; thus, there was an ample supply of open spaces (bombsites) to muck about in.

One night during the air raids, which regularly occurred throughout the war, several churches in the town had been hit. St. John's Church, just across the road from our new home, had been knocked about a bit and was sealed closed. Yet this was another place for exploration. One day it seems that one of the locals decided that the lead organ pipes were a good source of unearned income. Thus, on one of our visits, it was noticed the pipes had been *liberated* and never again to be seen in their original state of tune!

Talking of tunes; whenever the wind 'got up,' hundreds of tiles, which had loosened during the air raids, would clatter from the church roof and crash onto the mounting piles already building upon the ground. Sleep was therefore quite often disturbed. On reflection, our playtime in and around Bromley reminded us of the price which so many had paid for what was now being called 'peacetime'.

Even from those childhood years in Bromley, one had got the message that wheels with pedals or four little wheels on the bottom of your shoes were a far better form of transport than shanks' pony. The full range of wheeled transport available to a growing lad was given a go. I became a bit of an ace, riding a tricycle up and down Park Grove on two wheels. To own a set of roller skates *with double roller bearings and rubber tyres* was another pinnacle achievement for young Bailey. Strangely, I kept a special eye out for two-wheelers with engines!

During an afternoon wander about, I spied Kenny Drew's older brother, the brother earlier referred to, who used to go to Brands Hatch. He lived in the family home in Park Grove. Kenny's brother had parked his motorbike, which had a black petrol tank, outside the tobacconist shop in Freelands Road (I now know that it was a 500cc BSA A7 'Shooting Star').

Walking very slowly along the pavement and hoping; sure enough, big brother got on his bike, kicked it into life, spun round in the road, rode towards where I was ambling along and offered Kenny's little mate a lift back to his house. Oh boy, wasn't this living! Wind in your hair, a cold draught through your sandals, and leaning over around the corners. If there was such a thing as a motorbike bug, it had begun to nibble at my imagination. Yet, I wasn't even eleven years old.

There was a motorcycle shop around the corner in Palace Road. One day, propped up on the pavement outside the shop stood a motorcycle that was naked without lights or number plates. It had flat handlebars and the footrests seemed to be mounted further back than on a normal motorbike. Above the engine sat a silver and black petrol tank with triangular black shapes picked out along the lower sides. The exhaust was open-ended and finished in a kind of trumpet shape. There was no silencer, and the tank had the word 'Norton' painted in a regal script. I was looking at my first road racing, 'Garden Gate' framed overhead camshaft Manx Norton. I was too young to ask the man with the black beret standing by the bike questions, but about the right age for dreams to begin to form in the juvenile head. I learned much later that the *triangles* were the points where, years ago, the base of the tank was soldered rather than welded to the main body shape.

Growing up in Bromley, post-war, our home on Park Road was close to the local nick, sorry, Bromley Police Station (PR). This road was well used by police cars; big boxy Wolseley cars and police motorcyclists riding what I later learned were Triumph 5T Speed Twins. The riders' uniforms included heavy boots with leather gaiters, and the headgear comprised forage caps with Mark V111 motorcycle goggles. The goggle straps were stretched around the brim of the rider's cap. Years later, I was to learn that the thin flat metal strip fitted inside the cap brim was designed to keep the cap looking smart and rounded. It would have been shortened by these guys so that the goggle strap could fit snuggly around the brim, hold it (fold it?!) down, and keep the cap firmly *on his head.*

You must consider that before the days of motorcycle fairings and screens, the rider very much rode 'with the wind in his face.' Another trick, which I became aware of, was that the wearer could dampen the front of the leather headband (maybe with the application of a quickly *lubricated* finger) before putting his cap on. Said cap would be sealed to his forehead and better stay in place. I was also to learn that Traffic Patrol police officers performed both motorcycle patrol duties, as well as being car patrol drivers and authorised vehicle examiners. Thus, if you saw a policeman wearing a flat cap with a less than a firmly rounded cap edge, you could easily tell that he was a traffic man.

Many years later, I came to understand that before RT radios were fitted to motorcycles, two motorcycles would work as a unit with a traffic car. In this way, the theory was that communication would be maintained between the mobile traffic units. Such 'teams' were known as Traffic Accident Groups. Traffic Patrol cars in the job were always referred to as 'TAG cars' from then on.

As a lad, one was used to seeing my dad in Bromley Market Square, checking off the buses as they passed through the town. His little lad was proud to claim that his dad was a gold badge inspector with London Transport. During winter, before going on duty, a regular exercise for RA Bailey (Rab) was for him to cut out and fit a lining of brown paper into his uniform greatcoat. Thermals and all that kind of insulation were not around and being on a *fixed point* in the Market Square for hours on end was more than a bit draughty. Dad's family was originally from Rotherhithe, and since the late eighteenth century had been Lightermen on the River Thames. So Dad's job, working on the buses, was quite a break from the family tradition.

Mum worked on the edge of the City of London at 10 City Road, the premises of S.W. Wells, a men's wholesale outfitters.

As a treat during school holiday times, we would travel by train and tube via London Bridge and Moorgate Underground Station to visit and explore around that establishment. The building backed onto the grounds of the Honourable Artillery Company.

It was in Mum's office that one of the outfitters presented the lad with a tie which he proceeded to cut in half and stitch in two lengths of elastic with a connector on each end so that it was possible to fit and wear a tie without the requirement to laboriously make a knot every time. Very early on, new lessons were being learnt for the future when the frantic rush of getting ready for early turn duty beckoned.

Sundays were very special in the family. Church Service at 11:00 a.m. (the breaking of bread), Sunday school at 3:00 p.m. and after tea, the evening Gospel service. Quite often, we went out to tea, which was always a bit special because food rationing existed for some years after the war. *Going out to tea* usually meant that some special treats were on the table, just for the children!

Mum and Dad loved someone called Jesus, whom the Bible said was the Son of God. Apparently, he loved *us* even more! So 'going to the meeting' was quite normal for my sister and her little brother. We began to understand about God's love for the world and in fact, Dad, who before the war had commenced his career with the LGOC, left what had then become London Transport and began to work with a kind of missionary organisation, which worked in this country called the Christian Colportage Association.

Do you mean missionaries in England? Yep! Dear men went from door to door telling others about the love of Jesus.

So Dad would set off at an unearthly hour every morning and travel across London, almost to its northern edge, (Southern Railway then London Underground) arriving in Edgware at the head office of the CCA. He would arrive home fairly late in the day and on Wednesday evenings would push off to some church or the other to teach people lessons from the Bible. On Sundays, Dad was normally somewhere again, telling others about the love and teachings of Jesus. Mum would sometimes go with him and as part of the service, sing a solo about God's love.

If I went with them, the request was always, 'Dad, please tell us a story as well as just preaching a sermon!'

I was to learn many years later that dad had been telling people the 'good news' about Jesus from his youth, and that even whilst he was still 'on the buses', he was an honorary evangelist with this Christian mission.

One Sunday evening, as a twelve-year-old, I went with the family to the Gospel (Good News) service at our local church, Elms Hall in Great Elms Road. It was a 'tin tabernacle' style of building and is now long gone, with other buildings now built in its place. There I heard a preacher, Mr McConnell, a Scotsman who lived in Grove Park, a bit up the road from Bromley. He talked about the Lord Jesus; with which person I was becoming familiar; but now telling us/me that one day he, Jesus, would return to this earth and take those who believed in him to be with him in heaven

I had thought that because I lived with Mum and Dad and that they called themselves Christians, I must also be a Christian because our house was surely covered by a kind of heavenly insurance policy. This must-have meant that whoever lived there would be okay. I realised that evening that Jesus' love was a personal love (the love for an individual), which meant that I had to put my trust in him and take hold of that love, if I wanted to go to heaven.

There was in fact no fully comprehensive insurance policy that covered me, simply because I lived and mixed with people who called themselves Christians. The expression used then by people about their love for Jesus was that they 'had been saved'.

I went home with my mum and by my bed put my trust in the Lord Jesus Christ. Strangely, I was now a Christian. What is a Christian? My Bible tells me that a Christian is a person who recognises that Jesus Christ, the son of God, died on the Cross to save everybody (including me) from our sins. He paid the price (penalty) for our sin, the sin of the whole world. More than that; not only would we 'go to heaven,' but that He would be a real part of us, present and guiding our daily lives. That was another learning curve to follow.

2

The bug bites

Once, more we were on the move, this time to a new house to where in 1953 the family set up home in Upper Norwood. It was here that the race days at Crystal Palace in the early 1950s took place, and whether a car or motorcycle racing was scheduled, a relatively small amount of my pocket money was invested at the gate to the race circuit and found me occupying a seat in the open stands, just above and on the approach to the famous double-apex right hand Ramp Bend. From this position, on the outside of the track, one was able to look down just across the track into what in those days was the paddock area. The spectators could watch the drivers and their mechanics prepare for the competition. Here, at car meetings, among many other famous names, the exploits of Reg Parnell in his Ferrari and Les Leston in his 1100 cc V-twin powered rear-engine Cooper Jap, battled it out together as each struggled for supremacy on the track.

Another driver was Tony Rolt, driving his Connaught. A former reluctant guest of Herr Hitler in Colditz Castle, Major Tony Rolt MC was engaged in a more peaceful contest for victory. I can recall Colin Chapman competing in various marques of Lotus sports cars; cars which he had designed and built. Colin Chapman was able to develop and demonstrate the resultant car design improvements on the racetrack.

At the motorcycle races, men like Joe Dunphy, Mike

O'Rourke, John Surtees, John Holder, and many others, were admired as they battled wheel to wheel on Nortons, the wonderful Manxes but now with featherbed frames and double overhead camshaft engines, NSU's, Matchless G.45s and 350 7R AJS solos. Oh yes! The angry bees were in fact 50cc two-stroke racers and the 'strokers' (two-stroke engines) in the 125cc class.

The 'start/finish' line in those days was on the bottom straight to the right, just before the ramp bend and thus, the tension and excitement of both the start and finish of each race could be appreciated. This line, in later years, was moved to and situated on the top straight, at the top of the hill.

The intoxicating smell noted in recent times came from what was known as Castrol R, a vegetable-based oil used in racing engines. This oil was able to operate at higher temperatures than mineral oil and retain its lubricating qualities to a much more critical level. When hot, 'R' gave off its own unique aroma. Thus, in bike-talk among the lads, a guy riding anything 'running on R' took on the identity of someone rather special. The truth was that 'R' based oil was super expensive, so any motorcycle running on the public road which left a trail of 'R' in its wake had probably just had an oil can cap-full added to the fuel in the petrol tank. What a joy in later years it was to follow an 'R' burner up the by-pass, taking deep breaths of its exhaust fumes en route. Nowadays we can only complain about air pollution!

Having failed the eleven plus exam, and as a consequence not qualifying for education at a grammar school, I spent several happy years at Quernmore Secondary Modern School. Mum later scraped the pennies together and to give young

Graham a chance at taking the GCE exams (General Certificate of Education) and paid for me to join Clarks College, situated on Bromley Common. School days continued, not that I enjoyed them that much, but it is the burden which boys and girls have to bear! When we moved from Bromley to Upper Norwood, it would be necessary for me to travel back to my old hometown each day to continue my secondary education at Clark's College. Thus, it was felt better that young Graham be transferred to the Croydon Branch of Clarks College, with Croydon being much closer to our new home than Bromley.

Whilst at my *new* school, Croydon Clarks, I learned another lesson of life. Some folks can be very greatly affected by a simple glance or silent look exchanged. Even when no disrespect or malice is intended; at times, offence is taken. One day, sitting with the other guys and girls in the classroom and being lectured by a teacher of the French tongue, who in our presence never even uttered a sentence in French, it would seem that the look in young Bailey's eye deeply touched the dear lady's feelings. Very abruptly, and with no qualifying comment, the boy was curtly ordered to go downstairs and see the headmaster, the boy apparently pre-judged as being guilty of the offence of 'dumb insolence.' Here, another lesson of life was learned.

Matters claimed can easily be turned into *established facts* without evidence being produced or any statements being offered by witnesses. Mr Valentine, with no reference to the complainant, gifted Bailey with six of the best. The said gift was applied via a split-ended cane to the seat of Bailey's pants. Following this new experience (the Dickensian thrashing); in the privacy of the boys' toilets, he examined the weal marks and they felt like six impressions of the English Channel. Dad, was a man of peace but also from personal experience, a man of discipline. Without my knowledge, he paid a visit to the headmaster, and as I understand it, left him in no doubt about RA Bailey's views of truth and justice.

Very soon, young Bailey transferred again. This time, back to his *old* school in Bromley. As I have said, the bug of motorcycles had already bitten me. So, each Wednesday, as I travelled to school on the 227 bus from Crystal Palace to Bromley Market Square, I would sit at the back and pour over the pages of the 'blue 'un' and the 'green 'un.' These were the names given to the motorbike magazines, *The Motorcycle* and *Motor Cycling*. Within the pages of these 'weeklies,' I learned more about motorbikes, what made them go, and the basics of 'how' to ride them.

Each June I was particularly excited as reports about motorcycle road races held on *an island* were included. This was a small island in the Irish Sea, somewhere between Liverpool and Ireland, called the Isle of Man. These races were known as the TT races (the Tourist Trophy Races). As I looked at the sometimes for special effect, sepia printed photographs of famous racers in action on the public roads of the Island, the motorcycle bug bit deeper. These guys were racing on public roads, not on closed short circuit racetracks. It seemed almost impossible then, but a dream began to form in my mind!

As the magic age of 16 years approached, the time in life when a motorcycle licence could be obtained, my ambition increased to own and ride a motorcycle. As Mum and Dad were clearly not motorcyclists and because, as a schoolboy, I did not have the resources to buy or own a motorcycle; to achieve that ambition seemed almost beyond reach. I had tried to convince Mum that the Mobylette, a French motorised pedal cycle, was quite safe because it 'only has a 49cc engine.' Also, because it was produced in France, to me that seemed to make the plea sound a bit more convincing.

My dear father, nonetheless, being aware of my longing to have a two-wheeled machine with an engine, went with me to a local shop at the Crystal Palace end of Church Road, where I had stared through the window on many occasions at a pedal bicycle with an engine. These became known as *mopeds*, the motorised pedal cycle. In the window was a Philip's moped. The heavy gauge frame comprised that of a standard trade delivery bike with the front forks braced, a bit like the speedway machines of the era. Fitted in the space between the crossbar, seat tube and front down-tube, was a 49cc two-stroke engine. In addition to the normal pedal-operated drive chain, there was a second chain that connected the engine to the rear wheel, and a handlebar-mounted lever operated clutch. This lever had a ratchet on it so that if the rider decided to pedal without using the engine, the lever could be held in, and the drive disengaged. A small petrol tank was mounted on the crossbar. The whole machine was finished in metallic silver with red lining and looked the business!

Unbeknown to me, my dear father quietly purchased the machine. I think that the price was forty-nine pounds and ten shillings and it was mine! In actual fact, Dad had purchased it before my birthday and I actually rode it in the woods behind our house in Beulah Hill before the magic 16 years were clocked up. Thus, I was committed to my first hire-purchase agreement - with my Dad! It is not recorded anywhere whether I ever paid him the full amount and Dad certainly never sought after any interest on his loan.

Thus, equipped with 'L' plates, my school cap on my head and satchel strung across to my back, at the age of 16 years, young Bailey set off for school in Bromley.

The normal school run was now to be undertaken astride my Philip's moped. This machine took me everywhere, even on long return journeys down into Hampshire.

On one school day, whilst riding the faithful machine through Penge towards Beckenham, with our young ace smartly dressed in the Clark's College school uniform, the silencer and exhaust pipe parted company because the threaded rod securing the silencer to the exhaust had fractured. The very hot silencer dropped onto the road and bounced into the gutter. The exhaust outlet was now similar to the megaphone shaped open exhaust of that Manx Norton I had admired years before. Having reclaimed possession of this very hot part of the exhaust system and after waiting for it to cool down, the silencer was then stuffed into my blazer pocket. The lad then rode on towards Bromley. The exhaust note, emitted now, easily matched one of those earlier described *angry bees*; it was bloomin' loud!

Ahead of me at the foot of a dip in the high street, near the junction with Kent House Road, was the local policeman looking after the school crossing. He heard me coming from afar and stepped purposefully into the road with his hand raised. Prosecution seemed imminent. The observant officer noticed that part of the exhaust was clearly (purposefully) displayed, sticking out of the young fella's blazer pocket. He stepped back, and with a knowing smile, allowed me to proceed.

Sadly, the manufacturer had not factored into his design that small capacity high revving two-stroke engines simply bolted into heavy-duty bicycle frames, created a degree of high-frequency vibration transmitted throughout the machine. The fractured exhaust bolt was the first result of the vibration. As time passed by, metal bits of the bike became brittle and began to drop off. Dear old Dad, although not a motorcyclist and without me being aware that he had done so, wrote to the manufacturer and complained about my rapidly disintegrating two-wheeled asset.

The manufacturers, clearly aware that there were some shortcomings in their design and development programme, provided replacement parts and even supplied a set of real telescopic front forks in place of the braced standard front forks. For me, this was really something, a motorbike with telescopic front forks!

In the several years, which had passed since putting my faith in Jesus Christ, I had learned that Jesus had told his followers to 'believe and be baptised.' What was this all about? Was being baptised simply the matter of scoring another spiritual point in the church, or following a traditional way of doing things?

The realisation, as I learned more, was that baptism, being fully immersed in water, was an open and public demonstration of one's faith in the Lord Jesus Christ. The picture simply depicted was of one being buried with Christ (under the water) and rising (from the water) with Christ. I guess that to many, such a ceremony would seem strange and yet it was simply a public declaration of my trust that Jesus Christ loved and still loves me, died on the cross for my sin, rose from the dead and lives with me.

At the Baptismal Service conducted in Clifton Hall, Thornton Heath, coming out of the water in shirt and trousers, soaking wet, one could easily have heard a voice shouting out, 'Now get out of that sonny boy!'

The public act had taken place. The Witness had demonstrated and said what he believed. It could not now be unsaid.

That was another lesson that would be so important in life's journey.

The motorcycle bug was well and truly established. I wanted to move on to being a real motorcyclist, to have a motorbike with gears and without pedals. Each week, the classified ads in the motorcycle magazines were studied and eventually I saw a 1938 250cc Royal Enfield motorcycle for sale in Forest Gate, East London. The sum of thirty-nine pounds and ten shillings, what now seemed to be the standard second-hand price for an older motorbike, was required to be paid so that the sale could be completed for the machine. After a long bus ride from Crystal Palace across London, a deal had been done, and after several days, my new motorbike arrived, having been transported to my door on a motorcycle with a platform sidecar. I was in business!

This new beast had pressed steel front forks, a rigid rear end, that is, no suspension, and was clearly second-hand. I recall that a great deal of work to smarten up the Enfield was carried out in my little workshop. The petrol tank was sent up into the Midlands where a specialist company, Percival Bros & Webb Ltd, refurbished the tank. When it was returned, the tank was finished in a high gloss black with gold lining, and the official logo of *Royal Enfield* emblazoned on each side. In fact, the fuel tank was the smartest part of the whole machine!

Many miles were covered on the Enfield and one of my favourite summer evening rides was to go south along the A22 Eastbourne Road towards East Grinstead. I would stop at Blindley Heath by the village cricket ground, just beyond the humped back bridge, turn in the road and wait for a car travelling North back towards Caterham. After allowing the chosen vehicle to pass by and giving it five minutes start, I would set off in pursuit and see how long it would take before the faithful Enfield got close to our quarry. It must be realised that in the mid-1950s the roads were nowhere near as busy as they are in the twenty-first century. Nor was there a speed limit on the open roads. The de-restricted sign meant just that.

One was also well aware that my aged 250cc motorbike was not that quick off the start-line! One day, after such an expertly planned and ridden pursuit, I eventually caught up with my prey as we dropped down the winding Caterham bypass and approached Whopsys Lodge roundabout. Having just drawn alongside the car, which I had been pursuing and was about to regally sweep past; on the final strait, there was distinct clattering from my engine, which then stopped dead. As I grabbed the clutch lever, the worthy steed coasted silently alongside the car, with a dead engine!

With its rider, now enveloped in a billowing cloud of blue smoke, which trailed out behind, looking like a Messerschmitt 109, which had just been struck by a Spitfire; the driver of the car looked across at me from his open window with some amazement and calmly drove off towards the distant sunset. Your 'ace' rider, with his machine losing momentum, hung on grimly to the end as his bike coasted silently to a standstill. He then had to wait for some time whilst the overheated seized engine creaked and clicked as it cooled down. It was then kicked back into life with very little resistance due to the loss of compression in the engine. A cautious journey was made back to base and much repair work had to be carried out upon the sad engine.

3

No more school books,
now work for your living!

School days drew to a close and career plans began to formulate. The dream for many years had been to take up a life working in agriculture because the idea of working in an office or inside a building just did not appeal to me.

Young Bailey had managed to secure a place at an agricultural college in Surrey; all was set! It was a farmer, however, who quite clearly put the *mockers* on the fulfilment of that dream. Dear old Mr Oatway from Willesleigh Farm, Goodleigh in Devon, pointed out that such a career path was pretty much a dead-end trail to follow unless the would-be farmer was part of a farming family or had training in farm management. Many holidays had been spent on that farm and others in the West Country. Surely that was some kind of qualification? But it must be admitted that these holidays were always enjoyed in the warm dry weather of the summer months. Certainly, never in the cold dark days of wintertime.

So, it was back to the drawing board. With the idea of an outdoor life still in mind, the additional thoughts of doing a worthwhile job, which maybe could include a bit of excitement, I began to consider the idea of maybe joining the police force. However, at the age of only 16 and a bit years, that career could not be entered into. It was then discovered that the

Metropolitan Police had set up a Police Cadet Force. So, after filling in various bits of paper, an instruction was received for Mr G L Bailey to attend The Metropolitan Police Recruiting Centre at 40 Beak Street London W.1. *'On Friday 9th March 1956 at 8-45am in the morning precisely, for the purpose of being examined as to your fitness for appointment. This will comprise medical examination, educational examination and interview by the Selection Board.'*

Bailey (GL) was accepted into the force and became Junior Cadet 1390. The training course for the new boys, which was to take place at Hendon Police College, would be of one-month duration and then it would be a matter, if successful on the course, of going out into the world of the Metropolitan Police.

My faith in the Lord Jesus and the growing awareness that He was part of my life was something real to me, yet one was increasingly conscious of the reality that such a way of thinking did not suit everyone's taste. I knew, however, that many family friends, who needless to say were older than me and who had seen and experienced the events of the war, held an almost unshakable faith in the God who I trusted and that, despite having lived through what had been an almost unbelievable experience of the cruelty of man to man.

As I was preparing to leave home, put on the police cadet uniform and start a new life among those who would initially be total strangers to me, the advice came to me clearly from Ron Perrett, an old soldier, who had been through Dunkirk and El Alamein; who was an experienced serving Police officer 'My boy, make sure that you nail your colours to the mast, right from the start!'

Hendon Police Training School was situated in Aerodrome Road, just beyond the railway bridge and opposite the old RAF Hendon Aerodrome, now the RAF Museum. The sleeping accommodation for the new intake of junior cadets comprised single floored huts, or 'hutments' as one very precise Scottish sergeant used to describe them. These buildings were just over the boundary wall from the road and almost under the shadow of the railway embankment.

On my first night with the young guys with whom your scribe would be training, the reminder to 'nail your colours to the mast' was in my mind. So, it was then, for the first time away from home, that Junior Cadet 1390 got down on his knees beside his allocated sleeping place and prayed to God. No boots came flying silently across the dormitory, nor did any of my new comrades voice any abuse or make any unfriendly moves in my direction.

Life at what became known as TS was quite active, with plenty of serious training and quite a few bits of fun thrown into the mix. The picture is still clear in my mind of a full-length photograph of Brigit Bardot, fully dressed for the beach! She was displayed on the end wall of our hut, distant from the entrance door, yet in full view, for all to see and admire. This image had been printed across several pages, published in one of the higher quality daily newspapers and gave good cause for reflection.

Hendon was quite an interesting training experience in more ways than one. One day, a fellow Cadet and I were *carpeted* for a minor infringement of the rules. I cannot recall exactly what it was that got up Sergeant Williams' nose, but as we stood to attention in front of the 'guv'nor' (Superintendent), we were severely *admonished*. Thus, a new word was added to my vocabulary, but little sleep was lost as a consequence. Another lesson for life was added to my list, which would give help in times of trouble. Sorry, I'm not that clever - I cribbed that one from my Bible. Psalm 59 v 16 talks about God being a refuge in times of trouble.

At the end of our course, the newly trained junior cadets were transported by the green single-decker police buses to their different postings, around what we had come to know as the Metropolitan Police District (MPD). Yours truly was dropped off in London Road, South London, at Norbury Police Station (ZN). Now, in 2020, it is closed and has apparently been sold off. Oh boy, what a crazy world we live in.

My main duties were to be in the Clerks' Office upstairs. One regular task was to take up the awful responsibility of stamp licking to apply and stick-on envelopes. It was in the CID office just along the corridor that Cadet 1390 learned the skills of making 'a good pot of tea for the lads.' A hardened Detective Sergeant laid out the correct and only procedure to be followed to get a real result tea-wise. 'Never fill the first cup full and then go on to the next ones,' he said. 'Put some in each cup in turn and keep topping up the pot until they are full, or you'll end up with 'em drinking coloured water. Do it right and then everyone will have a good cuppa. Don't forget that rule, and you'll do alright son!'

Our Superintendent was named Lushington. He hailed from a place in Somerset called Chew Magna and spoke real posh. He had started off with the rank and by the mid-fifties defunct, of Junior Station Inspector (JSI).

Boy, wasn't I mixing with some special people so early in life? Seriously though, one was given the full run of the place and it was there that the perception of the work of being a Police Officer (peace officer) began to be grasped. To see Station Police Sergeant (SPS) Joe Gay in full cry – for this lad, it was a new experience. His build could be described as similar to a small well-constructed brick-built utility out-building. He was a pleasant and quiet kind of guy but customers presenting themselves at the Front Office counter who *tried it on* with a bit of lip, immediately discovered that his mind worked quickly and his vocabulary far exceeded theirs, both in eloquence and descriptive emphasis.

On one day of the week, junior cadets were all engaged at Kingsway Day College in Central London. The theory of the plan set out 'upstairs' at Scotland Yard, was that we were to gain more General Education. These days were not times of great academic advancement, rather a time to meet your old training school mates, make new friends and hear the latest news about what was going on about the metropolis.

We began to discover that some of the fellows 'had contacts' at the Commissioner's Office, which was the title of New Scotland Yard in police lingo. Following initial postings, it was the policy that after six months, junior cadets should be moved to a new police station or department. If you knew who to speak to, it was possible after your first six months to get a posting to almost wherever you wanted. Most of us were in awe of these guys with such insider knowledge, because the apparent power which they held to *get things sorted*, had been denied us.

We also learned that the 'plumb' postings were for a junior

cadet to be based at a District Garage, the home of the Traffic Patrols. Now, Traffic Patrols were the men who rode 500cc (5T) Triumph Speed-Twin motorcycles and rushed around in the Wolseley patrol cars; the very men who I had been thrilled about all those years before. To a young boy's eyes, they seemingly hurtled around the streets of Bromley.

To be posted to a District Garage was therefore something, which only those *close to the throne* could ever achieve. So, for us mere 'outsiders', it was a case of 'just dream on.' I had no contacts at CO, no mates in the know, and so, just dreaming about getting among the Traffic Patrols would have to do.

Needless to say, if one of the 'Trafpols' (a title which emerged in later life) came into Norbury nick, I did my best to talk to them. Being pinned down for most of my time up in the clerks' office under the watchful eye of Chief Inspector Bastone meant that there was little opportunity. Me, being in charge of the stamp box, *thus stamp licking, sticking on envelopes and recording postage* almost glued me to the spot!

4

Wheels set in motion

Soon came the six-monthly posting to another station. When and where I was to go was something about which I hadn't got a clue.

'You're going to DT4 on Monday, Bailey. I hope that you enjoy yourself.'

This was the message which I received from the Chief Inspector. DT4, you ask? District Transport Four!

'But that's Thornton Heath District Garage, Traffic Patrols?'

'S'alright, son. Off you go.'

That was something like the conversation but the response on my next 'educational' visit to Kingsway College for our weekly brain bashing was, 'Now, just how did you fiddle that, Bailey? Just who do you know?'

'I know Nuffin!'

There were personally no contacts at CO, so maybe Chief Inspector Bastone had sussed out my love for motorbikes, who knows?

Working as a Junior Cadet at DT4 was a whole new experience. Most of the blokes were either former wartime servicemen or had served their two years Conscription as National Servicemen. Each was a personality in his own right and many of them were real characters. It was possible even in a crowd to recognise each one of them by just noting the shape of the wearer's uniform cap (beaten up or guards regiment standard) or the rake of its position on his head. It never ceased to amaze me just how a standard police uniform forage cap could be personalised.

Remember the wire trick mentioned earlier? If you had placed all of the caps together on a canteen table; without doubt, one could have accurately named the individual owner of each one of them.

On arrival at the garage, I was put under the watchful eye of John Brewis, one of the older guys. Memories are immediately evoked of the strong smell of white-line paint. It was a special brew with an aroma of its own which spread like white treacle and was used to mark out on the garage floor the car parking and motorcycle bays This was kept in the store at the back of the huge garage and the store was John's office, a place to put things out of the way - - a general hidey-hole!

Initially, this was to be my base-camp, where Bailey learned the great skills of how to *flag up* the accident black-spot maps for Number Four District (that was a quarter of the whole Metropolitan Police District). Said map completely covered one wall of the table tennis room and each accident was marked with a flag, the colour of which depicted the seriousness of what was then known as a Road Traffic Accident (RTA). It was therefore sadly the fact that the location of each fatal accident was marked by a triangular black flag on a pin.

Now, Mitcham Common, which was on our patch, is a vast area of common-land inhabited by birds, bees, and various furry mammals. It was wandered upon by pedestrians walking dogs, playing golf, or even sitting on the grass fishing in the one solitary pond. Although the common is bounded by and intersected with several roads, it is easy on foot to be a good distance away from any of them, deep in the country.

The Guv'nor at the garage, Len Pearcey, Superintendent Grade Two (one crown on each shoulder), would regularly check out the accident situation. He would stand four-square with hands deep in his pockets and closely scrutinise the details of the map.

One morning, with a roar, I was summoned into his presence in the ping-pong room, which doubled as the Parade Room.

'What's this Bailey?' He said, pointing at a single spot deep within the unexplored foliage of Mitcham Common, well away from any public thoroughfare; a place where probably no human footprint had ever left its mark. Since the boy had last updated this important statistical resource, five or six fatal RTA's (road traffic accidents) had occurred in this unexplored area. That must have been the case because there was evidence clearly marked by a tight cluster of firmly planted black flags.

Guv' was not pleased, the boy was choked off and had to amend the statistics before he made the tea. And I recall that the cream doughnuts were on me that morning (*purchased from the bread shop across the road and supplied by!*).

Flags in the wrong place kept the lad on his toes and were one example of a certain constabulary sense of humour that was never vindictive, even though at times it must have raised the blood pressure of the victim.

It did not take long to realise that coppers knew how to wind up their mates, young green cadets; or even to demonstrate a viewpoint if one of the Skippers (Sergeants) upset them. It was known that one sergeant, nicknamed *Richard the first 'Dick the I'*, was not on very good terms with his next-door neighbour. He had also made some waves among the men on his relief. A full set of the twenty-four volumes of *The Encyclopaedia Britannica* was therefore ordered anonymously by some personage, to be delivered to said neighbour with a message to the carrier that, because Dick the I had ordered this set of twenty-four volumes and would be on duty when they were delivered, the neighbour was prepared to look after them until Dick arrived home!

Another Skipper, who had also caused some dissent, arrived home one day to find that a truckload of ready-mix quick-drying cement had been delivered and was establishing a permanent and mountainous attachment to the driveway. Funnily, I never learned what was the final outcome of these two events.

I began to value the privilege of working among men who, after all, had lived through much more horror and suffering than I could ever imagine, in their battles to bring peace to Europe and the world. Although they knew and respected discipline, these guys had little time for what they felt were petty-minded, self-seeking, more senior Supervising Officers.

I recall one day that Robbie Robson, the official Constables' Police Federation Representative (PC's rep), was engaged in a rather serious discussion on police matters with 'guv'nor', the Superintendent mentioned earlier. Robbie, an imposing figure of a man, who had seen armed service throughout the war, stood with his medal ribbons carried on the left breast of his uniform jacket.

At one point, Robbie was heard to say, 'Your problem guv is that you think that the crown is on your head and not on your shoulder!'

End of conversation.

Another daily task was for me to chase up the authorised police drivers when their driving licences were due for renewal. In those days, driving licence renewal was an annual requirement throughout the land for all drivers and motorcyclists. It also fell to the boy to update the monthly police mileage records and be prepared to tour the guv'nor's office with the aforementioned tea at the prescribed times. Talking of keeping records; computers were almost something of science fiction (ordinary mortals did not even have the word in their vocabulary), so pen and ink or biro were always resorted to when detailed statistics had to be compiled.

On the monthly mileage chart, each Traffic Patrol's total mileage was recorded. Black mileage was covered behind the wheel of a Tag Car and red mileage was the score added up on motorcycle patrol duty. I recall that as each month neared its end, some of the older guys had a bit of a struggle totting up their 'red' mileage, particularly if they had been posted on a car patrol and had not had to cover a motorcycle patrol for someone who had taken time off. If no black or red mileage was recorded in six months, the officer was suspended from driving or riding duties (ceased from being an Authorised Police Driver). He could then be required to travel across London to Hendon Police Motor Driving School (MDS) and submit to a 're-test; a fearsome prospect to be under the examining eye of a senior driving school instructor.

Hence, it sometimes became necessary to organise the frantic quick run around the block on a bike to make some red ink mileage before the Cadet updated the mileage record for the month.

Let's face it, on a cold, rain-swept November morning, to many coppers patrolling the rush hour traffic on a motorcycle around South London's Vauxhall Cross, just south of the River Thames at Vauxhall Bridge, was not the most fun experience. This was particularly the case in the late fifties and early sixties before pedestrian traffic light controls were put in place and the road builders had yet to devise a surface that gave tyres even a little bit of a fighting chance to grip its oil and rubber bound covering. Because of the nature of the approaches to this complex, a driver could have a good run at the junction 'chasing the amber' and find it difficult to stop! Thus, it was considered by some 'Trafpols' to be a sound philosophy that a third class (car) drive is always better than a first-class (motor-cycle) ride when it's raining.

I can remember being posted to that very same junction in later years, on what was known as STS (Special Traffic Scheme) patrols, parking his Triumph and spending hours directing the rush-hour traffic by hand as it bore down on him from four directions. The traffic would then whizz off onto Vauxhall Bridge, along the Albert Embankment, or under the railway bridge towards the Surrey's Oval Cricket Ground. Officers who were employed on that posting never required a laxative. Yet it is strange, as it was the 'peds' (pedestrians) launching themselves into the road and trying to outrun the motor vehicles who created the most anxiety. In their endeavour to get there first, these folks would ignore what the kind policeman was doing and with a seeming death wish, flood into the road. One supposes they had the subconscious feeling of safety in numbers. One soon developed the ability to emit a powerful fingerless whistle to stem the flow. Thankfully, there is now a footbridge to guide the 'peds' over the top of the traffic flow.

The bike bug had bitten me well and truly but as a mere junior cadet, there was no way in which I would be allowed to ride or even touch one of the maroon-coloured beasts, tethered in their parking bays. So, when the opportunity came, I just wandered about the garage, watching and taking it all in. The standard police Triumph 5T Speed Twins were fitted with sprung hub rear suspension and breathed through car type SU carburettors, unlike the civilian specification of an Amal carburettor. The blokes felt that the SU detracted from the overall performance of the bike and they were not over-enthusiastic about the sprung hub rear suspension unit, which was fitted into the un-sprung frame. This comprised a rear wheel with spring units inside a large diameter rear hub.

Riders who had been more used to 'feeling' the road through an un-sprung rear frame sometimes preferred that ride to the vague lack of feel transmitted by the sprung hub unit. The bikes were fitted with a saddle supported at the back by double coil springs and so it was easy to appreciate how an 'undamped' saddle and the sprung hub could fight against each other in some road conditions. Police service bikes were further equipped with steel legs-shields. Inside one was mounted the ubiquitous Pyrene fire extinguisher and on the other shield a zipped pouch where the rider's police truncheon was carried.

These machines, therefore, carried little excess baggage, were quite agile and could thus be chucked about. The well-worn lower edges of the leg shields gave clear evidence that a Speed Twin, under pressure, could give a good account of itself.

The garage was equipped with at least one machine fitted with a public address system (PA) mounted on a carrier over the rear wheel, for use when emergency or traffic messages had to be transmitted to the public. Only one, or maybe two of the machines, were radio-equipped and the riders were 'specially selected', because the R/T (radio/telephone) was a huge device of batteries, valves and other wireless bits carried as panniers on either-side of the rear wheel. The handset was above the rear wheel on the carrier and an aerial of vast length pointed skyward from the back of the equipment. Add that weight and imbalance to a sprung hub, sprung saddled Triumph being pushed hard on an emergency call, with the aerial whipping about the heavens and little imagination is necessary to realise that the riders could all tell tales of 'hairy' moments.

It was not unknown for a rider to *step off* at speed when the machine took control. Traffic Patrols speaking of a bike/rider being 'rashered' was enough to make one's eyes water! But they never fell off. The term was always, 'he rode it right down to the ground!'

5

'Tricks of the trade'

The faithful Royal Enfield continued to serve me well but the desire to find something more up to date with a bit more power was quite strong. There was a Traffic Patrol at Thornton Heath Garage who answered to the name of 'Hutch'. He was a smooth character and off duty, sped about the streets on a 649cc Triumph Tiger 110. Fitted with an aluminium cylinder head and with a higher performance specification than the standard Triumph Thunderbird; in the late fifties, it was quite a cool set of wheels.

One day, Hutch sidled up to and informed the boy that he owned a 1951 Vincent Comet, which he thought maybe I would like to purchase. 'A Smooth sales style' could, in retrospect, be used to identify his approach to the young lad, probably still wet behind the ears. Vincents were quite special machines, using their own hand-built 998cc V-twin engines. In fact, each complete motorcycle was selectively hand-built; that is, the engine internals and other moving parts were carefully selected to ensure precise tolerances and therefore that best performance was achieved. The end result was a special machine with the most efficient performance.

As Vincents were not mass-produced, they were very expensive. These Stevenage built beauties were not regularly seen on the roads being used as everyday transport. In the world of the fifties, normally a bloke would not be able to afford a Vincent for his daily ride to work but would rather go for a BSA Bantam or ex-WD machine (side-valve Norton, Ariel, Matchless or BSA M20, another side-valve engine machine).

The bike on offer was a single cylinder 500cc unit, known colloquially as only 'half a Vincent'. To me nonetheless, half a Vincent was better than no performance bike at all. The deal was done and over the following weeks, many happy miles passed under the wheels as I explored the local highways and byways.

Late one evening, however, with a mate sat up behind (John Collins; all 6'3' of him), riding homeward along the A22 Eastbourne Road, the engine suddenly gave up the ghost. After abandoning the bike, we had to thumb a lift to get a car ride home. When the engine was dismantled, it was discovered that at some earlier date, clearly following some serious damage to the valve gear in the cylinder head, the whole section of the exhaust outlet, valve seat, spring and rocker mounting had been machined out. An attempt had been made to shrink an aluminium sleeve into the cylinder head to enable a replacement exhaust valve, rocker, and exhaust tract to be fitted.

What anyone with the simplest knowledge of engineering would have known was that the aluminium cylinder head, when hot, had a certain rate of expansion. Fitting a sleeve of a different material with an unknown rate of expansion was a non-starter of an idea. A great amount of heat is generated in the combustion chamber/exhaust manifold of an engine. The re-engineered part had moved within the cylinder head as the heat of the running motor had caused expansion. Different materials expand at different rates, QED (quite easily done) I certainly had been!

It seems that the lad had been sold a pup. One more lesson was added to the list of life experiences. Needless to say, there had been no warranty or guarantee included in the original purchase. I guess that the seller had made quite a profit on the deal. It was interesting that Hutch did offer to give me a *genuine* lined fabric Vincent tank cover when I informed him of the engine failure. I wonder where that cover had come from in the first place. By now, a well-worn adage was adopted: 'buyer beware!' With the costly new cylinder head purchased and fitted, many more happy miles were covered on my half a Vincent.

A small group of us including 'Ossie' from Carshalton, David Symons from Thornton Heath, one or two other guys and I used to meet up on a Saturday afternoon and make our way out along the A3 Portsmouth Road to visit Comerfords in Thames Ditton. This was a large motorcycle emporium where one could simply wander, feast our eyes and dream about machinery which we would have loved to own. The return journey brought us back towards London along the Kingston-By-Pass. A 70mph national speed limit had not yet been brought into existence and so we all enjoyed a very brisk and some might say competitive ride home.

The present-day underpasses had not yet been constructed on this section of the A3, so major junctions incorporated round-abouts of differing shapes and dimensions. Negotiating these multi-junctions, one soon learned the need for reading the road, planning ahead, late precise braking and brisk changes of direction with early and smooth application of power via the twist grip if you wanted to avoid being last home!

The group would also take longer rides up to Silverstone for the BMCRC (British Motor Cycle Racing Club) *Silverstone Saturday* Race Meeting and settle down to watch the aces from our vantage point at Stowe Corner. One of the members of the group, who worked with David at 'Bailey Meters and Controls' on Purley Way in Croydon, would trundle up with us, riding his fully-equipped sidecar outfit and cook us a fried breakfast which we enjoyed sat on the grass on the edge of this very fast right-hand bend.

It was here that I first saw the great Bob McIntyre riding his Joe Potts 350cc Manx Norton. His face and record were familiar to me as I avidly studied the current racing reports published every Wednesday in *The Motorcycle* (the blue 'un). The news was that Bob was going to be riding his 'Joe Potts' Manx Norton at Silverstone. It would be fitted with the new Schafleitner modified six-speed AMC gearbox. Four-speed gearboxes were the norm in those days. A five or six-speed box would give the rider much more use of the available engine power. Highly tuned racing engines had a fairly narrow useful rev band and thus, six gears in the box meant that the engine power could be more efficiently utilised.

On the opening lap of the race, Bob was well into the lead and ahead of the pack as he rushed down the straight towards the right-handed Stowe corner. It was thought that the gearbox locked up (seized), Bob Mac was flicked onto the track at high speed. He smoothly slid out to the edge of the track, picked himself up and sat there on a straw bale, watching the rest of the race, apparently quite unshaken.

Here was a truly great rider.

Bob McIntyre

His was a neat unhurried riding style and Bob seemed to be quite undemonstrative. He became to me an example of what motorcycle racing was about. Needless to say, following every race day at Silverstone, the return ride towards London along the A5 saw scores of motorcyclists, inspired by the achievements of the stars and quite a number attempting to emulate what they had recently witnessed! The competitive bug was beginning to bite, but one was becoming conscious that the racetrack was the only place to play at racers!

As has already been said; in the Metropolitan Police in those days, before all the motorcycles were equipped with R/T sets (radio telephone/two-way radios), two solos operated with a radio-equipped patrol car and thus formed a Traffic Accident Group. So it was that even after all police motorcycles were fitted with radios, the name 'Tag Car' stuck and that was an easy way to distinguish a Traffic Patrol car from the ordinary Area Wireless Car which operated from a local police station.

Various external distinguishing 'marks' were evident on Traffic Patrol vehicles. A police sign was fitted front and rear, some cars were fitted with a public address (P/A) speaker on the roof. Later on, twin spotlights were fitted on the forward edge of the roof, one on each side. All police cars were fitted with a rather large silver bell for use when operating in an emergency situation. This was well before the two-tone 'donkey' horn was introduced, at which stage for some years the crew had the choice of both forms of warning of their presence.

Although cadets were denied the privilege of riding or driving police vehicles, a day spent working with a Traffic Patrol crew was a 'working period' when one could experience driving skill at its best. To learn 'on the wing' and be instructed, not only by what the blokes told you about driving skills but by seeing the broken bodies of road users who had tried their hand at the art or been knocked down by a driver of limited skill. An added perk for the young cadet would be to share with the crew as they took tea and toast early in the morning shift before things heated up.

One early turn, I was posted riding with a crew in tag car (Z17) which covered the Epsom/Banstead area. Around mid-day, one of the crew was taking 'time-off' so we returned to Thornton Heath Garage (DT4) and awaited the relief crew member's arrival. For some reason he was delayed and so the driver, Ron (Taf) Williams, *promoted* me to R/T Operator!

As we left the garage and entered Thornton Heath High

Street, an emergency call came over the radio. 'Personal injury (P.I.) accident, Ashley Road, Epsom Downs, just north of Langley Vale Road.'

'That's ours boy, we'll take it.'

From where we were at that moment, Epsom Downs could not have been further away. Without resorting to the headlights, horn, or the earlier mentioned police bell, Taf demonstrated driving skills out of the aces in the pack; four-wheel drifts in a Wolseley 6/90 under complete control and in perfect safety, gave an insight to a life's experience, which could be ahead. A slight hiccup meant that as we were moving at high speed along the A217 and rapidly approaching Banstead crossroads, the 6/90 wheezed, then died, and ran silently to a standstill with smoke filtering out around the edges of the bonnet.

In those days, when the weather was hot, cars driven under pressure would sometimes run out of steam because the engine-driven fuel pumps were not up to the task. The petrol would vaporise in the pump and not reach the engine. As I recall, with the bonnet raised and Taf's cap vigorously waved over the offending item to create a cooler atmosphere. We were quickly on our way!

6

Getting down to 'the job' proper!

Soon the time arrived for this young fellow to move on in his service and commence the full three months training at Hendon Police Training School; a course which had to be successfully completed before one could be attested (take the oath of allegiance to the Queen) to be a Constable in the Metropolitan Police.

Following these three months of training, I would become a Senior Cadet and be involved in more 'on the job' activity and further instruction 'out on the streets' until reaching the age of nineteen. At this point, a Senior Cadet or entrant would be accepted as a Constable.

The months of training were quite intense and involved gaining knowledge of police procedure, regulations, the law and how to apply it, as well as becoming skilled in self-defence and awareness of how to conduct oneself on the streets of London. Apart from physical training, there were periods during the weeks of strict drill training, marching up, turning around at the end, and marching back down again. We learned how to turn to the left, turn to the right, and upon the command, smartly come to a standstill and salute whoever required such an acknowledgement.

The drill instructor was a sergeant by the name of McMorran. He stood erect, using precise movements and clearly demonstrated previous experience in an army Guards' Regiment. In fact, the slashed peak and rake of his cap confirmed the position which he had previously occupied. His voice could be heard at the far end of the parade ground (probably even at Hendon Central Tube Station, a mile up the road) and there was never any doubt about the instruction which he had given.

At some time during our training, this Sergeant left the school. Apparently, for a period of time, he was going somewhere else on a course. Sergeant McMorran was replaced it would seem, apparently temporarily, by another Sergeant who had been posted in from Thames Division, the River Police.

The uniform of a Thames Division officer differed from that of a policeman operating on land. The uniform jackets of the guys who worked on the river were in the nautical style of a double-breasted reefer jacket and each lapel carried an insignia of silver metal lettering, the words identifying him as a member of Thames Division. These uniformed jackets and markings, to a degree, looked very similar to the uniform worn by drivers employed by Southdown Coaches, a large South of England coach company. The consequence was that his 'mates ashore', with tongue in cheek, often termed Thames Division officers as *Southdown Coach Drivers*!

Sadly, this new Sergeant had neither the commanding presence nor voice projection of the recently departed drill sergeant who he had replaced. It became clear that coppers, whether young recruits in training (a number of them probably former National Servicemen) or police cadets, seemed as quick as more experienced officers at assessing those around them. After all, coppers are only uniformed examples of the man in the street, who generally is as quick at 'reading the score' as the next person (remember the look in the eye?). Sadly, our new 'Sarge', because of his apparent lack of authority, although he often sought to enforce it using his *little black book* to note a particular incident, seemed to have begun to give some of the guys on the various training courses cause for dreaming up some form of quiet (or maybe not so quiet) mickey-taking.

All of those in training were required to assemble daily before instruction classes on the Parade Square behind the school swimming pool. A parade before and uniform inspection by the senior officer of the day was held as part of the early morning parade, and a second parade, without a uniform inspection, took place after lunch. The body of men on parade comprised thirteen classes of Constable Recruits and a similar number of Senior Cadet classes.

The Drill Sergeant, standing with his back to the swimming pool and facing the men on parade, would call the ranks assembled to attention. The constables were ranked down the right side of the square and the cadets on the left side; all facing towards the swimming pool. They would be dressed off, instructed to stand at ease, and then to stand-easy. The gathered throng would await the arrival of a senior officer, generally, the Chief Inspector walking from his office, who would approach down what was for the men on parade, the right-hand side of the swimming pool building. This officer would be approaching from behind where the Drill Sergeant stood ready to hand over the parade.

The Chief Inspector was more or less blind-sighted to all of us, save to that of the Constables' right-marker, who stood at the head of and right side of the constable ranks. His view was straight up the passageway along which the Chief Inspector was approaching. On seeing his approach, this Constable's job was to give the nod to the Sergeant who stood facing the parade but with his back to the approaching senior officer. On receiving the nod from the right-marker, the Sergeant would call the parade to attention, salute the Chief Inspector and inform him that the parade was all present and correct. So far, so good!

One particular afternoon and it must have been pre-arranged, the Sergeant, having brought his men on parade to attention, dressed us off and instructed us to stand-easy (legs apart, hands behind backs), stood ready, awaiting the arrival of the Chief Inspector. The rear-most two ranks of the twenty-six deep rows of cadets broke into song! The Sergeant, clearly surprised and angry at this breakdown in discipline, broke into a noisy hobnail booted march down the parade square, between the ranks of constables and cadets and towards the apparent source of the noise.

Before he had reached the targeted centre of the melodi-ous notes, the singing stopped. Having reached the supposed source of the noise, he dived among the men demanding to know what was going on, shouting plaintively that they were on parade. Whilst amid his tirade, the cadet ranks at the top of the parade square, the front row of the parade, took their turn to break out in song! The dear old Sarge, now clearly rattled, charged back to the front of the parade ground, at which point the singing stopped but restarted at its original source.

Telling the story so many years later, it all seems almost impossible. Yet it was one of the highlights of my days at Hendon. This, now clearly extremely upset Drill Sergeant, charged once more to the rear of the parade (sparks could well have been flashing from the hobnails of his boots). His voice raised in anger with the whole parade doing its utmost to hold in the explosive and obvious enjoyment of the moment. In the meantime, the Chief Inspector has arrived. The right marker has no-one to pass the signal to!

Said Chief Inspector, with a look of mystified and bemused surprise, walked to the saluting point and waited for the Sergeant. Various voices from the crowd advised the Sergeant.

'The Chief Inspector is waiting for you, Sarge!'

The Sergeant now doubled from the back of the parade square to the front, skidded to a standstill, threw up the required salute to the Chief Inspector and reported clearly; 'The parade all present and correct, sir!'

At which point, the Chief Inspector advised him that the whole parade was not standing to attention, as it should have been, but still standing easy!

The Drill Sergeant now had to call us all to attention and repeat his earlier report to the Chief Inspector. I have no idea whether there were any repercussions following this episode, but I just know that many recruits and cadets will have added the memories of that happy experience to their life's story.

Another lesson was also learned; son, it's going to happen to you one day. It doesn't matter who you *think* you are; someone in *the job* (the police) is going to set you up for a bit of a laugh at your own expense, and maybe put you in your place!

Three months of training were soon completed and I was posted to Streatham Police Station (ZM) where one spent more time on the streets with experienced coppers, became involved in doing the job and learning more about the skills of police duty.

My love for two wheels continued to grow and on one snowy night, one of the constables at the nick swapped with me. He took my Vincent and I was allowed to use his Triumph Speed Twin sidecar outfit. One recalls happy hours spent with my friend, John, riding through the snow, down into Sussex and back.

On that first ride, I simply put into practice what had been learned from the blue 'un about sidecar driving and developed it. The joys of sidecar driving added another colour to the experience of motorcycling.

7

Those boots are made for walking

Too soon, my 19th birthday arrived. In May 1958, young Bailey became PC 462L and was posted to Camberwell Police Station (LC).

In those days, which seem so long ago, the Metropolitan Police District (MPD) was divided into four districts, each District then being divided into Divisions, sub-divisions, sections, beats and localised patrols. Camberwell was in L Division and part of the Number Four District. The Divisional Station was Brixton (LD). Peckham (LP), about a mile and a half east of Camberwell, was a Sub-Divisional station and Camberwell was its Sectional Station.

Our ground comprised many beats (numbers eleven to eighteen) and a constable would be posted to cover one of those beats, patrolling on foot during his tour of duty. At this station, the full strength again compromised men who had either served and fought in the armed forces through the Second World War, had served 18 months to two years post-war as National Servicemen or were former war-reserve police officers. Ex-cadets, who had not done their 'National Service', were not considered to be 'up too much'; therefore, it took about six months before many of these older guys would engage one in any informal/friendly conversation.

The passing comment would often be, 'What you want son is a bit of discipline wiv a sergeant up be'ind yer! That would soon sort you out. Oh, and am I standing on yer 'air?'

Being the 'new boy' and a mere lad on the relief, the great responsibility to run our relief tea club was allocated to this young probationer (colloquial language: *he was lumbered wiv the job*). Thus, PC Bailey became the tea club secretary on the relief. Cor, Mate. What a privilege!

There were three reliefs and each in rotation performed early turn, late to turn and night duty. Because the police canteen was not open 24/7, each relief ran its own tea club. The relief tea club secretary was responsible for purchasing tea, milk and sugar; making sure at prescribed times that 'a brew' was always on the go whenever required. To operate this vast business empire, each officer would contribute four-pence per week. He would thus be able to imbibe tea by the cup full *at required times*.

Just inside the swing doors of the station entrance, was what was known as the Communication Room (reserve room). Against the window out into the street was the telephone switchboard, which provided inter-station communication and connected the outside world to the different offices in the building. After parading for duty, we would drop in to check on messages referring to matters to be dealt with involving our posted beat and also later return to record on the message pad any results.

The communications officer operated the switchboard and kept up the message records. He was also the Reserve Man, ready to give additional assistance should the wheel come off somewhere on our ground. On the wall, just inside the comms room door was fixed a grey electronically powered device which, when switched on, gave out a regular bleating sound. This gave an idea of any nuclear threat from an enemy source. We were instructed that should the note alter in its rhythmic timing, nuclear dangers were becoming more imminent! So, not more than fifteen years after the end of the Second World War, there was already fear that another conflict might be brewing up someplace. More important matters, however, were on my mind.

One Monday morning, at about 6 a.m., shortly after parade; in my official capacity as *tea club secretary*, I set about collecting the weekly four pence contribution due from each of the lads. This regular income was essential if our small business empire was to even survive the threat of a nuclear attack. John Simpson, PC 435L was standing in the reserve room, near the front doors which gave out onto the street. I requested the 4d required for his continued membership of our exclusive club.

John's response was, 'What do you want that for?'

I replied, 'John, it's for the tea club.'

'You don't want four pence from me!' John replied.

I insisted that he passed what was due into my financial control. John then took possession of my helmet, pulled out the three little wooden pegs holding the silver/metal Rose onto the top of the helmet and the three little wooden pegs securing the Metropolitan Police badge to the front of my police issue headwear. John then removed the Rose and the badge from the helmet, placed them with the six little pegs into the helmet, moved out into the entrance hall, swung open the double doors and threw the lot out into the centre of Camberwell Church Street, the A202 (main trunk route from Hyde Park Corner to the Kent Coast). The rush hour had just begun; thus, traffic was fairly heavy, and the young *helmetless* constable was to be seen scrabbling amongst the vehicles moving towards Kennington Oval, trying to find the missing bits.

Life lessons had been mentioned earlier. Nothing was said. I had been tested. John and I were soon firm friends and colleagues. Coppers became mates and were prepared to go through thick and thin together, but maybe not without checking the quality of the metal first!

But what about bikes? I was now looking for something better than *half a Vincent*. In due course, a visit was paid to Conway Motors of Goldhawk Road, Shepherd's Bush. This company specialised in the sale of Vincent motorcycles. As I walked through the showroom, my gaze was drawn to a feast of Vincents, all lined up in their livery black with gold-lined petrol tanks, aluminium mudguards, and beautiful V-twin engines. The engine/gearbox unit comprised the main member of the machine. On series 'B' and 'C' models, a tapered box-shaped oil tank unit formed the top spine of the bicycle; the forks were mounted on the headstock at the front of this unit and the dual seat attached via a spindle and bushed bearing at the back.

The rear triangulated frame was pivoted on a mounting behind the gearbox and the sprung suspension units ran from the top of the rear sub-frame to the lower rear end of the oil tank unit. The Vincent, designed before and soon after the war, so advanced for its time was relatively light (435lbs) and the frame was flex-free.

On the day of my visit, there were series 'B' and series 'C' Vincents on display. The series 'A' Vincent, known as *the plumber's nightmare* due to its external oil pipework, had ceased production before the war. A series 'C' Vincent Rapide caught my eye and ticked all the boxes; thus, I was soon riding off eastwards, heading for home on a machine which was a dream to ride. It was extremely smooth running and relatively slow revving. With a 998cc 50-degree V-twin motor delivering the power, this new toy would accelerate to the 30mph urban speed limit in bottom gear.

What followed were years and many miles of wonderful motorcycling experiences, covering the length and breadth of the U.K. When arriving for duty at Camberwell, my fellow constables' bikes were always parked on Wren Road, outside the back gate of the nick. A BSA Golden Flash with a sidecar also graced our little parking space.

One day, soon after I arrived at Camberwell, whilst out learning beats with George (PC Pudney), we were walking in silence and young Bailey, seeking to make conversation, respectfully enquired who owned the Flash. George's response comprised three short words; the last defining word was explicit but would not be used in good company or before the evening 9:30 p.m. threshold. His response did, however, confirm his ownership. I continued on my way with George, *learning beats* in silence!

The Vin would rest, firmly supported on its rear stand, the rear wheel raised from the ground. If I was feeling a bit lazy, I could kick the engine into life whilst the bike was still on its stand. Being a V-twin with almost 500cc capacity in each cylinder, a good swing on the long-curved kick-start lever would be essential to spin the engine into life. Mr Vincent had thought of this and fitted an exhaust valve lift lever on the handlebar. The drill was, by holding in the valve lift lever one could push down the kick-start lever and move the piston on one of the cylinders so that it was just past the top dead centre, the valve lifter having released the compression in the cylinder. Then it was simply a matter of taking another full swing on the kick-starter and the engine would spin through the exhaust and induction strokes of the piston until it came up against the ignition stroke of the other cylinder. Only then it would fire. It was important that the rider kicked-over using the 'correct' cylinder because one piston fired up and the second piston came up against compression-only fifty degrees afterwards and if you chose the wrong one, you would be up against compression before the engine was spinning. Thus, it was possible to kick all day and get nowhere.

Being only around eleven stone plus a couple of pounds and not much more than 5'8" tall, your scribe was not exactly a big guy. Yet, having got the knack for kicking the beloved Vin into life at the end of my shift, starting up the bike to go home was simple and quite straightforward. This was a bit much for some of my mates and one day 'Jock' Nichol, a much beefier type than me, who wished to demonstrate how easily he could fire up the engine, spent a great deal of effort trying to kick the bike into life. It was a fruitless endeavour and 'Jock' was soon quite red-faced and frustrated when he finally gave up. Honestly, I tried so hard to tell him how to do it, but as one discovers so often in life (and this was another lesson), the other guy always knows better than you do. So, just stand back and enjoy.

Five years working as a beat copper at Camberwell was quite interesting and had its moments. In Camberwell Road, on the far side of Camberwell Green, the local butchers operated under the name of O'Rourke. When I was on that beat, whilst sheltering between the sides of beef hanging in the shop, I was privileged to be able to talk to the son of the owner. His name was Mike O'Rourke. He, like his dad, was a skilled butcher. As you recall, I saw Mike racing at Crystal Palace. This guy was a skilled and experienced rider in the TT Races and was a true gentleman. I believe he quietly humoured this young strip of a copper, voicing dreams of one day following in his wheel tracks.

Mike O'Rourke beginning The Mountain climb

In the family's flat upstairs, this dear fellow allowed me to look at his TT Replica Awards; needless to say, awards won in the Isle of Man Tourist Trophy Races. Sometimes, when patrolling on foot, another guy used to ride past me along Denmark Hill. His name was Joe Dunphy, yet another Crystal Palace and TT rider. In the coming years, Joe became a wise advisor and encouraged me as I set out to achieve those TT dreams. I discovered that motorcycle racers were often real gentleman, friendly, and quite humble about their achievements.

Joe Dunphy Manx GP winner and TT ace

Moving on, as they say, life in Camberwell was fairly interesting. At one end of the ground (the term used in reference to an area covered by a given police station) lived the Richardson brothers. They operated from Peckford's Scrap Metal Merchants in New Church Road and it was suggested that they more or less ran crime south of the River Thames. History records that things went reasonably well for them until they began to poach north of the river. The Kray twins and the rest of East London were not very impressed. A king-sized confrontation took place in 1966 at 'Mr Smith's' Club in Catford, with fatal results. But that is another story.

At the other end of our ground lived Freddie Mills, one of the country's top-line post-war boxers. He was World Light Heavyweight Boxing Champion from 1948 to 1950. He drove a Citroen DS19, a car with a futuristic design that was well in advance of the times. This meant that whenever Freddie Mills was in the area, you could not help noticing him. He was a friendly guy, but history records that he suffered a tragic and violent end to his life.

When out on night duty, the first task was to 'do your shops' and check that they were locked and secure. The first lesson in this regard was that you always pulled the front door so that, had the shopkeeper not properly closed it when he went home, your gentle tug clicked the latch home. Job done, all secure. If on the other hand the lock had not been 'clicked' and you gave it a big push first, you were faced with an 'insecure premises'. This meant a lot of writing, sending for the key holder and hanging around until he arrived; maybe an hour or more later, even if no burglar was inside doing a bit of thieving.

So, at around 11:00 p.m. one night, I arrived at the row of shops in Denmark Hill just above where the Odeon Cinema, then stood at the junction with Coldharbour Lane. All was quiet as I gave the front door of the hardware shop a gentle pull. No click, therefore, it must be locked. OK, now give it a push, I thought.

The door swung open with a mighty metallic crash, hitting a tin bath that had been placed just inside to catch the early morning mail as it dropped through the letterbox. The galvanised receptacle skated at speed across the shop floor, until it was brought to an abrupt and noisy stop by several other metal items of hardware loosely gathered against the far wall. The owner, it turned out, was Mr Ted Broadrib, Freddie Mills' father-in-law, who lived above the shop. He was quickly 'on scene', suitably impressed by PC 462's dedication and rewarded his local Bobbie with a good cup of brew and a friendly natter in his flat above the shop.

One day, walking along Coldharbour Lane, I came across a young fellow in possession of a motorcycle, which, it turned out, he had earlier *liberated*. It didn't belong to him! In those days, one set of handcuffs was kept locked and secure in the station safe. None were issued to the blokes on the street. Personal radios (bat-phones) with direct communication to the police station hadn't been thought of, or at least, they hadn't told the blokes on the ground. Policemen were issued with a whistle on a chain, a box-key, and a wooden truncheon.

One night duty we carried a torch. Communication (calling for assistance) was thus limited to blowing your whistle and flashing your torch in the direction of where the next policeman might be lurking. For the rest of it, you were on your own. So, this skilled officer, being very clever, told the youngster to push the motorbike down to Camberwell Green to the police station. The pushing will keep him occupied, I thought. I strode purposefully alongside my prisoner, secure in the knowledge that he had felt a collar and my prisoner had his hands full!

As we arrived outside the nick, however, my new young acquaintance, rather more quick-witted than this young super-cop had anticipated, threw the bike at me, jumped over it, and was gone. This young copper, with motorcycle racing dreams in his head, then had to explain to the Station Officer that not only had he recovered a stolen motorcycle which was outside the station, but that the prisoner/'stealer' of the bike had run away! The advisory comments, clearly and succinctly voiced by my Sergeant should not be repeated in print in your select company presently reviewing my faithfully reported evidence.

On another occasion, whilst dealing with a hospital enquiry at Kings College Hospital (KCH), I noticed a 650cc Triumph motorcycle complete with rider and passenger, parked on the ramp outside the Casualty Department. Noting the detail, the fittings and accessories of this machine, it was clear that things did not match. Namely, that Triumph parts from a later year of manufacture were fitted to the older machine standing before me. The evidence was that the machine that provided the parts had been stolen by these guys. This time, I got my man safely to the police station. Enquiries revealed that quite a bit of motorcycle crime was tied up in this machine, but witnesses were needed to confirm the crime.

When the case subsequently came up at Lambeth Magistrate's Court, the supplier of the stolen machine turned out to be Gus Kuhn Motorcycles of Clapham. The boss, who was present at court, was Vincent Davey. Maybe I will talk more about him later. Alongside Mr Davey, was the representative of A. Bennett, a Triumph motorcycle supplier from the Midlands. Here was another man with whom I might have something to do in the future. The bottom line was that as a result of the arrest, PC Bailey received a Commander's Commendation for his, what would be called, 'detective ability.'

The Commander was the guy in charge of Number Four District. It must be said, however, that the specialist officers from C10 (the Stolen Vehicles Branch at Scotland Yard), had helped greatly and encouraged my efforts. Nonetheless, the response of the team was: 'This one is down to you, Bailey, you can take the credit.'

Mates doing the same job!

In later years, a Commander was placed in charge of a Division, a number of which made up a District. As has been said, the Met then comprised four Districts.

8

Is this lift-off time?

Off duty, one of my regular stopping-off places was at a motorcycle shop in West Wickham, situated on a superb site at the junction of Glebe Way and Wickham Court Road. The owner was none other than John Surtees, the World Motorcycle Road Racing Champion. John also became Formula One Motor Racing World Champion. His brother, Norman, ran the shop whenever John was away racing.

John Surtees

One day, I spied a brand-new BSA DBD34 500cc Gold Star Clubman racing motorcycle, which was on display in the showroom. This machine was fitted with all the extras which would be necessary to compete on the racetrack; even down to the rather special RRT2 close-ratio gearbox. (RRT2 signified that the gear-box shafts ran on needle-roller bearings). This bike stood resplendent in the window on the Glebe Way side of the shop. Around the corner on the Wickham Court Road side, behind another showroom window, was a second-hand Vincent Series C Rapide, the same year of manufacture and identical to my own. The BSA was for sale new, priced at four-hundred and twenty-two pounds and a few shillings. The Vincent was offered at the price of one-hundred and twenty pounds.

The dream of motorcycle racing was becoming clearer in my mind and a 'Goldie' to me was the obvious first step as I sought its fulfilment. Managing the shop on this particular day was John's father, Jack Surtees. As I soon discovered, he was a dealer of the old school. To make the finances work, I felt that if Jack would give me say £100 for the Vin, I could manage to raise the rest to buy the BSA. His response was less than encouraging.

'You can have sixty quid and that's it.'

Hang on; buy at £60, sell at £120? Someone is after a one hundred percent profit on that one! So, disappointed, I jumped on the Vin and rode home.

A week or so later, there I was once more, peering through the window at *my* 'Goldie'. Suddenly, standing beside me was John Surtees himself, dressed in a smart business suit. He was soon acquainted with my wish to have the Clubman BSA.

'Trouble is that your dad would only give sixty for my Rapide and there's no way I can make it work at that price,' I said.

'Let's have a look at it then.' said the boss. He swung his leg over my beloved Vincent, kicked it easily into life and was gone down Corkscrew Hill in his best business suit. Ten minutes later, having completed a circuit, John appeared along Glebe Way; smoothly drew to a halt and with eyes streaming as a result of the crisp run out said, 'OK, did you say that you needed £100? That's alright with me.'

As the deal was completed, we chatted and yes, even world champions are gentlemen. As we chatted, I learnt that John had developed his engineering skills at the Vincent factory. He thus knew more than most guys about Vincents and what made them rattle. On that day, I recall he filled me in on one problem from which the standard Vincent needle-roller bearing big-end suffered. At high revolutions, the needle roller bearings would skid rather than roll, bunch up, and try to twist, with the result of a seized-up engine. Thus, the racing Vincent Black Lightning was fitted with caged roller big end bearings. I was slowly learning. Also, I was aware that the Vincent works were established in Stevenage, Hertfordshire, well north of London. As Mr Surtees commuted daily on a Vincent, between Kent in the South and Stevenage in Hertfordshire, he must have known the fast route!

So, Bailey was moving closer to the bottom rung of mounting the racing ladder. Walking the beat meant simply that you were a police 'peace' officer. Walk, watch, listen. Keep the peace. Seek to prevent crime; help anyone who needed assistance and act when crimes were being committed or if the peace was being disturbed. One got to know the ground fairly intimately. One day posted on 14 beat, wandering through Canning Cross, which wound round behind the George Canning Public House, I found one of the lock-up garages open. A couple of guys were working inside. One of them, a tall slim bespectacled gent, I discovered was George Hopwood. The other, a fair-haired, handsome fellow was called Peter Butler. They were both motorcyclists. George owned a 650 Triumph Bonneville and Peter an AJS CSR Sports Twin. The Bonneville, I later learned, was an Ex-Eric Oliver Thruxton Five Hundred Mile Race machine. The three of us began a real friendship which has continued to this day with George. But sadly, when Peter passed away, having been struck down with Leukaemia, we all felt the loss of a friend, great sportsman, and regular guy.

The BSA Gold Star had replaced the beloved Vincent and covered many road miles both at home and abroad. Sadly, however, poor handling and an out of true front brake drum were evident and serious engine vibration was one of its main weak points. During a holiday touring through Europe, the beast finally cried enough in the middle of Freiburg and had to be ferried back to the UK and returned to the BSA factory. The management at BSA failed to honour any warranty or accept the slightest responsibility for the faults with their product, on the grounds that it was *a Clubmans Racer* and that I had used it on the public roads. When asked what warranty would be given if it *was* used on the racetrack as a 'Clubmans Racer', the response was that it would not be warranted because I would have been racing it. Needless to say, legal minds were brought in and the ammunition of Birmingham Small Arms proved to be ineffective.

My solicitor, incidentally, was named Peter Clarke. As a member of The Glider Pilots Regiment, in 1944 he had flown a glider into Arnhem and knew a bit about 'doing battle.' As an afterthought, one was beginning to live through and experience just why the British motorcycle industry had apparently *taken its eye off the road to the market* and had begun to lose out to those foreign piano manufacturers (Yamaha), who built two-wheeled products, for the customer, rather than to suit their own traditional ways. During a later visit to the BSA factory, where I was greeted by a friendly senior management person, I queried why the factory had adopted such a silly after-sales stance regarding their thoughts on *when is a warranty not a warranty*. The view was expressed that Gold Star riders were of the 'leather jacketed' type. My response was that surely the warranty policy had little to do with the style of the jacket which the buyer was wearing, as he stood *cash in hand* at the till. It didn't matter whether he wore a leather jacket or a policeman's helmet; the money was just the same. Awkward silence and departure for home. I became aware that, sadly, in the early sixties, the British motorcycle industry was beginning to lose its market. It appeared that the customer was not important. The customer seemed not to matter. One began to appreciate why some folks become campaigners.

My dream of racing was still burning bright and to fill the gap, as the BSA was brought back to life up there in Birmingham, John Surtees sold me a brand-new Triumph T20S Tiger Cub with a power unit of a mere 199cc. These Tiger Cubs were a versatile machine and were used in a variety of guises in motorcycle competitions. The T20S was a model designed for Trials (mud plugging) competitions. Therefore, my new machine would need some modifications to be applied if it was to take to road racing. The Midlands contact, met previously at

Lambeth Magistrates Court, as we know was connected with the well-known Triumph Specialist A. Bennett of Nuneaton. Their motto: *'The Authority on Triumphs'.* They supplied me with a set of close-ratio gears to convert the gearbox to road racing specification. The complete set of gearbox parts with the addition of a new front wheel spindle came to the grand total of seven pounds five shillings and sixpence! Written in ink alongside the total cost was the word 'approx.' Written at the foot of the bill was a note:

I understand that you are competing in The Southern 100. May I wish you every success. Always willing to help.

Yours faithfully, A. Bennett.

What a privilege it was and remains, that there were many folks, some complete strangers, who were prepared to sponsor young dreamers as they sought to realise those dreams!

I was able to purchase the appropriate racing camshaft and the motorcycle, with various modifications, began to take on its road racing identity. Peter Turner, who owned the cycle shop in Church Road just round the corner from The Crystal Palace racetrack (and was the son of the local undertaker), used his skill to 'gas flow' the cylinder head. What this means is that the fuel/air mixture will enter, burn and exhaust from the combustion chamber more efficiently, thus improving the performance of the engine. George and Peter had to listen to my chattering on about going down to Brands Hatch, our local motor racing circuit, on a Wednesday practice day, spending a fiver on an afternoon of riding around the course. I would ride the Cub down to Brands, fit a larger main jet into the newly fitted Amal Carburettor, remove the silencer and fit the factory-supplied exhaust pipe extension.

Both George, with his Triumph, and Peter, aboard his CSR, came down to Brands one afternoon and we all had several sessions blasting around the circuit in the company of *real* racers. George decided that preparing and tuning the machine was more his scene, whereas Peter clicked! The rest, as they say, is history. Peter A. Butler became one of the top-line Production Machine racers of his day. In later years I was able to beat him to the finishing line, but only once! George (GAH) became and is still renowned as one of the best Triumph motorcycle builders/tuners/preparers around the place.

Returning to my 'day/night' job, in the days when the man on the beat looked for leadership, several skippers (Sergeants) and guv'nors stood out. At Camberwell, we had one particular Station Police Sergeant. The SPS rank was recognised by the three chevron stripes surmounted by a crown on each uniform upper sleeve. The Station Police Sergeant was one step below the rank of Inspector. He had passed the exams and the two inspector pips on his shoulder would be next. This SPS, Ray Anning, was *a policeman's policeman*. He'd been there, done it and had they existed, 'worn the t-shirt'. One cold night duty, whilst patrolling, the SPS tiptoed into a card school-being conducted by some of the chaps, in a place where no sergeant would have thought of looking (the boiler room underneath the Odeon Cinema at the junction of Denmark Hill with Coldharbour Lane). Been there, done that – if you know what I mean?

The only station based mobile police units on our sub-division in those years comprised the Area Wireless Car (L2), the station police van (Morris Commercial), with bench seats running down the sides of the bodywork, the general-purpose GP car (Hillman Minx), and the beat cyclist.

On our relief, Len Blake was the pilot of this powerful gent's pedal-powered law enforcement machine and his was the only wheeled form of transport at our nick. The motor-powered units already referred to were based up the road at Peckham (LP). It was decided by those in charge that the speed and efficiency of Camberwell nick would be enhanced by the be allocation of a Beat Duty Motorcycle Patrol.

In the early sixties, the machines used were LE Velocettes, fitted with 192cc water-cooled horizontally opposed flat twin-cylinder side-valve engines. The motorcycle was constructed from a one-piece pressed aluminium frame, with leg shields integral with the main bodywork, a windscreen and metal pannier boxes. The power was delivered through a shaft drive to the rear wheel and the earliest models had a three-speed hand lever operated gearbox. Very well silenced, these machines could trundle about the streets almost unheard and seemed to fit the bill quite well.

As of yet, the wonders of radio communication were not thought necessary for the beat duty motorcycle rider, which in earlier days in outer London areas had been 500cc Triumph 5T Speed Twins. His uniform headwear was the peaked forage cap. The rider still carried his 'issue' whistle on a chain with key, truncheon and torch attached (if he went out after dark).

The Velo rider now was issued with a safety helmet which appeared to be identical to his mate on foot duty but was more robustly constructed to give more protection. The Noddy rider was issued with a heavy-duty motorcycle Macintosh in case it came on to rain. A Great Coat (British warm) was issued to be worn, should the temperature drop. These strange-looking machines soon became known as 'noddy-bikes' – Enid Blyton, please note.

It was quite a thrill for young Bailey to be selected with some of his mates to go on a 'noddy course' to the place, which to drivers in 'the job' seemed to be the centre of the universe; Hendon Motor Driving School (MDS).

The three-week course, having commenced in the 'class-room' with all the theory stuff, then progressed to Hendon Aerodrome, just across the road from the Driving School. You will be aware that today this former RAF Aerodrome is the home of the RAF Museum.

As part of our training, on the first day out on the road, the squad of riders had to walk the bikes across the Aerodrome Road into the airfield, just to get the feel of the weight and balance of a dead motorbike.

We were soon given the lowdown on riding slowly, changing gear and manoeuvring at slow speed. Then we were allowed to ride up and down the runway to get the feel of things. Soon, becoming bored with this seemingly basic stuff, the young ace from Camberwell sorted himself out a little circuit using part of the perimeter track and went off on his own.

Len Chatterton, one of the Sergeant Instructors soon focused upon the errant tearaway away in the distance, slid alongside on his Triumph 5T and enquired as to my movements in the vicinity. He began advising, in very basic English, on my future driving plans.

Bailey obediently re-joined the party. Something about discipline, I think. Having duly qualified as a top student on the course, scoring equal points with a sergeant, ended the first of many great experiences at Hendon.

Back at Camberwell, it was around 1:00 a.m. one cold winter night-duty. I was posted on the noddy bike and as I walked into the Front Office to report the outcome of an errand I had recently completed, I noticed that my SPS was seated at the front office desk, deep in conversation with a young lady standing at the counter.

She was dressed in a blue, light summer coat. The pallor of her face was blue with the cold, almost matching the colour of her coat. She was clearly in some distress.

'462! This young lady is locked out of her flat. Her husband is inside with someone else, we think. Will you go and let her in please?' He asked. 'I'll send her along with Charlie in the GP car, OK?'

'Yes, Sarge,' I replied.

He looked straight at me and said no more. Yet, I was aware that there existed, in the unwritten books of knowledge, one law known as the *Ways and Means Act*.

The look in his eye confirmed its authority and indicated it was of necessity that I clearly understood and applied that particular set of rules.

After a quick ride along Camberwell New Road in the direction of Kennington Oval, I then parked the bike up and soon found myself checking the location of the lady's home. It was situated on an estate comprising blocks of LCC flats (London County Council). I soon discovered that, fortunately, she lived in a ground floor flat in one of the blocks.

A quiet walk around and some gentle investigation (remember checking the shop doors for security?) revealed that a sliding sash-chord window had not been fully secured. Gently lifting the lower section and climbing over the bath, which had thoughtlessly been built directly below the window, I stole silently in my sized nine boots from the bathroom, then went across the hall and quietly opened the front door to let the dear lady in.

My attention had been drawn to a securely closed door, just off the hallway, which led into a room from which emanated muffled sounds of joyful satisfaction.

Opening it, I noticed that Hubbie looked up from his diligent activities with some surprise.

'Good evening mate, just to let you know that your wife has come home,' I said.

PC Bailey then left through the now opened front door and rode back to the nick, reporting my visit to my Station Sergeant and recording the result on the message pad in the reserve room, with a note attached 'NCPA' (No Further Cause for Police Action).

The next night, Inspector 'Timber' Woods, the Duty Officer, took me to one side and in serious, supervisory and sombre tones informed me that the husband of a lady in a flat off Camberwell New Road had made a complaint against the police for breaking and entering his flat the previous night.

'This complaint against you will be investigated!' He said.

A week or so later, the same inspector, with some difficulty but seemingly with grace, informed PC Bailey that no further action was being taken about the complaint.

My response to this kind *No Further Action (NFA)* was, 'Thank you, Sir. I lost a lot of sleep over that!'

One of the *Primary Objects of an Efficient Police Force* calls for a peace officer, where necessary to adopt 'tact and conciliatory methods' and I felt that one of the requirements of the *Ways and Means Act* had been fulfilled that cold winter night.

My SPS, Ray Anning, was a truly straight-up honest 'copper's copper'. You will go a long way with a good leader. He later became commissioner of the Royal Hong Kong Police Force. That too is another story.

9

Approaching the start line

As a young Christian, I felt quite convinced that racing motorbikes on a Sunday did not set a good example for anybody.

To say one thing, to claim to believe something, then to live what appears to be a contradiction, as in, to do something to *contradict* that claim, seemed pretty pointless. After all, there were six days in the week to do whatever I liked, but surely Sunday was a day to remember and worship the God who loved me that much that he sent his Son Jesus Christ to die on a cross for my sins and the sin of the world.

I can hear you saying, 'Well that is a *naff* idea that falls flat. You being a copper and all, having to work on Sundays! Get out of that, matey!'

One is reminded of the event recounted in the Bible (Matthew Ch.12). Jesus went into the Synagogue and healed a man who was sick. It was the Sabbath. The Pharisees (the top guys in the Synagogue) really took Jesus to task for what they held was an unlawful act.

His response was, 'If any of you has a sheep and it falls in a pit on the Sabbath, will you not take hold of it and lift it out? How much more valuable is a man than a sheep? Therefore, it is lawful to do good on the Sabbath.'

OK, so there weren't many sheep loose on Camberwell Green on a Sunday, but there were always plenty of folks who might need me to be around the place, as a copper. The local villains didn't take weekends off either!

After numerous practise days at Brands Hatch and having secured my Motorcycle Competition Licence from the Auto Cycle Union (ACU) the motorcycle sport governing body; on August Bank Holiday Monday 1961, I entered for the 250cc race at the motorcycle race meeting to be held at Crystal Palace, as you recall, just down the road from where I lived.

The 'Goldie' was still nowhere-near ready for use and so my little modified Tiger Cub would be the 'debut' machine and was going to try to *growl* at 220cc Desmo Ducatis and similarly high-performance *real* racing bikes in the chosen event.

Come race day, my fairly recently purchased £5 set of racing leathers were bundled up and stuck atop the petrol tank. The box of tools was lodged on the seat and the Tiger Cub began its walking pace journey under 'one person power' from my home in Beulah Hill, along Church Road and down the slope of Anerley Hill into the circuit.

One of John Surtees' mechanics from the shop in West Wickham had kindly come along to give this *racing person* a hand and some moral support. I had always been a fan of John Surtees, so copying the basic design of this helmet, mine was similarly painted but with red markings rather than John's blue striping. In addition, I had added the BMCRC badge and the logo of my favourite machine, the Vincent.

A few years later, as the pudding basin helmet was replaced by the 'space helmet', the design was modified adding the flowing design worn by the great Swiss sidecar ace, Florian Camathius.

As I recall, practice went fairly smoothly and come race time, with the drop of the starter's flag, young Bailey set off in a roar of noise and exhaust fumes, each rider seeking to 'out' accelerate his fellow competitor.

Crystal Palace as a racing circuit was an exciting place to be, particularly on my first race day. More so because, for a number of years, having sat and watched with amazement stars of two, three and four wheels competing on this circuit, I was now *actually* doing it myself, following in their wheel tracks. Only 1.39 miles in length, but filled with twists, turns, climbs and descents.

Today we are made so conscious of how rider/spectator safety on racing circuits has improved with run-off and vast 'no go' areas. The problem with Crystal Palace is that The Palace estate is set on the side of a hill and the builders of the Nineteenth Century hadn't considered that one-day motor vehicles would be racing about the place! Thus, they had not left much room for safety run-offs to be 'built-in' to what were then avenues and pathways.

So, it was a matter of either not falling off or being aware of the railway sleepers, trees and concrete walls which lined the track. But that was what road racing was all about and so, very early in my motorbike racing days, one was subconsciously becoming aware of and preparing for the potential dangers which would be faced in days to come, when this dreamer began attempting to fulfil the seemingly impossible fantasy of riding around a mountain set on an island in the Irish Sea!

Oh, yes. The 250 race.

The twitch of the gentle left and sudden tightening right turn at North Tower bend came and went, followed by The

Glades, a twisting rush through trees and undergrowth with little room for error.

Round the right-hander of Park Curve and down the steep drop of New Link onto what had during my early visits been the start and finish strait.

At the end of the strait, we all rushed towards Ramp Bend, a right-hander with an uneven and tightening radius and a high concrete wall on the outside.

Not an inch of space for any mistakes here!

Then followed the Anerley Ramp and the twisting climb up Maxim Rise, towards the right-hander of South Tower Bend which took us onto the top strait. This was now the start and finish strait.

How many, if any, laps Bailey managed to complete cannot be recalled. Suffice to say that he recorded a DNF (did not finish) on the results sheet. The ignition system on The Cub comprised a cylindrical tube-shaped contact breaker/distributor assembly which was set into and protruded vertically from the timing chest on the right side of the engine. This unit supplied the essential sparks to fire up and run the engine. To achieve the correct ignition timing, it was necessary to rotate this unit in a clock or anti-clockwise direction and then to lock the unit in the correct position with the long screw/pinch bolt recessed in the timing cover.

At some stage, this screw either came loose or fractured, the timing shifted as the unit rotated, oil began to pump from the screw hole and the motor ran out of steam! It was the end of Bailey's great debut and he set off on what seemed to be an even longer push to get back home!

As you will already have been made aware, the racing bug had bitten deep. Several months before my 'debut' at The Palace, having dreamed about it for many years, I had actually travelled to the Isle of Man for the 1961 TT (Tourist Trophy) Races. This event is held in late May, early June and has taken place every year, from when it was established in 1907, except for the years of the two devastating World Wars.

The BSA Gold Star was still lying *somewhere* in the BSA factory, awaiting treatment for its ills (the repairs having been prompted by the legal efforts of my former Glider Pilot Regiment pilot and Morris Mini racer, Peter Clarke).

My transport for the journey up to Liverpool and throughout the holiday, of necessity, had to be the faithful Tiger Cub. A great deal of preparation had already been undertaken to turn this would-be trials bike into a road racing machine.

The footrests, footbrake and gear levers had been mounted further back on the machine and suitable dropped handlebars had been added so that the proper racing ride position could be adopted.

You will recall that the engine had been prepared and fitted with a high lift racing camshaft and close-ratio gears. To help the engine breathe more efficiently, the cylinder head had been 'gas flowed' and a larger Amal carburettor now replaced the standard unit.

As I set off for my great adventure to The Island, it had not been possible to obtain the high compression piston needed to make full use of the various engine modifications. And so, the Cub had to be run using the standard, low compression (trials) piston. I was not sure just how well this little bike would perform on the long run-up to Liverpool, the port of departure for the Isle of Man Steam Packet Company ferry. But amazingly, it flew along, gobbling up the A5 and A41 highways with ease.

The time spent on that beautiful island was a completely new experience. My eating and sleeping arrangements had been booked earlier, thus, I was to be based in a pleasant household in Douglas, the main town of the Isle of Man.

My Hostess was the wife of a retired Isle of Man Constabulary Police Sergeant who was, at that time, employed with the harbour authorities in Douglas.

Various other racing enthusiasts were also staying at this address and one of them in particular, looked down his nose at the fellow who was riding a mere Triumph Tiger Cub. His disdain was heightened because the little machine was dressed up to look like a racer. He was a Velocette owner, after all!

As I explored the island, it was soon clear that this was a place of great beauty, with sandy beaches, coves, steep cliffs down to the sea, narrow glens through the hills and a central moorland area where one could hear the enchanting call of the curlew.

The highest point of this area was the mountain named Snaefell (the Norse name is Snow Fell). Snaefell, at 2034 feet, could be clearly seen from many points around the island, when it was not shrouded in mist. From the summit, it was said that you could see six kingdoms: the Kingdoms of Man, England, Wales, Scotland, Ireland, and the Kingdom of Heaven.

Quite a wonderful place to visit, where one seemingly could almost reach out and touch these different parts of Britain and Ireland. They seemed so close.

Thus, the TT circuit was known as 'The Mountain Course'.

The TT racing course I discovered, ran around the island and circled The Mountain along public roads for thirty-seven and three-quarter miles. Watching the various races, one was amazed at the speeds at which the riders were travelling over these 'ordinary' roads, some steeply cambered with pavements, high curbs, roadside lamp posts, stone walls, and all sorts of hazards to negotiate.

Could I, would I, ever be able to compete in this place?

The racing bug had bitten deep and even to compete in any motorcycle race was still in the future; yet here I was, dreaming about riding in the TT! Therefore, of course, it was necessary to ride around the circuit, as it were, to *learn the course*, to find exactly what it was like from the riders' point of view. You never know, the knowledge might be of use *someday*.

Needless to say, to obey the speed limits, abide by the law, and keep to the correct side of the road, meant that one could never really gain what the competing racers' eye view of the circuit would be at racing speeds. They were able to use the whole width of the road and straighten out single bends, or more importantly, find the best line through series of bends, which put ordinary *open road* mortals at a bit of a disadvantage. Nonetheless, I thoroughly enjoyed this new experience of riding along what was a genuine road racing circuit as fast as I considered was safe.

One afternoon, having set off from where the race start line was situated on the Glencrutcherry Road above Douglas, moving off just ahead was a Velocette with a rider and pillion passenger. These two folks were dressed in what was then recognised as *European* motorcycle gear. They wore plain white crash helmets with a slightly darker coloured strip running around the base. We rode almost as a team, never having even met or spoken to each other, yet following the same route as we travelled along the course. Needless to say, the Velocette, which was a 500cc Venom, even two-up had more *get up and go* than my little 199cc Tiger Cub.

The rider of the Velo clearly knew his way around the course, but using his apparent knowledge as my guide, I was able to stay with him. We shared an enjoyable and fairly quick ride around the whole of the TT circuit. The Cub showed an impressive turn of speed and with its lower compression ratio had pretty good pulling power and acceleration from low engine speeds.

Arriving back at the start and finish point of the TT circuit, having propped our bikes up on their side stands, we got into a friendly conversation. I discovered that the rider was Rudolf Glaser, a German motorcycle championship racer who had quite a record on various European racing circuits, including DDR 500cc Solo Champion for the three years from 1957 to 1959. He graciously complimented me on my ability and the performance of the little Tiger Cub.

Suitably encouraged and perhaps with more confidence in my own ability than was due, on the evening before the Wednesday racing programme I set off from Douglas along the course in the opposite direction from that followed by the racers. Leaving Hillbury Corner and climbing towards the Mountain part of the circuit, the plan was to look for a good place from which to watch the Junior Race (350cc) the next day.

Most of the route from Douglas was a long steady climb.

As I approached the left-hand turn at Creg-Ny-Baa full of confidence (if I were racing it would have been a fairly tight dropping right-hand turn), I swept into the bend, cranked the bike over and proceeded to demonstrate my riding skills to the many motorcyclists enjoying their evening, standing outside the Creg public house.

Sadly, the bend, which was a climbing turn, tightened up and Bailey found himself running out of road.

He clouted the bank on the right side of the bend and ended up in a heap on the floor.

The Tiger Cub bounced across the road and thumped a stationary BSA Bantam, which had been leaning innocently and inoffensively against the opposite bank.

Somewhat dazed, still spread-eagled on the road, I spat two broken teeth into my gloved hand, focused my eyes and saw immediately in front of me two pairs of shiny black boots. From a lying position on the road, it became evident that the wearers of the boots were a Constable of the Isle of Man Constabulary and his Supervising Sergeant.

They asked me who I was and requested to see my driving documents. No enquiries were made as to my physical condition and although I didn't even know what time of day it was, I then stood there and supplied the pieces of paper which were required. Among other items kept safe inside my driving licence was my membership card for the Metropolitan Police Motor Club (MPAA Metropolitan Police Athletics Association).

'Oh, so you are from the Metropolitan?' They asked.

I replied in the affirmative.

Once the details had been recorded from the documents, they were returned, and I was left to my own devices.

At that moment, having bashed my head on the ground, I didn't really know where I was, what time of day it was; even that I was on the Isle of Man, *where I was to go from here,* wherever this place was?

Eventually, things came together and deflated, Bailey eventually made it back to his digs. A somewhat second-hand Tiger Cub was restored to my possession and the now toothless owner sat and licked his wounds.

Two days later, a summons was served for Bailey to appear at the High Bailiff's Court in Douglas on Saturday morning. Aware of my predicament, the dear hostess at the digs advised me to visit the police station down in Douglas and seek an audience with the Chief Constable, being sure to tell him that I was a guest of her husband one of his former loyal Sergeants.

The visit was made; I guess that the Chief Constable had better things to do, and thus, a conversation with a lowly Chief Inspector took place.

I was asked whether I was going to plead 'guilty' or 'not guilty' to the offence of Dangerous Driving. My response was that a plea of not guilty would be made because it was felt that a defence could be offered. More importantly, the young copper standing before him could see any future career in the Met Police being at an end. My job depended upon it!

His response was, 'Then you had better go and find yourself a good Advocate!' Interview terminated.

I exited the police station and wandered the town looking for a *good Advocate.*

As I recall, on a Friday, traditionally the Senior TT (500cc) race day saw your scribe wandering along Athol Street in Douglas, where I discovered a solicitor's office opposite the Courthouse. Here an interview took place with the solicitor where I recounted my sad tale, making the point that my job could be on the line.

At the end of some discussion, the legal gent suggested that he crossed the road to the Courthouse where he could speak to the Court Inspector.

Some minutes later, upon his return, I was advised that a 'plea of guilty' to Careless Driving would be accepted by the court and that although it would be required for me to attend the court, I would not be called to enter the witness box.

The Bailiff duly fined me the sum of ten pounds and gave me *time to pay*. My driver's licence was to be endorsed to the effect that I had been found guilty of Careless Driving.

One had to acknowledge the quick service, which was made available to those of us who misbehaved on the public roads of the Isle of Man. The legal process was conducted in such a way that any wrongdoer would be well and truly *sorted out* before the ferry, which would take him back to the mainland, left Douglas Harbour.

This ended my first memorable and mainly enjoyable visit to the Isle of Man. It must be said that the boss of Gilbert Harding, the main motorcycle emporium in Douglas, had already rolled up his sleeves, gone into the workshop and straightened out the bent front forks by skilful use of a bench press and a set of rollers. Mr Harding didn't even charge this silly person much for his efforts.

So, this young would-be-racer returned home; his circumstances straightened in more ways than one!

It was back to the grind, walking the streets of Camberwell. My dream had always been of exchanging, walking the beat, wearing a pointed hat for the much more interesting job of becoming a Traffic Patrol. Because the police force was a disciplined organisation, one of the requirements of the Discipline Code was that, should any legal process be entered against a police officer, the officer must declare the matter to his senior officer. Thus, before many weeks had passed, 462L *stood on the carpet* at Brixton police station in front of the Chief Superintendent.

In those days, the Chief Superintendent was the senior officer in charge of a Metropolitan Police Division.

He sat and listened to my tale of woe and in so many words confirmed that I had been a bit stupid to fall off my bike at the feet of officers of the Isle of Man Constabulary.

His formal gentle 'choking off', however, was made easier to take when the guv'nor made the passing observation that he was aware that when a Met officer travelled out into one of the Constabularies (that is, a police force out of London), he would be 'fair game' as far as any Constabulary was concerned.

Being made aware of the ambition to become a Traffic Patrol and concern that my recently acquired driving record would *put the mockers* on that plan, the Chief Superintendent observed:

'Of course, things might be slowed down a bit.'

So, there it was, the awareness that *you've messed up, son. You'll just have to wait and see and learn from your stupidity.*

An interesting tailpiece to this story was that my driving licence was never endorsed for the offence committed in the Isle of Man because, at least in those days, the endorsement by a Manx

Court could not be attached to an English driving licence. Breathe again!

Years later, as a Sergeant at Brixton nick and chatting to a colleague who had served in the armed forces during the Second World War, it was discovered that there was a *history* between the Met Police and the Isle of Man Constabulary.

During those years, The Island was a place to which Aliens had been sent. There were certain restrictions in place upon the movements of Aliens, which to a degree, some of those temporary visitors to the island had been able to circumvent. Maybe a weekend trip on the ferry to the mainland. This had necessitated the Home Office sending a group of police officers from the mainland to take over and supervise 'travel' and other arrangements.

This detachment, it would seem, comprised Metropolitan Police officers. Had your scribe been aware of this when he rode his bike down to the feet of the local law enforcement officers, he would have been aware of the irony in the rhetorical question, 'Oh, so you are from the Metropolitan?'

My racing season post-Crystal Palace progressed with rides wherever I could find them.

In August I had a ride on the Club Circuit at Silverstone when Bemsee (British Motorcycle Racing Club) staged one of their club meetings. It rained and was rather damp!

By September, the Goldie had returned from its 'treatment' at the BSA factory in Birmingham and was entered in the Production Machine Race, again, a Bemsee event at Silverstone.

The Gold Star was conveyed to Silverstone on the sidecar

platform, alongside my newly acquired Norton 19S, a 600cc single-cylinder plodder. This was the Bailey racing transport. The Cub came along for the ride in the 250cc class. This little fellow was somehow shoehorned in alongside Chris Goodfellow, as he drove his car to the meeting.

Chris was a former RAF type who had done his National Service and, as with the other older coppers at Camberwell nick, had become a friend and was a fellow 'mucker-in'.

Production Racers were road-going machines, which had to be fitted with lights, silencers, registration plates and all the accessories necessary to make it street legal. No 'go faster' parts could be fitted unless they were catalogued for that machine by the manufacturer.

We enjoyed a great ride. The Goldie pulled well from 4,000rpm, red-lined at 7,000rpm (engine revolutions recorded on the rev counter) and was going well with good acceleration. Halfway through the race, along the Club Straight changing up through the box and into top gear, there came a sudden vibration through the footrests. The exhaust note increased massively and the engine now had to be kept at high revs because there was nothing at 4,000.

Nonetheless, we managed to secure second place in the 500cc class. The silencer, which on a Gold Star leaves the exhaust pipe into a megaphone shape and is then formed into a parallel cylinder finished with a tailpipe, had fractured (remember my concerns about vibration). I was left to complete a rather noisy race, running on an open megaphone!

Of course, the carburation would have been negatively affected and the motor would have run weak.

I was experiencing what was known a *megaphonitus*: reluctance to run at low engine speeds.

The organisers, thinking that I had 'engineered' the *mid-race modification*, disqualified Bailey from the results.

On reconsideration, having viewed the real evidence (oh, boy, I've heard that one before) of an actual metal fatigue fracture, they then re-instated the result and we returned home with a great result in what was my first season as a 'racer'.

10

Shift work plus

As my length of service in the job added up, observations of how things worked began to increase my knowledge of the world of policing. *Things worked;* matters not referred to in the Metropolitan Police 'Instruction Book' (I.B.) or Police General Orders (The G.O.).

One October morning I was posted as reserve 'coms man' (the Reserve Man, official title; Communications Officer) for the early turn shift. The duties of the coms-man comprised keeping on top of telephonic communications in and out of the nick at Camberwell, a Sectional Station.

The means of communication was simple: the telephone. Teleprinters were operated from Sub-Divisional and Divisional Stations. It was essential to keep a clear written record of who or what was being dealt with and ensuring that the Station Officer knew what was going on. At the appropriate time, the coms-man was responsible for making the tea and ensuring that the troops outside in the cold did not go thirsty.

Using the official title, the reserve man was simply just that; standing-by as a reserve officer as has been said, should *the wheel come off* out on the streets.

He was also responsible for looking to the welfare of any 'guests' resident in the cells situated on the other side of the charge room.

Having been posted, I went about the regular morning

task of giving the prisoners their breakfast, brought hot-foot from the canteen across the yard. One of the guys, who had been nicked for *putting in* a shop window the day before and committing one or two additional fairly minor offences, had planned ahead.

'Well, mate, I'm set for the winter. I'll probably get three months for this and will be in Wandsworth. I've got a mate in the kitchens, so I've got a job sorted in the warm.'

A *Plea of guilty has been entered in this case, your Worship*.

As I have already said, QED. Similarly, 'suspects' could be detected by CID officers and brought in for questioning, simply because they were resting on a bench in the middle of Camberwell Green without any fixed abode.

One day, a new posting was allocated to 462L. Street Betting, a 'one-month posting'.

I was to work with Mac, a former serviceman who had fought in the Far East. Mac had very clearly declared negative views about the men from the Orient who had opposed the Allies following the attack on Pearl Harbour in 1941.

We worked in plain clothes. On one day, Mac sent me off down a pathway behind the houses in Camberwell New Road. Our task was to detect and apprehend street bookies and book-makers, who in those days were conducting their business unlawfully (betting shops had not at that time come into being).

What was required was evidence that street betting was taking place. Evidence of a group of local citizens gathered around a gent who would have some cash and betting slips, which they had handed to him. We needed enough evidence to prove what he was up to and establish that his activities were unlawful.

Mac packed me off down the footpath with the instruction that 'he' would be found halfway along with all that was necessary for me to nick him.

A positive result followed the instruction dutifully obeyed; a good arrest.

As the weeks passed, my catch of 'bookies' increased, with Mac pointing the way down various back streets around the Camberwell area.

The bookies all seemed to come quietly without any real bother, except for one irate guy up a side street off Camberwell Road who was incensed that a 'bleedin' schoolboy' had been sent to nick him, but I *had* started to shave – honest, guv!

At Lambeth Magistrates Court, a *plea of guilty* was always entered, but I soon became aware that if a *plea of not guilty* had been entered, Officer Bailey would be struggling to prove his case beyond reasonable doubt.

The realisation dawned that I was being involved in *put-up* jobs, whereby the principal bookmaker, safely in his office someplace else, would put up a runner to 'carry the can' and thus keep the local constabulary off his back. 462L didn't need to apply too much further consideration to what was actually going on.

It was clear that I was being involved in something, which was not quite right; that someone, somewhere, was pulling the strings.

As a young Christian, the only recourse was to let them upstairs know how I felt. To 'tell the truth, the whole truth and nothing but the truth.'

It was well known that the *guv'nor's men* were about the place and that matters discussed in the canteen at grub time could easily reach an ear upstairs. So, as conversations took place and thoughts were exchanged with fellow constables, it was not long before a decree was issued for PC Bailey to attend the guv'nor's office at the Sub-Divisional Station in Peckham, a mile or so up the road.

The nick was in Queens Road, a couple of hundred yards from Rye Lane.

They say that good news travels fast. The Superintendent had passed my case one rank down to the Chief Inspector. Oh well, never mind, you might meet the Queen one day!

The CI was not impressed by my stand and expressed his views quite clearly. Another lesson learnt, but don't allow principles or beliefs to be shaken by finding the easy way out.

It's funny that several weeks later, 462L was again posted to bookies, but this time, working on Peckham's patch.

Duly kitted out in my 'civvies' gear, I began walking at a steady pace towards the targeted street betting site, around the back of Meeting House Lane. Then, silently, along came 'Nobby' Clark, the Skipper in charge of the bookies' team.

Slowing his gents' ped to a walking pace, he called, '462, you're back to ordinary duty!'

Well, there you are then; something about the left hand not knowing what the right hand is doing.

I was back on to uniform duty. Maybe *him upstairs* had forgotten to tell the Duties Sergeant till after the starter's flag had dropped, and I had been posted to Peckham.

Not being a student of the finer points of law and aware that there was nothing written about it in any official police publications, this observer came to realise that there were different types of processes when it came to law enforcement.

There were 'straight-up jobs', 'put up jobs': a bookies runner is waiting for you to arrest him. 'Set up jobs': for instance, where say a car is placed as bait for a thief to liberate for personal use. Then sadly there were 'fit-up jobs': to solve a crime by putting (moulding) someone into the frame as the guilty party.

Looking back, as life went on through my time in 'the job', it became apparent that there was often someone who wanted to make a name for himself or gain a position, and that often it was deemed essential to make a move or take an action, sometimes involving someone else, to achieve that goal.

In reality, in many walks of life in the great world outside, one can observe that similar moves are often made to gain power, riches, or recognition. I am not going to start preaching but a Police Officer is a *peace officer* serving the Queen and the duty is to keep the public peace and maintain law and order, without fear or favour.

My motorcycle racing life was beginning to take-off and for the whole of the 1962 racing season, whenever or wherever there was a race meeting that was not on a Sunday, I would send off an entry to compete in the 250cc class.

To qualify for an International Competition Licence, a rider with a National Licence would only qualify and establish his experience, if he had scored sufficient points in National Events. Until then, the competitor was restricted to Club or National competitions.

As a newcomer to the sport, that licence was a passport into the future.

The 1962 season began with a ride in the Easter Monday National race meeting at Crystal Palace. Over the winter, with the advice and help of my friend and ace race tuner George Hopwood, a number of improvements had been made to the faithful Tiger Cub. For instance, the front forks had been shortened to improve the weight distribution, balance and steering of the machine. The efficiency of the standard Tiger Cub front brake had also been improved.

The race, as I recall, was run on a wet surface. The advantage was that my Tiger Cub, with less power than many of the other machines, was not as handicapped as the more highly tuned and powerful bikes where the riders of which had to be more careful with the twist-grip throttle control in such conditions.

My Cub was also fitted with a very basic straight exhaust pipe, unlike the machines which ran with megaphone exhausts and this helped to give my engine more flexibility and torque than a more finely tuned engine. A newly acquired dolphin fairing completed the set-up.

The result, as I passed the flag at the end of the race, meant that the Cub earned me sixth place in the 250cc race and the princely sum of £3 in prize money.

Under the heading of work still to be done, advice was taken 'on board' from those more skilled in engine tuning than Bailey.

On one of my visits to John Surtees' shop in West Wickham, I was able to seek the advice of John himself.

'With a standard exhaust valve, you are going to be in big trouble,' he said. 'In serious competition and at sustained racing speeds, the standard exhaust valve will certainly overheat and 'drop in' *known colloquially as a blow-up*! (The valve head would detach from the stem). Get hold of a Nimonic 80 steel exhaust valve somewhere and machine it down to fit the Cub.'

He invited me to drop around to his house and he'd see what he could do.

At a later date, after a ride to his home in Foxley Lane, Purley and a tentative knock on the door, I found myself speaking to the World Motorcycle Champion on his doorstep.

Upon reminding John of his suggestion, he disappeared from the doorway and a few minutes later, re-appeared with a superbly engineered Manx Norton Nimonic 80 valve, brand new, and wrapped tightly in blue engineers waxed paper.

'Here you are. That should do you. I made it for my 350 Manx,' he said.

Fishing my wallet out of my pocket, I prepared to pay the price for this masterpiece of engineering.

John simply responded, 'No, It's yours. You wouldn't be able to pay what it cost.'

Have you ever been given something, which was of value and had cost a great deal to manufacture, *as a gift* that was really beyond your reach?

It should be admitted that the valve, which is such a beautifully machined and polished masterpiece of John's engineering skill, has remained hidden in my sock-cupboard to this day!

Once more, without seeking to be preachy, a reference to the Gospel of John Ch.3 v 16 reminds me of a gift that can't be paid for.

For God so loved the world that he gave His one and only Son,
that whoever believes in Him shall not perish but have eternal life.

Sometime later, Mr Surtees, having visited the USA, returned with a special aluminium cylinder barrel, made specifically to fit a Tiger Cub. The cylinder bore matched that of a piston used in the twin-cylinder 500cc Triumph 'Tiger 100'.

Needless to say, the Tiger 100 had two pistons, which answers your question, how can that work?

With the piston skirt suitably reduced in-depth, it would match the stroke of the Cub crankshaft and thus, the barrel could be fitted to a Tiger Cub and the bike's capacity would be increased to 239cc. More gee-gees on tap.

Following John's trip, this one-off barrel was featured and described in detail for the readers to study in *The Motorcycle* magazine.

Guess what? John later sold it, unused, and brand new to the young dreamer of a copper. John's price did not strain the Bailey bank account!

Mr Surtees later made available a superb Lyta aluminium petrol tank, which fitted the Cub perfectly.

Was it back door sponsorship?

To me, it was a reminder of what a great sport it was to be involved in, even for an impecunious dreamer of a novice racer, that even a World Champion would give one a leg up the ladder of ambition.

As I am putting these thoughts together, the world is mourning
the passing of the man known by many as 'Big John'. John Surtees

passed away on Friday 10th March 2017 and one is reminded of what a great man John was. No one has ever equalled nor probably ever will achieve his place as holder of both World 350cc, World 500cc Motorcycle and World Formula One Car Championships. In addition, he established and ran his own Surtees racing car construction operation. That same man quietly helped your scribe to realise a dream. I wonder how many more benefitted from his quiet 'get things done' approach.

In addition to being a member of BMCRC, I also joined the Bantam Racing Club and enjoyed race meetings organised by them at the Snetterton Circuit in Norfolk. The dream to 'do the TT' was always in focus and so an entry was secured to compete in the 250 race at the Southern 100 race meeting on the Billown Circuit outside Castletown in the Isle of Man. OK, so it's not the TT, but this might be the nearest that you'll ever get to it boy!

By now, the Bailey racing transport had been updated to a new Austin Mini pickup truck, bought new from Steele Griffiths, in Camberwell New Road (13 beat). VAT had not yet been invented, although purchase tax was well known. In the early sixties, 'commercial' vehicles were still sold without purchase tax being added to the price. Small but beautiful! I therefore now owned a new set of wheels with a 1000cc power plant. Full racing equipment could be carried; one bike or two, tools, a tent and cooking gear. My new Mini could also be used as everyday transport. Thus, equipped, *we did The Island. We* being one of the R/T Area Car drivers from Brixton nick, who was an outstanding trials rider, accompanied yours truly as spanner man.

The Billown circuit was a completely new experience because to race on what were public roads presented new skills to be developed. There were twists, bends, cambers on the road and varying surfaces, which one did not normally find on former airfield circuits or tracks that had been developed specifically for motor racing.

The first challenge, soon after one left the start line on an almost straight piece of road, which comprised a very fast downslope and uphill gradient, was a right turn that took the rider past stone walls, between a cluster of very substantial-looking buildings and on to a downhill swoop out into the country.

After a rapid descent through a series of high-speed bends past fields that were protected from us by roadside banking, one arrived at an acute, almost double back right turn, near the village of Ballabeg.

Riders then rushed past some roadside cottages and as I tried to learn the course, I realised what a new and challenging experience real road racing was going to present.

The required qualifying practice laps were completed the day before the race, on what I was by now well aware, a genuine road course!

On race day, the 250cc riders lined up for the start and at the drop of the flag, the field, they set off in a normal run and bump mass start, riding from set positions on the grid. Because the Cub, with its straight pipe and 239cc capacity, had plenty of low-down acceleration, unbelievably I was quickly up at the front of the field.

With the realisation that maybe this little Triumph was competitive, I was quickly getting stuck into the race but, as we rapidly approached the first fairly tight right-hand corner and I braked and changed down through the gears, the engine stopped and the Bailey transport coasted to an ignominious and silent standstill!

The race, my first race in the Isle of Man, was watched by a thoroughly disconsolate would-be racer, sitting on the wall among the spectators on the outside of the same corner. Yet, to the folks watching who gathered round, Bailey was treated as though he had achieved something great!

What is the cause of the engine crying enough? The pushrods had jumped off the cam followers and the valves had stopped going up and down! Had this boy-racer changed down through the box too quickly and over-revved the engine? I think so. Yet another of life's lessons, but this one had been abruptly underlined. Machine sympathy, sonny!

Various events followed as the season progressed and once again the Cub galloped at a couple of rides at Snetterton.

Dickie Fifield, a fellow police constable from Peckham nick, gave me a ride on his 50cc racing Itom. An amazing little racer. A two-stroke engine with a megaphone exhaust, three-speed handlebar gear shift and very narrow tyres! We had a good day out but I do not recall what results were achieved, except maybe ringing in the ears from the two-stroke's bee-like 'zinging'.

Working the beat with Dickie around Peckham was always a joy. He was very well-spoken and cultured in tone, thus it was a joy just to listen as he joined in any conversation. The greatest pleasure was when, as tended to happen out on the streets, one of the local lads gave Dickie a very basic mouthful of 'the verbal'! His response, always delivered with a *cut-glass* accent, using a range of vocabulary beyond the reach of many, generally left the vocal assailant speechless and Dickie's colleague laughing into his helmet!

The police officer was taught about the advantages of tact and conciliatory methods. Dickie had that by the helmet-full

I was happy to go anywhere to 'get a ride' and so when the opportunity came up to compete at the Barbon Manor Hill Climb, the entry form was rapidly despatched.

Barbon Manor is near Kirkby Lonsdale, Cumbria, in the north of England. The course, one of the shortest on the hill-climb calendar at only 890 yards, uses the original driveway to the Manor House. Chris Goodfellow, my fellow Camberwell officer (the former RAF type who, unlike Bailey, actually did his National Service) and I set off in the Mini pick-up for a long run-up to Barbon Manor. Chris was chief mechanic, tent erector plus cook and we were set for a great couple of days.

After Bailey had passed the test of having his police helmet stripped and *come good* in various other checks by the older guys at Camberwell, these men had become mates who would stand by you if things on the street got ugly. Yes, we even became friends. We competed with the Cub and having asked around the Paddock, I managed to secure a place as a sidecar passenger with Roger Willoughby. My task was to keep down the third wheel of his Vincent sidecar outfit. Although in practice, because I failed to get over the back wheel early enough and we climbed the bank on the last right-hander, he forgave me, and we secured a third-best time up the hill in the sidecar class.

11

At last, a real Trafpol

Eventually, after five years at Camberwell, in 1963 I was successful in being selected to become a Traffic Patrol officer. Traffic Patrol police officers, needless to say, were primarily employed on any duty involving traffic situations on the streets of the Metropolitan Police District. They dealt with road traffic accidents, (RTAs). This comprised damage only accidents (DOs), personal injury accidents (PIs), and fatal road traffic accidents (FATACCs). Other than that, they were trained to be specialists regarding traffic matters and the mechanics of motor vehicles. Yet they were still Police Officers and were as responsible as the foot-duty officers were for keeping the peace and enforcing the laws of the land.

'THE PRIMARY OBJECT of an efficient police is the prevention of crime: the next that of detection and punishment of offenders if the crime is committed. To these ends, all the efforts of police must be directed. The protection of life and property, the preservation of public tranquillity, and the absence of crime will alone prove whether those efforts have been successful and whether the objects for which the police were appointed have been attained.'

Sir Richard Mayne, 1829.

So, whatever branch or speciality department of the police force you were attached to, 'the primary objects' were the foundation of your service.

At the time that a new chapter in my life adventure was unfolding, a fully qualified Traffic Patrol Officer was colloquially referred to as a 'triple one'. He would be a Class One Advanced Motorcyclist, a Class One Advanced Car Driver and an Advanced Traffic Patrol. This final qualification was because the officer would have undergone and been successful in training regarding more technical and mechanical matters. Thus, an advanced traffic patrol would be termed 'a vehicle examiner' and be called upon to examine vehicles that had been involved in serious injury or fatal road traffic accidents (RTAs/FATACCs) to establish whether any fault or defect in any vehicle involved could have caused or been contributory to the accident.

Life's journey was continuing and another ambition was moved into the *ticked box*, police service-wise. It was the beginning of another adventure but with a great deal to learn.

Later in my traffic orientated life, the speciality of accident reconstruction became another skill I had to learn. Accident reconstruction was simply that; *to reconstruct*, using detailed evidence of damage to vehicles, roadside property, and road markings, to build up a picture of what had happened.

For instance, quite often a driver is too badly injured to help, the accident resulted in a fatality and or there were no witnesses as to what caused the accident. With the absence of a witness, the physical evidence: tyre/skid scuffing markings on the road, damage to the road surface relating to damage to a vehicle or vehicles involved could/would provide important information.

Before I could even commence duty as a Traffic Patrol, this lad needed to achieve some basic qualifications for this specialised department.

Another foot-duty mate and I attended Hendon Motor Driving School for a motorcycle test to assess our abilities. The man to check us out on the road was none other and the famous Sgt 'Bomber' Harris, a name revered in the police motorcycling/competition world.

Neither of us came up to the standard required by Sgt Harris to be authorised as police Traffic Patrol motorcyclists. Therefore, it was required that we would successfully complete a full Standard Motorcycle Course.

Speaking to the Traffic Patrol guys in the canteen at Camberwell, being made aware that 462L was soon off on the planned motorcycle training course, they quietly advised the lad to simply give 'a good steady ride' whenever he was out on a run.

'No need for fireworks,' they said. 'Then you'll be OK, son.'

Thus, at the end of February 1963, I again reported to Hendon MDS for Standard Motorcycle Course number 285. For three weeks, three squads of three young coppers were trained in the skills of riding a motorcycle to 'the system'.

The instructor on my squad was another one of those Sergeants, famous for their motorcycling exploits, not only on duty but also off duty, like 'Bomber', *cross country* and trials riders. His name was Len Farmer. A former RAF serviceman:

His initials were LMF! But that derogatory RAF term nowhere fitted Len.

Apart from the classroom work, basic slow rider training and obstacle course practice on the *school road*, there were plenty of 'long runs'. Here, the squads would cover considerable distances around the country during each day, all with Len sitting up close behind with his front wheel alongside the rear wheel of the leading rider. That way he could gain, as near as possible, the same view of the situation ahead that his student should be focusing upon.

Len would clearly see and note any rider errors. If the student was getting into a bit of bother, Len would be close enough probably to get him out of it; certainly, to thoroughly bend his ear afterwards!

Each member of the squad had his 'time up front', and there was no escape from Len's analytical attention. A suggestion was made that perhaps Bailey was a bit too steady and could have pushed on a bit harder. I managed to complete the course successfully and was established as a Standard Police Motorcyclist.

The remarks in the final report from Superintendent Max Newman stated:

'PC Bailey can now give a very sound brisk ride to the system. He has the right pattern and as this develops, he should be ready for advanced training after 10,000 miles. His Highway Code and Road Craft marks are disappointing for a prospective Traffic Patrol.'

Who's such a clever clog now? Plenty more work to be done yet, son, I thought to myself.

The System: Metropolitan Police 'Roadcraft'

The system of motorcycle/car control is a system or drill, each feature of which is considered, in sequence by the rider/driver at the approach to any hazard. It is the basis up which the whole technique of good riding/driving is built.

A hazard is anything that contains elements of actual or potential danger.

There are three main types:

Physical features, such as a junction, roundabout, bend, or hill-crest.

Those created by the position or movement of other road users.

Those created by variations in road surface or weather conditions.

So, there you have it. Keep to the system, son, and you'll be alright.

1967 On patrol in Lewisham: approaching 'The Mountain'
Courtesy of the Daily Express

12

A new season-a new experience

R. L. Knight, Ray Knight, was a motorcycle sports jour-nalist; a keen and skilled competitor who knew his stuff. Ray was supported by Stan Brand, of Hughes Motorcycles, a prominent Triumph motorcycle dealer in Wallington.

In the 'Club Racing' world, riders became friends and shared each other's ups and downs. Sometimes they even swapped parts, should a rider have broken something on his machine during practice.

Of the many and various machines, which he competed upon, Ray also owned and rode a Royal Enfield twin-cylinder machine, which was called The Red Plum. Ray and I became friends and many of us shared great times of social jollity at his home down in Kent. Yvonne his lovely wife, always laid on the goodies, so we never went hungry. Ray was *an Isle of Man person* and so the place often came into the realm of our chats as the fellows shared their dreams.

Around the tail end of 1962, I became aware that Ray and a Bemsee member, Pat, were playing about with a Matchless G45 500cc racing bike.

I seem to recall that one practice day at Brands Hatch, having been introduced to Pat, I was given a lap of the short circuit on, what to me was an amazing, genuine racing machine, not a souped-up road bike.

Most privately-owned racing bikes in the Junior and Senior Class were single cylinder 350/500 Manx Nortons, the 350 AJS 7R and single cylinder matchless 500 G50s. The 125 and 250cc class had some more exotic two or four-stroke machines of Italian, Spanish, East/West German, or Czech manufacture. The British built offerings comprised one or two exotic one-offs specials but were mainly tweaked road bikes as per Tiger Cub or older pre-war racers which had been updated and made to go well. James, Royal Enfield, Greeves, and others began to manufacture some two-stroke racers, but we were at the beginning of this new era.

The G45, to me, was something else. It looked right with a big lump of a power plant, slab-sided fuel tank, narrowed at the rear to allow the rider to tuck his knees in and, neatly tucked in twin exhausts with reverse cone megaphones. The exhaust note was something else, and just a lap round Brands was an exciting new experience for the boy.

As things developed, Pat later produced an early post-war 350cc 7R AJS. 'See what you can do with this,' he instructed me.

The bike, which arrived was completely dismantled and I recall that it had a bolt-through fuel tank fixing, which indicated the earlier style 7R than that which was currently on the track. Most of the winter of 1962-63 was spent putting the Ajay together.

I recall that one day, having spent many hours very carefully assembling the twin leading shoe front brake, it was then fitted into the front wheel and spun on its spindle. It became clear to me, a skilled technician, that he/I had succeeded in assembling *a twin trailing shoe* front brake. As in, I had assembled it the wrong way round. Back to the drawing board, sonny, and next time think before you bolt I thought to myself.

As the 1963 racing season approached, the Cub was readied for the fray and my pudding basin crash helmet was exchanged for the new 'space helmet' style, which was going to give riders more head protection.

I still had the original set of one-piece leathers, purchased for £5, which were rather bulky but had to do the job. An outing at Snetterton on a rather cold day in March saw the Cub secure fifth place and the 250 class. A photograph from that event provides evidence that a heavy pullover was worn over the leathers to keep the cold at bay. It must be said that Snetterton, in Norfolk near the East Coast of England, could experience some cold winds blowing from the east off the North Sea.

The Easter Monday event at Crystal Palace approached. Pat produced a 350cc Manx Norton for me to enter in the race. Now, a Manx Norton is something else and quite a step up from a Tiger Cub. This particular bike had been the mount of Geoff Tanner, the man who had ridden to Junior 350 and Senior 500cc victories in the 1955 Isle of Man Manx Grand Prix!

To be given the use of such a bike with the pedigree of race winner in the 1955 Junior Manx Grand Prix; that was for real racers, not this dreamer boy. Maybe that mountain I had dreamed of conquering was developing into more than just a lively flash of imagination. Nonetheless, there it was. I turned up at the Palace, raring to go.

I recall that as the Norton was being readied in the paddock before practice for the race, the Castrol R vegetable-based oil had to be warmed up on a primus stove before it was poured into the oil tank. Racing machines were quite sophisticated and to even 'run-up' an engine with cold oil in the system was asking for trouble.

Practice went quite well and one was quickly aware that a Manx handled to perfection. It followed and held to the chosen line 'pin-point' so precisely. The 350 came on to the Mega at 4,000 rpm, the engine came alive, smoothed out and accelerated rapidly to the top of the rev band at 7,000 rpm, which then called for a quick upward change to the next gear.

When it comes to the race, the rider must be on the ball. He must place his machine in the correct place allocated on the starting grid.

Then the first gear needed to be selected and the machine pulled back in gear with the clutch engaged. Thus, the engine was pushing back against the compression of the piston (remember Jock trying to start the Vincent).

The rider usually stood on the left side of the machine, although some such as Ray, would stand on the right side. The bike would be resting on his hip. He would now apply his full body weight forward on the handlebars but with the front brake applied, so that at the drop of the flag and release of finger pressure on the front brake lever, the brake would be released and the machine should leap forward using the stored-up energy applied by the rider. The clutch lever would have been pulled in to disengage the drive.

As soon as the starter's flag was dropped, a quick hard running push, bounce side-saddle onto the seat, engage the clutch, the engine should spin, fire up and we should then be off!

While the machine was accelerating away, it was then necessary, having firmly placed your left foot on its rest, to swing your right leg over the seat to find that footrest, get flat on the tank and go for it. That's the way it was, folks!

What a machine. What a new experience. I was riding up against the best.

All went so well.

The left kink and tightening right turn into North Tower Bend came and went and the rush through the sweeps of The Glades which passed in a blur, down and through New Link, along the bottom straight and into the double right apex of Ramp Bend. What an experience of speed, noise, tempo and the atmosphere filled with the aroma of hot Castrol R.

All was going so well as we climbed through the twists up from Maxim Rise until the Manx thundered into South Tower bend, a quite severe right turn following the rapid approach. This bend required firm braking on the approach, and it was the first occasion on the lap that really heavy braking was required.

The Manx was neatly tucked in tight on the left side ready and following braking, was to be flicked right into the apex of this comfortably cambered bend.

As I held a straight line and went for the brakes, it became more than obvious that the Norton's front brake was nowhere near the standard required for racing speeds.

Practice, OK. Racing? No way!

It just was not up to the job.

Having failed to lose enough speed, I was forced offline.

The bike and the disappointed rider ran wide and completely

missed the apex. I, the rider of the machine, racing number 10, began thinking some fairly negative thoughts as I pushed on as hard as the lack of a decent front brake allowed.

The ride was an enjoyable experience on a machine with superb performance. To ride a Manx Grand Prix winning Norton was an experience that raised the dream to a whole new level of expectations for the future, and the Manx was so clearly in a different league from a tweaked-up Tiger Cub!

Sadly, however, upon my safe return to the paddock following the race, as I, the disappointed jockey recounted to his helpers the lack of an efficient braking experience, there was some coughing behind the hand and many apologies.

'We had been a bit worried about that!' They all said.

Another lesson I learnt. Thorough and complete machine preparation is essential, even on Easter Monday!

The next event for the Manx was to be at Aberdare Park in South Wales. This was a National event, organised by the Aberaman Motorcycle Club, with many top-line riders competing.

The Tiger Cub was entered for the 250 race and the Manx for the 350 event. Bailey, now equipped with his own racing transport in the form of the Austin Mini Pickup truck, was ready to go. The Cub was prepared, the Manx again made available for me (front brake having been sorted) and so, loaded with two bikes and tools, plus my tent, primus stove and other camping gear, the fairly adventurous trip to Wales commenced.

On arrival at Aberdare Park Paddock area, I found a good spot to set up. The tent was erected, and the food was prepared. A young local lad showed interest and promised to keep an eye on things while this fellow was out on the circuit.

As the winter of 1962-63 had been quite severe, the country road surfaces had been affected and in places, broken up by the cold conditions. Aberdare Park was simply just that, not a public road. In retrospect, it might be that the events which were to occur had some connection with poor weather and resultant road surface conditions; but I guess we'll never know.

There was little time to familiarise myself with the circuit, save to say that it was a fairly short lap.

I recall setting off on the first exploratory lap of practice. Part-way around the circuit the road climbed and took the rider into a climbing left-hand turn.

Suddenly, the Norton ran out of drive and was running wide, as in going straight on. Ahead of me was a solidly constructed and firmly bedded park bench built of a concrete vertical framework with a wooden slatted back and seat.

It was protected by several straw bales!

Bike and rider hit the bales which disintegrated, immediately coming into firm contact with the park bench.

I can still see the picture as I first saw the tree, ground, sky, then the tree again, but this time closer. Then another complete rotation of my body with final contact head-on with the mature and solid timber trunk.

On hitting the ground and attempting to stand, using my right hand and arm to push myself up, the amazing discovery was made that Bailey boy now had two right elbows which both folded, under bodily pressure.

The Marshals rescued this fallen rider from the track laid him gently on the grass and began to straighten out the crumpled, now ex-racer.

One of the experts from the St. Johns Ambulance first-aid team was quickly on the scene.

'Don' take his 'elmet off in case his head falls in 'alf!' He said in his clear South Wales accent.

Confident as to my future care, I relaxed in a messy heap and awaited further developments.

Outcome: fractured right radius and ulnar, with a smashed left heel/foot.

Lesson to note for future reference: never attempt to cartwheel at high speed from a fast-moving vehicle because the bits at the end of your flailing body tend to hit the ground hard before the main structure makes contact!

Later examination revealed that a stone had been thrown up from the track and lodged in the exposed primary chain so that when said stone arrived at the engine pocket, it wedged the chain, which then snapped. The drive thus disconnected and the bike took the 'straight ahead' route, rather than being powered through the bend. Well, that's what I was told but as I never saw the dear old Manx Norton again, these mechanical details were never confirmed.

The seven-mile trip ambulance to St Tydfil's Hospital in Merthyr Tydfil was far from comfortable because every undulation on the road surface transmitted its shock waves via the broken bones, trapped in the flesh of my arm, the ends of which rubbed together.

Arriving in the Orthopaedic Unit and settling into my place, I became aware of guys in a far worse state than myself. Welsh coal miners, one of whom had been trapped on a coal conveyor belt and suffered a horrible leg break. I recall that he had noted that the emergency pull-wire, normally running by the belt, had not been operating at the time. As I recall, it was not even in place! Something was said about future interest by the Miners' Union, but in those days, the magic term 'health and safety' had not been coined.

Five weeks were spent in that place. The local Constabulary was extremely helpful and hospitable. When my ever-patient mum arrived from London to check up on the boy, she was well cared for by the team at the local nick. One day, I recall a visiting police officer casually asked me what type of fruit I most enjoyed. Sometime later the local greengrocer walked into the ward dressed in his brown overall. It seems that he had been advised of my choice by the lads from the nick. He sincerely apologised that my favoured fruit was not in season but was nonetheless armed with a goodly supply of alternative flavours for the boy, which he *hoped* would suffice!

During my stay, I was visited by members of the Aberaman Motorcycle Club; total strangers who came to see how a fellow motorcyclist was getting on.

There is a camaraderie among motorcyclists, which stretches far beyond national and international borders. It must be admitted that the only face which I would and still recall after many years, was the beautiful black-haired young Welsh lady club member, dressed in a stunning white polo necked sweater. Talk about ways to help a young fella's recovery!

I was so impressed by the friendliness of the local law, Clubmen and fellow racers. Unbeknown to me, my bikes were sorted, the camp dismantled, everything was loaded onto my Mini pickup and taken back to my home, way down south near Crystal Palace.

Lying in a hospital bed, long before mobile phones had been discovered, communication with the outside world was restricted. As the surgeon and hospital staff spent their time fixing me up, the world outside became a distant place. Things went from one's mind as I replayed thoughts about current problems. Sadly, as time went by, saying thank you went 'by the board' under the heading of, sorry, but I forgot! I am ashamed to say that I can recall that the only 'proper' thanks I made were to one group of 'helpers', the local Constabulary. More about that later.

The surgeons attempted what was termed 'a closed reduction', where they tried to get the broken ends of the bones to line up without opening up the damaged arm. It was then necessary to go for an 'open reduction' procedure. This resulted in several titanium plates being inserted in the broken arm to secure the now aligned broken bones in position.

After five weeks of great care by the staff of St. Tydfil's Hospital and the many visits from a number of the friendly people of South Wales, the boy, accompanied by a charming St John lady, travelled by train back to London. There I became a resident at Westminster Hospital. Here, under the watchful, very caring and skilful eye of Sister Hutchings (known by many as 'The Hutch'), I was sorted out. This time the surgeons took some slivers of bone from my left hip and grafted it into the broken bones of my arm.

I learned that bones are 'sticky' at the broken ends and they mend if the broken ends *tack* and are held together. Bailey's tacky bits lost their qualities of adhesion too early in the recovery proceedings up in Wales, so it became necessary to resort to a more technical procedure.

How did I get to Westminster Hospital? My older sister, Joan, was a Staff Nurse at Westminster Hospital. She may have done a bit of *asking* on behalf of her little bruv!

There followed several weeks of convalescence down in the Kentish countryside per favour of the National Health Service. One day, on the ward, I received a telephone call from Les Wise (Les's wife Pat was a very competent racer on her own Velocette).

'Graham, where is the Norton?'

'I don't know, Les,' I replied. 'It was brought down from Aberdare after my off, but I haven't been told who these great mystery helpers are.'

'Well, the problem is that it is entered for our rider in the Manx Grand Prix. It's our bike and had only been borrowed for you to use. We need to find it and get it sorted,' he insisted.

Sadly, to this day, I never discovered the detail and outcome of that mystery. Nor for many years did I discover who the kind rescuers of my bikes and gear were.

Whilst still licking my wounds, soon after the Welsh adventure, a personal hand-written letter dated 19th May was received. It had been penned by the guv'nor, the Superintendent at my Traffic Unit (DT4) in Thornton Heath; a dear Christian man, known very respectfully as 'Daddy' Horne. Rupert Horne, a senior member of Rye Lane Baptist Church in Peckham, spoke of his sadness about my accident and wished me a good recovery. As the letter drew to its close Mr Horne wrote:

Don't think me too old or out of date if I offer a word to you— think seriously about the racing and trials. You may think on reflection that the motorcycling in the job will suffice. I feel sure that there are channels into which our Lord and Saviour could utilise your energies and courage, to his service and glory. I shall not mention this point again unless you raise it yourself. With all good wishes and the good hand of the Lord upon you.

Yours very sincerely, RW Horne.

Oh dear, was this the end of my dream?

I began to wonder whether, as a Christian, racing motorbikes was really the sport to be involved in. Of course, there was plenty to occupy my life working as a young Traffic Patrol; learning the trade and developing my skills as a Copper.

Maybe, whatever that *mountain* was, simply represented a figment of my imagination.

Racing motorbikes was pushed to the back of my mind and contact with motorcycle racing was limited to the regular study of *Motorcycle News* plus the old favourites of the green 'un and the blue 'un (Motorcycling and The Motorcycle).

13

A new chapter

Nonetheless, the motorcycling bug, which had bitten deep, still held a firm grip, and one day I saw a 1949 series B Vincent Rapide advertised in Motorcycle News (MCN), with the registration mark KUC 97. The asking price of ninety-five pounds was attractive and with a friend, who just happened to own a minibus with fold-down seats, I visited the owner of the machine down in Richmond, Surrey.

The advertised Vincent was standing lonely and forlorn, draped under a waterproof sheet in the back garden. Long strands of grass were growing up and twisting around the spokes of the wheels, quietly drawing the bike into the undergrowth. Yet, I noticed that the bike was fitted with twin 'Electron' front brakes. These were only fitted by the manufacturer to a Black Lightning Vincent!

The Black Lightning was a specialised and fairly rare Vincent racing machine. It could be clearly seen that what appeared to be a standard Rapide V Twin engine unit had been fitted with two front cylinder heads! The front head of a Vincent had a better gas flow and therefore better combustion than the rear head. It was considered a good move by those *in the know* to fit front heads on both cylinders. The carburettors fitted to this machine were Amal Monoblocs, which were more advanced than the standard 'inch and a sixteenth' carbs and with a larger bore. There were clues that this bike was far from 'bog-standard', and thus, maybe a bit special!

My newfound acquaintance took my pal and me upstairs to his bedroom, where he showed us several additional Vincent parts which he had stored but didn't want his dad to know about.

Having recently been disqualified from driving, the Vin was of no further use to this young man!

Very quickly, the sale was agreed upon.

The machine KUC 97 was purchased with the various additional Vincent engine and cycle parts, plus a set of Black Shadow crankcases included in the sale. Everything was loaded into the back of my friend's minibus and carried home.

Investigations revealed that this particular Vincent had many parts fitted within the engine, which had originated in the Black Lightning model. The price was right but it became clear that I had gained more for my money than had been anticipated. The gearbox was fitted with a set of close-ratio gears; the bottom gear allowed my *new* Rapide to comfortably reach 60mph without changing up to the next gear.

On the open road, the young competitor in me on one occasion, whilst waiting at a junction controlled by traffic lights showing red, noted the posh fella with a flat cap in his E Type Jaguar, sitting proudly alongside, arrogantly blipping his accelerator pedal in a modern-day *laying down the gauntlet* manner. On 'the green' it was easy to *leave the lights* abreast of the driver, who was giving his Jag full wellie and frantically changing up through his gearbox, then simply pull ahead, still in bottom gear. How silly we are, at times.

Following my tumble at Aberdare and having only recently returned to work at Thornton Heath Garage (DT4); one day, having been 'posted' to *light duties* for several weeks, whilst making my way across the garage area, a 'job' truck arrived, loaded with four new motorcycles. They comprised a Featherbed framed Norton 750 twin, (The Norton Atlas), a BSA Lightning, a Royal Enfield, which I believe was the new 736cc Interceptor, and a Triumph 650 twin.

The Atlas was Norton's move (go-between) from the well and long-established dominator towards their later development, Norton Commando. The Lightning was a 'sportier' development of the older BSA A10 Golden Flash, and the Interceptor was a step up from the 700cc Constellation. It was clear that they were all fitted with single carburettors, and thus, probably mechanically set up for police operations, which required a flexible yet powerful performance. The only *new* bike in the collection was the Triumph, which looked quite different from any previous Triumph I had ever seen.

It turned out that these motorcycles were for 'evaluation'; to be ridden and tested by experienced Traffic officers, simply to check out which would be best for Traffic Patrol duties in the Met.

Only one make subsequently came into service. The Triumph 'Saint' had arrived. The registration mark of the test bike was 89 FYE and, as I recall, its Fleet number was 2449T.

Moving forward in time; this actual bike was issued to and based at Lewisham Garage (PTU). As it was for some time the only Saint at the garage, it became the much sought-after mount for one or two traffic guys, your scribe being one of them. When, eventually, it was taken out of service, it was used by the Speedometer Testing Department at Lambeth ('Speedos Lambeth'), and last seen by the writer, many years later, lying unloved in a shed at Hendon Training School. Obviously, it was being used as a 'prop' when training young coppers in the correct procedure when reporting and dealing with road traffic accidents. It is now in the safe hands of an enthusiast who knew what he was looking at.

On 16th March 1964, only 13 months after my Standard Motorcycle Course, Bailey, now PC 762Z, was sent off to the Driving School (MDS) for Advanced Motorcycle Course 204.

The 10,000 miles of road mileage, which had been set for the boy to complete (in fact, this was the requirement for all Traffic Patrols) before being considered a suitable candidate for an Advanced Motorcycle training course, had not been achieved. Seemingly, it had been forgotten. Perhaps 'them upstairs' had decided that an earlier Advanced Course would help to see what the youngster was made of following his 'big race-track off', and bring him up to scratch.

The job, in many ways, was a unique organisation comprising thousands of officers subject to fairly strict discipline. Yet, as one experienced over the years, it was an organisation, which put quite a lot of thought into looking after the lads (note that letter from my guv'nor).

Our Instructor this time was 'Bomber' Harris himself. A man of few words but able to communicate very clear and precise instruction.

At the end of the course, in addition to the written and practical mechanical examinations, each student had to demonstrate his abilities to the Inspector in charge of the motorcycle wing and undertake the anticipated *Final Ride.*

Success in both the written and practical tests, provided that the *final ride* came up to the mark, would secure the qualification of Class One Advanced Motorcyclist.

The guv'nor of the motorcycle wing, Inspector Whitten, set me on the road. Aware that only a year ago it had been suggested that Bailey could have *got on with it better,* it was decided by this student, to go for it!

My machine was the standard police 649cc Triumph Thunderbird. The ride, comprising both built-up areas and country roads, was a practical examination and required the rider ample opportunity to demonstrate his abilities. Seeking to obey all the rules of the road as we threaded our way through the built-up areas, upon reaching the country part of the route, Bailey rode as hard as he could!

We were returning to the school on the final leg of the run and were near Mill Hill, travelling along Watford Way, the stretch where the A1 and A41 run together for a short distance.

Inspector Whitten was tight on my tail, right up my exhaust pipe!

Following the pause for traffic at the roundabout at the junction with The Broadway and after giving it everything as we negotiated and left the intersection, I skilfully changed up from first to second gear, missed it, and found neutral.

I attempted to select another gear, missed third gear and found another neutral! The next one up was fourth, the top gear!

Inspector Whitten shot past me on my nearside, looking more than a little mystified. My super-swift police motorcycle was now laboriously chugging along in top gear.

Having eventually recovered the gear appropriate to my now rapidly reducing speed, I regained the necessary momentum to ride down Aerodrome Road, thus, arriving at the Driving School.

As Inspector Whitten and I discussed my performance out on the road, he seemed fairly satisfied with my ride, but he observed, 'It is okay to scratch your bottom but it's not so good to tear great chunks out of it!'

My written efforts in the final examination were just about passable. The practical stuff and final ride, however, seemed to have put on enough shine to ensure the final outcome.

Superintendent Max Newman once again added his comments to my final report:

PC Bailey is a brisk and capable rider who tends to be overconfident. He is inclined to take the easy way out and could do with more perseverance. He would do well to remember that a good rider relies on his skill to keep him out of trouble, not how to get out of trouble.

You have a long way to go, Bailey boy if you are going to get to the top of that mountain!

N.B. In the events that followed, as *the mountain* was looked for when riding Triumphs at racing speeds, one learned how easy it was to miss a gear. The recognised problem with Triumphs was that if the selector spring in the gearbox was not set precisely and its operation was thus not fully effective, missed gears were easy to find. Call George Hopwood. He'll sort it for you.

So, it was back to Thornton Heath Garage and *normal* duties. The Standard Car Course followed with another visit to Hendon. PC Bailey became a Class Three driver and was authorised to drive R/T equipped police vehicles, provided he was crewed with a Class One Advanced driver.

The new model of police specification Triumph motorcycles was beginning to be brought into service at Traffic Patrol Garages. Just like the bike seen sitting on the 'job' truck. It was again fitted with a 650-twin cylinder engine but was a much tidier motorcycle. It was no longer fitted with the tin-bath rear bodywork, had an aluminium cylinder head, plenty of low-down acceleration and went like the wind.

The machine became known as 'the Saint' (Stop Anything In No Time). This term was coined at the Triumph Factory at Meriden by Neale Shilton, the International Sales Manager of Triumph Engineering. It is recalled that he wore the legendary 'Saint' logo on his motorcycle helmet (the Saint, a fictional character created by the author Leslie Charteris).

Although the standard 3134 cams were fitted, the cylinder heads had been gas flowed and certainly, the exhaust system (smaller bore exhaust pipes) was quite different from that fitted to any other standard Triumph machine. The silencer/expansion boxes were of a larger diameter than earlier models; they were greater in length and the cylindrical shape was attractively formed. Herein, I believe, was a secret ingredient.

The silencers terminated in short, fairly large bore tailpipes. As preparing racing engines became a bit of a pastime, growing knowledge revealed that for the power unit to work to maximum efficiency, the combustion chamber and the exhaust system of any petrol engine must be in tune with each other.

It is no good to simply stick a *noisy silencer* on the end of the exhaust to make the bike go better *'cos it's nice and loud!* Triumphs knew this and certainly demonstrated it with the tuned exhaust system of the Saint. It must be said its exhaust note was quite distinctive, deep, and a bit growly.

The proof of the foregoing observations became clear to your scribe following the death of Sir Winston Churchill on 24th January 1965. Many 'Saints' were going to be pressed into service to escort VIPs to and from airports and other locations, as they arrived in London for the funeral of this great man. These machines would also be in the area during many public events, as a consequence of Sir Winston passing. The Triumphs were quickly taken into the various police workshops and returned to service with Triumph 'mutes' fitted into the tailpipes. Needless to say, the exhaust note was distinctly muffled but more so, the torque, sharpness, and power of the engine, namely the overall design performance, was greatly reduced. Sadly, *the mutes* remained as standard equipment in these machines thereafter. Something about cutting off your nose to spite your face!

Various changes were made within Traffic by 'them upstairs', and this meant that while a skeleton strength was left at DT4, the rest of us were pushed to Traffic Units nearer to Central London. A number of us reported for duty at Barnes Central Traffic Division Garage on the south bank of the River Thames. The travelling from home to work was now extended from one mile to eleven miles, nine of which were over the ground where Thornton Heath Garage (DT4) had formally patrolled. Yet we 'Thornton Heathers' were now patrolling most of the ground which we had previously covered, at the literal personal cost of covering nine extra miles each way from home to duty, only to travel most of the way back on patrol.

Central Traffic Division had been created! Needless to say, Bailey got into hot water for voicing what was considered to be a *logical* point of view, with the message being quietly passed down by our Superintendent that my *facetious observations* could cost me dear. A mere Constable with a point of view, whatever next?

Several years later, following promotion to Sergeant and being posted to Brixton Police Station, a foot duty posting, I was quietly informed, *on good authority*, that my former boss at Barnes (your facetious observations) who had risen higher in the senior ranks to the Commander of TD, would never permit my return to Traffic Patrol duties. Talk about climbing mountains!

During his posting to the unit, PC Bailey, now 362TD, was taken on to the team, which comprised the Special Escort Group (SEG) known in the job as *The Queen's Beasts*. My first posting was working with a seasoned SEG Traffic Patrol officer. We were given the task of escorting Archbishop Michael Christodoulou Makarios, the President of Cyprus, around the Metropolis during an official visit to the United Kingdom.

The political situation in Cyprus at that time was a little precarious, and thus, security surrounding our visitor was at a premium. Our duty and responsibilities were to ensure that special care had been given to our guest. My colleague, who clearly didn't think much of a youngster being teamed up with an officer of his experience, clearly made his sentiments obvious within the first hour as we set off from our base at Barnes Garage, crossing the River Thames at Hammersmith Bridge and riding east to Hyde Park.

The early morning journey to Park Street, located just behind Park Lane, where we were to pick up our VIP from his hotel, took us via Hammersmith along the West Cromwell, Cromwell and Brompton Road, through Knightsbridge to Park Lane, in the thick of the rush hour. Traffic was heavy and slow-moving. We were set upon what is known as a *crisp ride*. I closely followed my senior colleague nicknamed 'The Widget' as we passed the slow-moving traffic. For most of the journey, he managed to time an *over-take* of slower vehicles and then tuck quickly into a small space between them so that his companion was always left 'out in the cold' staring at a Keep Left island dead in front of his machine. This term was recognised as 'feeding him one' and the aim was to 'drop him' as *in it* and leave him behind.

Not having been given the precise location, the lad was dependent upon the senior guy to get him there. I managed to pass this surprise test but was made well aware that 'esprit de corps' was not a completely universal mindset throughout the job. Nonetheless, the posting of around four days was safely completed. The only hairy moment was when a car tried to beat the Archbishop's chauffeur-driven Roller at a crossroads junction off Park Lane, shooting from the left across its bows as we entered the junction. The Archbishop's limo braked sharply to avoid the pretty certain collision and it was quite interesting, riding as *tail-end Charlie,* to notice through the rear window and observe how the Archbishop seemed to bow very deeply and respectfully as his car rapidly lost speed. It was a joy during one tea break, sitting with Special Branch and other officers, to talk to the Archbishop's rep about his view of the Lord Jesus Christ.

At the end of a very interesting four days, the team, which comprised uniform and Special Branch officers, was duly rewarded by the Archbishop. Each one of us received a delicately embossed silver bowl, supplied, according to the binding around the box, from G.S. Stephanides, Son & Co. Jewellers and Silversmiths, 73 Ledra Street, NICOSIA.

The second posting in May 1966 saw the team escorting Chancellor Bundeskanzler Ludvig Wilhelm Erhard of West Germany when he paid an official visit to the Metropolis. The remaining memory is of circumnavigating Hyde Park Corner one cold wet evening. We were on a journey from the German Embassy to the Guildhall for an official dinner. It would seem that time was pressing and they were running late (maybe the call 'Schnell, Schnell!' had been ignored).

Bailey's Triumph motor-bicycle was thus being closely pursued, as in pushed, on a wet rubber and oil-streaked road surface by a German Embassy Merc in a hurry, yet firmly supported by four wheels. Riding a snaking Triumph motorcycle slithering about on two wheels was good for freeing up the digestive system. At the end of that official visit, we were each awarded a silver coin date stamped '1963' with the Chancellor's effigy embossed thereon.

After some time had passed serving at Barnes Garage, I was posted further south to Lewisham Garage, formally DT8

(District Traffic Eight), but now renamed PTU (P Division Traffic Unit). Here, once more, I was privileged to serve alongside men who had come through the war and seen more horrors than most of us could have dreamed of, even in our darkest nightmares.

I particularly recall Reg Perreton from Devonshire. A former Devon County Swimming Champion, Reg had joined 'the job' in 1939, and in 1943 Reg served with 'the Devons'. His passion for flying meant that Reg turned down the offer of a Commissioned rank and transferred to the 22nd Independent Parachute Company, the Special Air Service (SAS), attached to the Sixth Airborne Division. He held the unique honour of being the second man to *touch down* on the Normandy Invasion. Reg had earlier *Roman-candled* into Italy during his 50th parachute drop and lived to tell the tale (*Roman candled* is a term which describes when a parachute fails to fully deploy and the collapsed canopy, complete with its 'chutist, rapidly descends to the ground in a twisting, spinning motion).

Reg was a great guy and spoke with a lovely, soft Devon accent.

Another guy with whom I was privileged to serve was Jim Harding. Jim, known in our unit as *the Sabre-Toothed Tiger*, had joined the army as a boy soldier. As the war progressed, at one point he was in the North African Desert.

One day, as instructed, he was on his way to pick up more ammunition for his gun crew, when over the hill (sand-dunes) appeared the 'Jerries'. Jim was captured and moved as a POW to Upper Silesia. Towards the end of the war, he was force-marched with thousands of the allied troops to Regensburg in

Southern Germany. If you stopped, even to tie up your boot lace, you earned a bullet.

I understand that the march took three months to complete. I recall Jim once telling me; 'Boy, there was only one sentiment in your mind through those months. No other thought but survival!'

Horace White, *Chalky*, known as *the Romford Cavalier*, was another character. He was quiet, seemingly quite severe. He wore horn-rimmed spectacles which were certainly not the then *required* 'job issue specification' and was always immaculately turned out. (It was established that 'job issue specs' should be the only style worn on duty)

Chalky, as a military man, served throughout and had survived the horrors of the war. Young Bailey felt so honoured to work with such men; guys who had 'been there and done it' but never talked much about the horrors which they had experienced fighting an enemy on behalf of their fellow countryfolk. Yet, their uniform worn medal ribbons, quietly displayed, spoke volumes.

I was privileged over many months, as we patrolled the South London suburb, to be able to chat with these guys. As I talked with Jim, very gradually and through quiet conversation, I learned more of his war experiences. This twenty-something or other lad once had the temerity of suggesting to Jim that I could, with his input and factual advice, write a book about the events and hardships of his war-time service.

'No, you bloody won't, boy!'

And that was it! So much of the history we owe is buried deep in the minds of those who *were there* and who subsequently said nothing; or even when under pressure from an inquisitive youngster, said very little!

As quieter moments of patrolling in a Tag Car allowed, we would discuss, our opinions of the guv'nors, the cost of living, the negatives of shift-work, most other subjects under the sun; and generally put the world to rights!

As the opportunities came, I was so privileged to be able to talk to one and another of my mates about my love of the Lord Jesus and my trust in Him. Reg would quietly, in a very friendly manner, 'take the mick' out of young Bailey.

One Sunday, after early turn, having had given him a lift in the family VW Beetle, I dropped Reg off near his home in Hayes. As Reg left the car, he mentioned that he was experiencing headaches that were bothering him.

'Probably been reading in a bad light and strained my eyes,' Reg said, as he bid me farewell and closed the passenger door.

Ten days later, after a short illness, Reg passed into eternity.

Chalky was a quiet professional and undemonstrative man, clearly a deep thinker. One Sunday morning when we were patrolling in P17, out in the Kentish countryside near Knockholt, Chalky and I had quite a serious discussion about Christian things. I recall talking about the Apostle Peter, *the big fisherman.*

At one point, Chalky quietly said, 'I wish I had your faith.'

I tried to explain how faith starts like a tiny mustard seed that grows and becomes stronger as it is fed. But being aware that I was only a lad, what did I know about the lives that these guys had really lived through and suffered so much, while I was happily collecting shrapnel off the pavements in Bromley?

Sometime later, Chalky was crossing the yard at Lewisham Garage in Ladywell Road. He collapsed, and several days later, passed into eternity.

At different times, soon after their sad loss, both of the dear wives of these men, one of whom I had never previously met, asked me to visit them. It was my privilege to meet each lovely lady.

The question put to me on each occasion was whether or not their dear husbands had gone to Heaven. What answer could I give, but that 'God is not willing that any should perish' (2 Peter, Chapter 3, Verse 9).

What a privilege to talk to them about Jesus' love. If we honour and seek to live for Him, we read in 1 Samuel, Chapter 2, verse 30, 'Those who honour me I will honour.' In John, Chapter 14, verse 6, we read that Jesus, comforting his frightened disciples said, 'I am the way, the truth and the life. No one comes to the Father except through me.' Then, further on in verse 16-17, Jesus says to his disciples, '...I will ask the Father and he will give you another comforter/Counsellor to be with you forever...the Spirit of truth.'

We can see that God's love, through his Holy Spirit, remains with us. Look at Jesus' response to the man, the thief on the cross crucified with him.

The dying thief had said to Jesus, 'Jesus, remember me when you come into your kingdom.'

Jesus said to him, 'I tell you the truth, today you will be with me in paradise.'

You can read about it in Luke, Chapter 23, verse 41-43. Maybe the thief's call was made when he knew that he was on his *last knockings*, but Jesus was and still is, listening out for the call. Yes, God's love is so great that He is there, even to the end.

14

Scandinavian adventure

For many, 1966 was the big year. England won the Football World Cup. GB's big year, however, was to be a planned trip to Norway, a land which had been visited before and a country which I had come to love.

This time, however, rather than set up as had been done before in the luxury of a hotel for two weeks, the plan was to equip the beloved Vincent with off-road (trials) tyres, fit the carburettors with air filters, fit a lower geared rear wheel sprocket plus other items and organise a bit of a tour around Western Norway.

Why all these additional special bits and pieces, you are asking? Simply that at that time, if you left the towns and cities of Norway, the roads were primarily un-metalled (not tarmacked). The problem was that in wet weather the roads would become cut-up and long ruts would form into the surface. Gravel and earth would pile up on curves and create banked turns. In dry weather, however, the roads would be quite dusty and in places, particularly on bends, the surface could become loose. In either wet or dry conditions, the roads could be quite an experience to ride on two wheels. To maintain them, at intervals a huge tractor with a giant transversely mounted dog-comb would scour up the rough road surface and a clean firm surface would be cut by a very wide, shallow steel snowplough formed blade, fitted further back on the vehicle.

Arrangements were made at London Docks and the Vin was duly delivered to and loaded aboard a cargo boat bound for Bergen in Western Norway.

Following later, using the SAS airline (Scandinavian Airlines System), I flew from Gatwick to Bergen, which was the easy part, spending several days with the Arviddson family at Michael Krohnsgate 36 in Bergen, waiting for my ship to come in!

During that time, the Football World Cup Final between England and Germany was broadcast live on Norwegian Television. My friend Liv's father and I thoroughly enjoyed the anticipation and enjoyment as we shared the excitement of the match. He couldn't speak English and I was unable to converse in Norwegian, yet we both knew that we supported the same side. Something about 1939-1945.

It was unbeknown to me that at the same time, some way south of Norway, a young State Registered Nurse and Midwife from University College Hospital London (UCH) was working with her friend, Ann, also an SRN, in a Refugee Camp at Espelkamp just North of Lübeck in Germany. The site was a former arms dump and the buildings mainly comprised Nissen huts. The young ladies were involved in caring for people living in the camp and on the day of the World Cup Final, were both watching the match with the folk resident in that place.

I understand that the support for the English team was somewhat limited to two quiet cheerleaders. The outcome decided in England's favour, apparently resulted in a formal to cold, with a clipped *Auf Wiedersehen,* farewell as the guests left the television room!

The Norwegian tour took the Vincent and me to the inland tip of the Hardanger Fiord, at the head of which are three smaller fiords: Ulvik, Osa and Eidfiord.

The plan was to cross to the east side of Norway, travelling in the direction of Oslo. The journey required a trip by car-ferry down the Ulvik Fiord. It crossed the Osa Fiord and entered the Eidfjord. The route took me via the Eidfjordtunnelen, up onto and across the Norwegian Plateau via Geilo, Gol, through Gjovik, and across the Mjosafiord to Hamar, which is north of Oslo. I then turned North to Lillehammer and when the Vincent brought me to Otta, we turned west to climb and cross the Jotunheimen Mountains.

Whilst still east of the mountains, during an overnight stop, I met John Morton, Eastern Collegiate Cross Country Ski Champion from Middlebury College, New Hampshire, USA.

We hit it off immediately and John travelled pillion across the Jotunheimen Mountains, via the Sognefjord and back to Bergen. We enjoyed a great ten days together. (In 1969 John took part in the Winter Olympics and was a member of the US Biathlon Team. He completed a tour of duty in the Vietnam War and was awarded a Bronze Star).

The Vincent loved the whole trip, ran trouble-free, without missing a beat and with such good low-down torque, gobbled up the steepest and loosest of climbs.

Although not exactly *the mountain* dreamed about, the Jotunheimen Mountain range was a place not to be missed, with its beauty and grandeur.

15

Sheep on the mountain

That mountain was slowly being climbed and the racing bug still had a stronghold on my dreams.

One day early, in the 1967 motorcycle racing season, my friend George (GAH), of Triumph fame, suggested that maybe it would be a good idea for GLB, as he called me, to enter for a Production Machine race organised by the Bantam Racing Club at Snetterton in Norfolk. The only machine which was then in Bailey's possession was the Vincent and it was not quite up to the mark as a competitive mount for the Production Machine class. What was to be done?

With the earlier feeling that, as a Christian, motorcycle racing was perhaps not on; quite frankly, I prayed about it. The prayer went something like: 'Dear Lord, if racing is not in your plan for me, please show me.'

Bailey, nonetheless, did his best to prepare the bike for a ride at Snetterton. Trial tyres removed, air filters taken off, gearing altered etc. Do you know what I mean, guv?

We all arrived at Snetterton on the day of the Bantam Racing Club event. The Vin was as well prepared for competition as possible.

On any race day, we were set to complete the necessary practice laps which were an essential requirement to qualify for a start in the race. The big V twin sounded good and was rapidly gobbling up the first few miles of practice then, all of a sudden, bang!

All the mechanical bits ceased from playing at racers, the rear wheel locked solid and it was necessary to grab the clutch to disengage the drive so that its rider didn't finish up on his ear in the dirt.

End of practice!

Bailey GL. DNS (did not start).

Oh well, that's a dream gone up in a smoking rear tyre! The gearbox had seized solid and big money was going to be required to sort that one out, even to put it back on the public roads.

OK, Lord. Message received; racing is out.

Several weeks later, George gave me a call and suggested that I entered for the Production Machine race at the next Bantam Racing Club meeting; again, at Snetterton.

'It's no good, George,' I said. 'The Vincent is up the pictures! There's no time to get it fixed by race day and I have no money to buy another bike. It would be a total waste of time to enter!'

George responded quietly, 'GLB, there will be a bike for you to ride. Enter!'

There is a story in the Bible (Judges, Chapter 6) about a man called Gideon. He was quite an ordinary guy, worked on his dad's farm and considered himself to be the *least* in his family.

Verse 16: 'Yet God called him to lead his people, the Israelites, to save them from their enemy the Midianites.'

Gideon didn't feel quite up to the task and asked God to make it clear that he had *chosen* this ordinary farm worker.

Gideon arranged with God that he would lay out an animal's

fleece overnight to check that he had received God's message correctly. The deal with God was that if the wool fleece was wet, covered with dew overnight and the ground around it was dry in the morning, Gideon would know that what God said was the way for him to go.

So, it turned out that the fleece was wet and the ground dry. But Gideon was still not sure about God's idea for this ordinary guy. He asked God not to be angry and to allow him to reverse the process the next night. If the fleece was dry and the ground wet, then Gideon would be sure of God's plan for him. And so it was; the fleece was dry, and the ground was wet.

We read that Gideon *then* led his people in the defeat of the enemy (Judges, Chapter 6, verse 36-40).

Just what has a story from the Old Testament of the Bible got to do with racing motorbikes at Snetterton or anyplace else, you might ask? The answer is simply that I got down to it and prayed again.

'Lord, if you never, ever want me to race a motorcycle again, please, you can show me just what your plan is,' I prayed. 'I am not going to make any attempt to get hold of a bike. Amen.'

Easy answer: no bike, no more motorcycle racing.

As the race day approached, George gave me a call.

'Okay, GLB, I've got you a bike for Saturday,' said George. 'Peter Butler is riding Boyer's Tiger 100 in the Barcelona 500 Endurance Race in Spain. So, as he won't be needing it, you are down to ride his Thruxton.'

Peter A. Butler was, by that time, one of the most competitive and successful Production Machine riders on the racing scene. His Boyers Triumph Thruxton was the next best thing to a 'works' bike and would take Peter to the winner's flag in the best company whenever he raced. And Bailey was going to race it at 'Snetters' on 22nd of April? As hard as it was to believe, we duly presented ourselves for machine examination Scrutineering at Snetterton.

All the 'proddy' guys knew the bike and had a good look at the bloke who seemed to have possession of it. Who was this *ordinary* stranger marked down as the rider? There's got to be some mistake, they must have thought. Strangers don't ride Peter Butler's bike.

The result was that the lad was able to mix it with the top club Production Machine racers. I seem to recall that after three races the Boyer Thruxton secured its pilot 3rd, 2nd and 1st positions.

Events began to take off as the year progressed, and I came to learn the truth of the Bible verses that had been given to me years before.

Proverbs, Chapter 3, verse 5-6: 'Trust in the Lord with all your heart and lean not on your own understanding; in all your ways acknowledge Him and He will make your path straight.'

That's what Gideon did. And like him, this boy also required a lot of help from the God of love.

16

Don't come back if you break it!

*This next chapter of events, the 1967 Isle of Man Production
Machine TT, with some later editing, was written within
weeks of the experience and thus, is as up to date and accurate a
report as is possible of the 'personal mountain' experience.*

We – certain conspiring friends and I – had often dreamt of a
standard Police Triumph competing in one of the long-distance
Production Machine Endurance Races.

A good crisp ride to the system, just to finish, would have been
the aim.

When it was announced that a Production Machine TT
Race would be included in the 1967 Golden Jubilee TT at the
Isle of Man, the conspirators joined in a good earnest debate.

The TT races run every year from late May into the first week
of June. Peter Butler, with George's skills as his mechanic, was
an early entry. GLB offered his services to go to The Island with
them as general 'goffer' and pit crew member.

One day, George said, 'GLB, why don't you give 'Sid' Shilton
at Triumph a ring and ask him whether he could lend you a
Saint? Then you could enter the Production Race as well!'

'I thought his name was Neale Shilton, George,' I replied.

'Yes,' George said, 'but everyone there calls him Sid!'

Neale Shilton was an International Contract Sales Manager at the Triumph Engineering Company in Meriden. At the time, he was responsible for the sales of police motorcycles worldwide and was also responsible for sales to the armed forces. He really was Mr Triumph!

The amazing fact was that he didn't simply put motorbikes into wooden boxes and send them off to the buyers. Neale Shilton would *ride* the product hundreds of miles to the prospective buyer, demonstrate it, and ride it back home again!

My response was; 'But, George, Neale Shilton won't pick up the phone, take a call from a copper in London and lend him a bike for the TT! It doesn't work like that.'

'Give it a go, GL!'

Sometime later, after a great deal of thought, I picked up the telephone and rang the number which George had given me.

'Neale Shilton here. Can I help you?'

'Er, Mr Shilton. My name is Graham Bailey. I'm a Traffic Patrol policeman from London. I wondered whether you might be able to lend me a Triumph Saint to ride in the inaugural Production Machine TT in June. The idea would be that it would be a kind of reliability ride, to demonstrate the Saint.'

'Well,' he replied, 'the problem is that I have three bikes out for the Welsh Two-Day Trial, and the others are committed elsewhere.'

He paused for a moment of silence.

'But the Saint, which I have recently ridden to the Hanover Police Exhibition, is in for a service,' he continued. 'What exactly do you want?'

The machine turned out to be a 1966 Saint.

It had seen some life, which had included the recent high-speed trip to the International Police Exhibition at Hanover in the hands of the still enthusiastic Neale, although he was over 50 years young.

Bailey was now stunned that this quite important guy was actually talking to him and even enquiring about the specifications required by a *total* stranger, for a standard police bike to be given into his care!

'Would it be possible to fit a close-ratio gear-box cluster and maybe also a 19-inch rear wheel so that an Avon Grand Prix tyre could be used?' I respectfully suggested.

The standard rear wheel on a Saint, at that time, was of 18-inch diameter. Not ideal for a competition type tyre.

'Leave it with me,' replied Neale. 'As I said, the bike is in for a service. We'll see what we can do. I'll be in touch.'

The final part of the arrangement was that I could borrow his demonstration Saint for the TT, provided that I was prepared to do some work to prepare the machine.

With my head spinning, it was necessary to start thinking seriously about entry forms, securing an International Competition Licence and generally getting sorted.

I very quickly discovered that Neale Shilton could *see a story* from miles off, even with a passing glance or by just receiving a telephone call from an ordinary Copper in London.

A day or so after our conversation, I received a call from Leslie Nicholl, a sports correspondent for the Daily Express.

'I understand that you are riding a police Saint in the Production Machine TT,' said Leslie.

Not long after the chat which ensued; on Friday the 12th of May, the story of Bailey's planned adventure appeared in the *Daily Express,* titled 'Here Comes the Saint'.

A call from Neale Shilton informed me that the bike was ready for collection.

George and I drove up to Meriden with George's trailer hooked up behind the family Beetle. We were ushered into one of the workshops and there stood the Saint. We were thrilled to see that it was fitted with a twin Carburettor cylinder head. Although specified by several police forces throughout the world, twin carbs were not familiar to the standard Met patrol bikes. Yet 'better breathing' would give the Saint more of a chance among the quick bikes. A close-ratio box had also been fitted, plus the requested 19-inch rear wheel.

One of the mechanics pointed to the dropped racing handlebars which had been fitted on the bike.

'They are the same pattern that Percy uses,' said the mechanic. 'He likes them well tucked in, so we thought that they would be just the job for you.'

Percy Tait was a Triumph works tester and a top-line Triumph road racer.

'Don't come back if you break it!' said one of the mechanics as a friendly parting shot as we took our leave.

So, with these words ringing in our ears, we bid farewell to an extremely positive and friendly team of Triumph guys at the Triumph Factory; in possession of a machine which I hoped was to carry me for 100 miles or so round an island in the middle of the Irish Sea and at high speed. They had done their bit and expected me, at the very least, to do my best. We returned home, now fully aware that quite a bit of preparation was required in the weeks ahead.

A few days later, I received a call from Mr Shilton. He had been on to his friend, Doug Mitchenall, from Avon Fairings, and a racing fairing would be delivered to my home address.

'Also, drop in at Hughes Triumph in Wallington,' he said. 'I've had a word with Stan Brand, the owner. He's organised to fix you up with a set of rear-set footrests and foot-brake assembly, a racing seat, and a set of Thruxton exhaust pipes and silencers.' This exhaust system was much more efficient and would give a little more ground clearance, which was good news, as I was not too keen to dig some part of the bicycle into the deck and *ride it down to the road* on The Island!

Your 'young dreamer' had spent hours fitting and adjusting the various accessories and bolt-on goodies that Neale Shilton had indirectly provided.

I had been privileged to become acquainted with Joe Dunphy. He was one of the local racers who had inspired this would-be racer at Crystal Palace, several years before. Joe had won the 1962 Senior Manx Grand Prix riding a 'Francis Beart' Manx Norton; and so he knew the way around the TT Mountain Course.

In quiet conversation, Joe described many of the tricky parts of the course, such as the braking points and the correct and safest racing lines to take. Long before the actual Island experience, I was learning that riding the TT course was not simply a matter of blasting down the straight bits and going steady through the twiddly sections. There were series of bends, which, if the first curve was not approached with the machine in the *correct* position, travelling at the right speed, with the appropriate gear engaged, the rider would be completely off-line for the succeeding bends, travelling relatively slowly at best, and potentially ending up in the hedge or worse.

One classic example I came to know but has since been straightened out, was Quarry Bends on the way to Ramsey. It was a tight and continuing series of twists. If the first right-handed kink was approached off-line, the rider would end up rather like a tennis ball being bounced between the walls of a narrow passageway.

These were Joe's instructions for the fastest route up Creg Willey's Hill.

'As you climb the hill and get to Sarah's Cottage, hug the wall on the left. As the wall ends, aim directly for the right-hand bank on the right-hander, immediately ahead of you. Your speed will take you just clear of the apex. Now, aim for the telegraph pole up the hill straight in front of you. As you approach it, the road goes right. Flick right and aim for the next telegraph pole, the road goes left. You're now absolutely on the correct line for the top of the hill. OK?

'As you approach Kirk Michael, hit the small yellow mini-manhole cover on the left as you approach the right-hander,' he continued. 'As the telegraph pole on your right lines up with the telegraph pole on the left side of the road on the exit of the bend, which you will see over the wall, *chuck the bike in* and you'll be set up for the run through the village.'

That was a bit more of Joe's wisdom, quietly imparted to the young wide-eyed Copper. I soon discovered that it worked!

It is safe to say that, many years later, in the early 1980s, now retired from racing; when engaged as a TT Travelling Marshal, this Police Sergeant, on his first lap of duty, arrived at Kirk Michael and *they* had taken the telegraph poles away! Oh well, back to the drawing board.

I was posted as a night duty reserve man at Lewisham Garage during the week before we left for The Island. My duties involved working with the night duty Garage Sergeant, entering and keeping up to date with the various traffic reports, dealing with bits of paperwork and *of course*, duties included making the tea and looking after the shop, should the skipper be called out to some incident on the Division.

The Sergeant, known as Toby Jug, allowed me, after the paperwork had been completed, to wheel the not yet fully prepared 'Saint' into the office and make the necessary final adjustments.

PC Bailey was entered in the Production Machine TT as a representative of the Metropolitan Police Athletic Association (MPAA) and had been given several days *Special Leave* to cover my absence from London.

The evening of Friday the 2nd of June, found a small convoy of solos pushing along the M1, Liverpool-bound. Yours truly ran-in on my Saint, trying to get the feel of this now potent looking police bike.

The little party included our number one mechanic, GAH, and Peter Butler, our friend and well-known Production Machine specialist, who was destined to finish in Fifth Position in the Production event. We set off from Liverpool on the Isle of Man Steamship Company ferry. Our 5:30 a.m. arrival in

Douglas, the main town of the Isle of Man, was accompanied by heavy and depressing rain.

'Is this here for the week?' I thought.

There was a fair amount of work to be done in final preparation for Practice and this included the fitting of racing tyres and competition brake linings, checking over all the nuts, bolts, chains and clearances. Then, of course, it was necessary to take a few exploratory laps around the circuit. The family heirloom, my old Vincent, was used for this purpose together with the coach trip, compulsory to all new competitors and conducted by the Chief Travelling Marshal, Peter Crebbin.

All the new boys were guided around the Mountain Course by this lovely former rider before Official Practice was permitted. We had begun to gain a vague idea about the layout of some of the twiddly sections from *a racing*, as opposed to *open roads,* perspective.

Soon Monday evening arrived and having gulped a quick cup of nerve steadying tea, the Saint was presented for pre-practice examination. All too soon, I was in the line-up waiting my turn to start the first practice lap, on what was to be the realisation of an extremely long dream.

Ignition on. Petrol on. Don't forget both fuel taps, I thought.

After a light tap on the shoulder from the official starter, a quick swing on the kick-starter, the welcome roar of 649cc, first gear selected and I was plunging towards Bray Hill.

The Mountain Circuit is thirty-seven-and three-quarter miles to the lap and includes just about every type of road condition one can imagine. It climbs from almost sea level, high up to Snaefell Mountain. In fact, at one point, the road climbs from twenty-four feet above sea level to one-thousand three-hundred and four feet in just over five miles. It snakes and twists through woods between walls, clefts and rock faces; dives through villages and at times hangs above precipitous drops with only a strand of wire between.

Bray Hill is the rider's first hint of what is to come. The sensation is rather like sliding down a shoot and finding that someone has removed the bottom half. The hill drops left, right, left and right, gently at first and then steeply, plummeting between houses and pavements, complete with bus stops and lamp posts. The rider straight-lines the hill as far is as is possible and as the machine hits the bottom, your chin is sent crashing towards the tank top which of necessity is supplied with a padded rest. The essential line to take at the foot of the hill is to place your machine just clear of the right-hand kerb and thread it between the kerb and a manhole cover, which is inches away from said kerb. Fail to do this and you are on the wrong side of the road in danger of coming unstuck on the undulations caused by the camber at a side road joining on your left.

No sooner have you recovered from this abrupt change in your anatomical attitude, than you're climbing and then dropping towards Quarter Bridge (the first real corner on the course). The machine would then spend some of its time executing neat little rear-wheel 'wheelies' over the bumps caused by more side road intersections. Here, the brakes undergo their first test as you hook your way into bottom gear and cast your machine onto its right footrest as you aim for the double apex, the second of which is unsighted until you are well committed to your chosen line. Then comes the quick dash to the sharp left, right over Braddan Bridge, then a left past the church, a slight climb, then a left kink, tight left, then drop downhill towards Union Mills. Then it's a sharp right and left-right again, and a left through the village.

One can go round and round a road racing circuit on 'open roads', study maps and books on the subject, but it is not until the course is followed at racing speeds that one begins to see things as they are.

I arrived at Union Mills in my first lap, trying hard to unravel the sinuous succession of bends when Percy Tait, on a Triumph Daytona 500, rushed past violently braking and cranked well over for a left-hander.

Union Mills is a blur of faces, houses, and straw bales after which you settle into the full-bore rush to Ballacraine with the succession of fast sweeps, bends and undulations taken at much more than 100mph, which throw you out of the protection of the fairing into the gale-force winds which seek to snatch you away.

At Ballacraine, as you turn right you traverse the Laurel Bank and Glen Helen section, then climb Creg Willey's Hill to the Cronk-y-Voddy strait, you realise that this is The Island.

The twists and turns are beyond description and the notoriously bumpy Cronk-y-Voddy Straight demands complete confidence in oneself and the machine. Together you leap from bump to bump, the handlebars snatching violently in your grip and the engine screaming in anguish as the rear wheel repeatedly drives on thin air. The front-wheel also takes its turn in pawing the atmosphere.

As you approach the end of the straight, the road ahead disappears from your view over a small ridge. You remember that it went towards the right when you looked last time and so tucking in tight left, blur past the small cluster of houses at the crossroads with its attendant group of stalwart marshals, then heave the petrol tank between your knees over to starboard.

Now you rush on towards Kirkmichael where there is a brief glance at the sea over the houses on the approach to the village. Don't forget Joe's instructions here.

Ballaugh Bridge, the much-photographed leap, passes under the singing wheels and is just as exciting as was imagined. The challenge of Quarry Bends is cautiously met as one hastens on towards Sulby with its own bumpy and extremely fast Sulby Straight. Then to Ramsey where all too soon one turns south and begins to climb The Mountain.

After the difficult turns of Ramsey Hairpin, Water Works Bend and the Gooseneck, you bore on upwards toward the cutting past Guthrie's Memorial and into the Mountain Mile. Here for the first time, you're alone. You realise it in the barren wilderness of the bracken and rock with a roof of low scudding clouds just above your head.

Here, for the first time, there was a brief moment to ease concentration and listen to the labouring note of the engine, wondering if ever this course will be mastered by you.

Suddenly, the American Lance Weil passed me on his much faster Bonneville. I found myself fully occupied with the task of keeping him in view, around the four right-hand bends of the Veranda taken in a count-down.

One: left of centre-line. Two: on centre-line. Three: just over the crown. Four: now dive across to the right and aim for the apex.

Weil was still in sight as I counted down the three right-handers before The Bungalow, climbed past Brandywell and dropped towards the Thirty-second Milestone. There were three succeeding left-hand bends, which I felt cautiously around and noted for future study!

I then went down to Windy Corner, and there he was in the distance. Through Keppel Gate, past Kate's Cottage, then into the heart-stopping blind left-hand drop which leads into the switchback downhill straight for Creg-Ny-Baa.

One might cry, 'Brakes, brakes, my kingdom for some brakes!', as you throw all your effort into slowing this plummeting monster from its headlong charge for this bottom gear right-hander.

With a close ratio gearbox, bottom gear is quite a high ratio. All is well as you pour on the coals away from this point and rush towards Brandish Corner along one of the fastest sections of the course.

Now you go left, down the long drop to the extremely fast bumpy right sweep at Hillberry. It is here that Weil disappeared into the distance. Signpost Corner, Bedstead Corner, Governors Bridge and The Nook before the Saint bursts onto the Glencrutchery Road and the first lap is completed.

We had arranged to run three laps off together as that was going to be the Production Race distance on Saturday. All the people at the pits got a glimpse of a crouching off-duty 'Pecon' and the roar of his engine as number 23 disappeared down Bray Hill on its first flying lap.

The evening wore on and I was slowly gaining familiarity with Mona's wiles, revelling in the low-speed torque of the engine and the perfection of the gearbox, which could provide a gear for every need, smoothly, and with a featherlike application of the foot change lever. It took some time to decide which gear was best for this bend, that corner, or a series of bends.

Ballaugh Bridge came and went. Ramsey Hairpin seemed different each time and with each succeeding lap, the clouds over the Mountain Road lowered.

I climbed from the worthy steed, finding my ears ringing and deafened from the prolonged wind roar but was happy with the first taste of mountain 'lappery'.

The qualifying time was 34 minutes. The first practice lap completed by each rider was not timed but my second and third showed 27 minutes 39.4 seconds at about 82mph, and 27 minutes 44 seconds. So, on the first evening, I had managed to ride the three laps, two of which had to be inside the 34 minutes required. The qualifying hurdle was safely behind me.

Tuesday was taken up with various tasks of preparation. It must be appreciated that three laps (113 miles) of the Manx Circuit represents the equivalent of several short circuit race meetings, so the machinery must be checked thoroughly after each practice outing.

The earth-bound Saint was made ready for the next practice session which was to be at 4:45 a.m. on Wednesday. The police machine had finished its first stint, free of any traces of oil, save for a weep around the kick-start shaft, and only required washing down to remove the many pulverised flies, which had failed to properly judge the speed and distance.

Unless you have crawled from the comfort of your nocturnal resting place at 4:00 a.m. in the darkness following a rain dampened night, to ride a bike around a mountain, you cannot begin to realise what 'nutters' some people are!

By the time I pitched bleary-eyed towards Bray Hill, the sky had brightened and the damp roads were drying in the fresh dawn breeze. Again, three laps were aimed at in a bid to learn yet more of the course. This was managed, only after several stops around the course with the rider mystified by an intermittent misfire. Each time I stopped and *ran up* the engine it would rev freely, yet as soon as it was driven off, the motor would repeat its malfunction.

The bike ran out of petrol near the end of lap three but after running it up a bank and slopping the remaining drains of fuel to the back of the tank, the engine was coaxed into life. The misfire was traced to the main high-tension lead which, when travelling at speed, was being blown back onto the hot balance pipe connecting the two exhausts and semi-welded itself up, causing an intermittent short circuit. Yet another anxiety was quickly dispelled.

Days were now spent in feverish preparation with our highly efficient and methodical mechanic, George Hopwood, quietly guiding us in the various jobs which had to be performed. It was a history-making event for a policeman to ride in the TT races and this had caught the imagination of various journalists. It must be acknowledged, however, that 'Dinger' Bell a Traffic Patrol at *Eltham District Garage,* well known and respected by me, with vastly more police service, had ridden in the September Manx Grand Prix races several years before the writer had visited the Isle of Man. In that sense, Bailey-boy could not claim to be the first. In fact, it is believed that a future Detective Sergeant in the Met had also raced in the Manx Grand Prix, but those details are not known.

We took the day off on Thursday and went up The Mountain to watch the traditional Thursday afternoon practice and admire the fast boys training. The sun blazed from the clear blue heavens and soon the air was rent by the banshee wail of Mike Hailwood's Honda screaming down from Kate's Cottage to Creg-Ny-Baa, picking off lesser machinery as though they were going backwards.

Seeing the Honda man sweep past a group of slower riders on the sharp right-hander of the Creg, looking perfectly safe and relaxed, is to see a man who is a master of his art; a mastery which cannot be bought but is surely inbred.

Another thrill that afternoon was to lie on the roadside verge on the drop to Brandish Corner. This is one of the very fastest sections of the course where Hailwood was electronically timed 156.6mph. The fastest sidecars were slow at only 125 miles an hour! We watched some of these three-wheeled projectiles from our lowly vantage point. Several of the fast men practising that day were really moving and even with the steering becoming wayward, they were maintaining *full chat*.

It is said that mountain 'lappery' in the dark is a good way to learn where the road goes and when! One night we took a ride in a van suffering from an obscure ailment in the gearbox, which persisted in dropping into neutral at the most inappropriate moments. You can perhaps imagine struggling over the mountain, climbing through a thick wind-blown cloud, with one hand holding the gear lever in place and with the other, endeavouring to keep between the narrow bounds of the almost unseen road.

On one of the long light evenings, I stood on Douglas Head, high above and overlooking Douglas with the darkness of night falling across the sea to my right and a bright glow of dying day still in the sky above the hills. As the lights glimmered one by one below me; across the water from the other side of the vast Douglas Bay came a distant scream of one of the works MV Augustas being run-up. As this stirring sound bounced from hill to hill, I was reminded of the tremendous amount of work that goes into the brief few hours of endeavour seen by the spectator, as each mighty factory strives against its opponent manufacturer for the top honours amidst the dusty and oil scented classic racing circuits.

Brian 'Ginger' Phipps, a fellow Met Traffic Patrol and BSA Bantam racer, arrived in the middle of the week and was soon recruited into our little team.

On Friday evening, the final practice for Production Machines, we were given the opportunity for two more laps and the final bedding-in of a new chain and other bits and pieces; just to check that all was well for the morrow and that the mountain had not moved!

As familiarity increased, my lap times improved to 26 minutes, 44.4 seconds, and 26 minutes, 58.8 seconds. This session was not without incident, however, as when I was approaching Laurel Bank in the Glen Helen section, I changed to a lower gear at one point and felt no corresponding sensation from the rear wheel. This was due, I later discovered, to the rear wheel being momentarily airborne over one particularly notorious bump in the road. However, I was concerned that some transmission fault had arisen or that I had missed a gear and found neutral. My concentration was sufficiently interrupted so that when I arrived at Laurel Bank, my line of approach was a little ragged!

The sight of a row of startled faces disappearing like the line of fairground targets behind the bank, which seem to be dead in line with my course, was quite comical although at that precise moment I was testing the Triumph brakes rather thoroughly! All was well and with a quick and apologetic wave I pushed on towards Sarah's Cottage.

There is a section of road near Milntown, a few miles from Ramsey, where the machines become completely airborne on a large ripple which is followed by a very abrupt flick to the right. It was, therefore, necessary to jump, land and be stable in the right place on the road, if the right-hander is to be taken in the best manner.

On that evening I was able, just about, to have that one taped ready for Saturday. The evening taught me a little more. As my geographic knowledge grew, the jump was recognised as being Milntown Bridge. If ever the machine someone is riding becomes airborne due to ground conditions, it is possible to control the attitude of the bicycle by the delicate use of the throttle. Obviously any thought of steering whilst in-flight must be forgotten to prevent what could be a lurid result; but by keeping the throttle open by the correct amount, it is possible to keep the tail down, 'floating' the bicycle on the throttle and prevent a front wheel, *nose first* landing. In this manner, as the top line cross-country riding exponents illustrate, using a rear-wheel landing; drive and steering control is recovered as quickly as possible.

After the Friday evening practices, groups of riders and their friends stood in the grassy area behind The Grandstand, exchanging notes about the events of the evening. The Triumph factory team, who throughout the week had been incredibly friendly and helpful to this young dreamer, were also gathered, chatting about how things had gone with their works riders. Doug Hele, the Chief Development Engineer at Triumphs, was in the group. Arthur Jakeman, one of the Triumph works department wizards, was standing with Mr Hele. He then spotted me.

'Doug, this is the policeman who's riding the Saint,' said Arthur.

'You're wasting your time,' said Doug, as he fixed me with a serious eye. 'Don't bother. You're going to look stupid. The bike's not competitive!' ('Works' machinery clocked speed at The Highlander: 132mph. Saint: a mere 116mph).

My humble response was, 'Well, I'm going to do my best.' Conversation over!

Saturday the 10th of June. The big day dawned bright and fair. Bailey could be found toddling around in proverbial circles, chewing on a plug spanner, wondering what he had forgotten and whether the bike would last the course; whether he would be able to keep awake for three laps and whether it was not just a fantastic dream from which he *would* awake and be thoroughly disappointed and whether… it was nerve-racking.

Who would ever dream of being given the chance of competing in the Isle of Man TT and of making history, as the first Police Officer to ride in this event?

The team discussed the starting drill and other details. The race was to be started with a Le Mans-style line up. The mechanics would support the machines, lined in echelon at one side of the road and with the fall of the flag, the riders would sprint from the other side, start their mounts and rush away into the distance.

We decided that Brian, 'Ginger' Phipps, would support the Saint from behind, with the rear wheel against his left leg and with his right hand, hold the folding kick-starter in the best position for me to give it a swing; Brian, having already taken up the free play on the ratchet. I only hoped that he wouldn't mind too much if I kicked him in the face as I swung aboard and crushed his fingers with my descending boot! Of course, after the run across the track, there might not be enough puff left in the rider to even climb aboard when he got there!

The afternoon was spent in warm sunshine, presenting the competing machines for the official Weigh-in, when each bicycle is checked for safety and conformity to its declared specification. As Production Machines, each had to conform to the exact specification laid down and published by the manufacturer for that particular model. Optional extras, offered for sale by the manufacturer for the machine, were permitted, but that was it.

Each entry was lined up in the collecting area, in race number and Class order (750cc, 500cc, 250cc), sealed off from everybody until the riders were permitted to take them and warm up the engines before the start.

The start was to be at 6:30 p.m. and we were permitted to go to our bicycles at 6:00 p.m. The machines were finally re-fuelled and run so that they could warm and circulate the oil thoroughly. The tank capacity of the Saint was so small that there would not be much fuel to spare over three laps at racing speeds. Therefore, we made sure that every last pint of petrol was squeezed through the filler.

It was announced that the two 'works' Norton Villiers Atlases had been withdrawn from the race and when John Cooper collected his BSA Spitfire, the clutch was found to be inoperative. So that was three places I had gained before leaving The Paddock!

There was an awful lot of really fast men left, though as interest was being shown in the lone Thunderbird/Saint, I was determined to ride steadily and finish the race. It was encouraging to know that there were a fair number of 'Trafpols' from the various Metropolitan Police Traffic Units scattered around the island. I know that they would've loved to have climbed aboard and helped me around.

The opening ceremony for the TT Week was underway and the flags of many nations were unfurled, fluttering in the warm air, but I was more concerned with the movements of the *inner* butterflies than listening to speech making.

All too soon, the 'stop engines' sign was displayed and we began to wheel our now silent bikes out in procession to the starting line on Glencrutchery Road. Tony Godfrey, who was making a welcome return to The Island after several years and was to ride a very standard looking Norton Atlas, arrived to find that he was too late to warm up his 750. This meant he was going to have to start with a cold motor. His position, number 24, was next to me and it was a very worried Tony, who stood in the line beside me.

The minutes slipped by on the big clock over the scoreboard, below which our Patrol Bike stood waiting for its fastest tour of duty yet.

A moment to look about me and I saw that the spectator stands were full under a perfect sky, hushed I imagined in expectancy of the battle to come.

To my right were the 500cc machines, which would start five minutes after the 750cc class and then the 250cc machines five minutes after that.

The butterflies had fled as I sat on the pit counter, aware of a strange calm. At that moment, in retrospect, I knew that things were going to work out.

Two minutes, one minute; check on my target. Yes, there was Brian, resplendent in his intercontinental gents' wear (a striped fisherman's T-shirt).

There had been a certain amount of concern among some of the competitors, not least of all me, about the massed start. It was thought that Bray Hill might prove a little tricky with what was to be quite a hoard of mobile hardware, forming a high-speed traffic jam on this first section. No time for these matters now, as I poised with seconds to go and ready to run across to the waiting Saint.

The Union Jack swept earthwards, and the hush was broken by the urgent pattering sound of eighteen 750 class starters sprinting for their machines.

I made it quickly and swung aboard, everything happening around me now.

I prodded the kick-starter before gaining proper balance; no time to complain about my clumsiness.

Calm down and try again!

They must all be gone by now. Swing again. Alright, yes, the motor is running, into gear and *screw* the throttle out into the mainstream. It is singing as we plunge amidst others to Bray and I'm able to kick the folding right footrest down into its proper position.

The hill looms ahead, and there must be slower riders than the Saint pilot because traffic is quite light.

Tony Godfrey howls past on the hill. That oil won't take long to warm up now, old chap!

I tucked in behind him and let him be the *red leader*.

Quarter Bridge, which foils impatient riders, was cleared alright, blast down the straight to the flick over Braddan Bridge.

I'm glad to have opted for dark lenses because as we swept away from the town, we were running straight into the full glare of the evening sun. Things were thrown into bold relief in its brilliance.

I hurtled towards Union Mills and after a pack of fast boys rushed by, I discovered that it was possible to keep this bunch in view, as we dropped through Crosby Village and had time to see who the company was. There was the American Lance Weil on his Elite of Tooting Bonneville. He was to finish fourth. Tony Smith on the works BSA Spitfire was there and was booked for the third place. Tony Godfrey finished sixth. Griff Jenkins on the fantastically swift Dunstall Norton disappeared into the scenery and as I followed my companions into the twists of Greeba Castle, Paul Smart on the other Dunstall came past at an even greater rate of knots. He had suffered a poor start and was trying hard to recover. The machine was banked well over and snaking quite visibly.

As we rushed through Greeba's Bend, one became so aware of the rapid and distracting movements of the rear suspension units of the bikes just ahead of the Saint. I arrived, just behind my little pack at Ballacraine, and as I'd not got the Glen Helen section quite fully taped, I was happy to let the others draw out of sight around the bends ahead, lest I be drawn into something by watching the dancing machines ahead rather than the road.

By the time the Saint reached Creg Willey's Hill, I was quite alone and able to settle down to a steady ride. The correct line on entry was essential if I was not to plant myself into an adjacent field. The winding hill with its roadside banks seeming to overlap each other at each turn, took me sharply up to the Cronk-y-Voddy Strait. The Saint rider was able to put into practice Joe Dunphy's advice regarding the climbing of Creg Willey's Hill.

It is difficult to describe the ride adequately in words.

The drop-down Barregarrow before Kirkmichael is beyond the skill of my pen. The machine drops through a left-hand kink at full bore, down the straight hill, which is bounded by and made tunnel-like by high banks. At its foot, the road disappears left around the corner of the white house on the apex at such an apparent angle that one must certainly ease off.

Just around the bend, the width of the highway increases considerably, and the sweep is much faster than it appears.

Really fast men keep their chin on the tank and remain on full bore all the way around. I followed my course and plunged down the slope, the engine screaming its familiar war cry, tight against the right-hand kerb.

Aiming the front wheel at the white house on the left, I flung the bike across the apex. My courage denied the use of a full throttle on approach to the bend, yet I comforted my chicken heart with 'winding up' the twist grip as the Saint swept, cavorting and writhing into the following straight, scything close to the outside bank as if trying to enforce its own will upon me.

Kirkmichael loomed up rapidly as I cogged down and swept right into the high street, which at normal times swings lazily left and right in the series of sweeps, but today, it rushes past, snaking viciously up towards you.

It is possible to straight-line much of the village road and as you tear through accelerating beyond three figures, shop fronts seem to brush first your right and then your left elbow in a fantastic blur of glass and brickwork.

The faithful Thunderbird rocketed me out into the country, past the de-restriction signs and into the right-left of Rhencullen. The left-hand part is taken in third with the bicycle on the full bank. Yet again, the machine leaves the ground here. There is a plaintive scream from the motor but the machine remains quite steady as it returns to earth. Indeed, a tribute to the Police Triumph, which is fitted for the race with standard forks, springs, and damping, as well as using standard rear suspension units. Digressing once more, the handling was pretty fantastic at all times when you consider that it had not been modified for racing.

After the following fast straight appear the orange marker boards on the approach to Ballaugh Bridge, which I arrived at very quickly indeed and as I had three laps to go, I was braking in good time.

The Saint was tucked into the bank on the right with hard braking applied, changing into bottom gear. I was now watching for the farm gate set into the banking. This was the peel-off point from whence the bike was flicked left towards the brow of the humpback bridge. The correct racing line, I had been instructed, is found by lining up a telegraph pole on the other side of the bridge with the upper window in the house beyond.

This was done as we hit the brow and I heaved the machine upright, poised back a little on the footrests and *floated* the Triumph on the throttle, feeling the smoothness of flight and the satisfying jolt of the rear wheel landing. I then flick right through the village, flat out to Quarry Bends. On approaching these bends, I passed the local old gents, who were wisely and critically observing the proceedings, sitting in the sun, supping their glasses of ale.

I wondered whether I could get around again before they ordered the next round!

Safely through the bends, I exploded onto the Sulby Straight, past another local (it was thirsty weather this evening) and arrived at Sulby Bridge. Here, coasting to a halt. waving me disconsolately past was Ray Knight on Hughes Bonneville, which had holed a piston. That's where the butterflies went to!

I went on and on, past crowds in Parliament Square Ramsey, through the town and on to the Mountain Climb.

At the Waterworks Bend, the view must have been good on such a fine day but there was no sightseeing for me.

Beyond the bend, another fancied front-runner, in the form of my friendly adviser Joe Dunphy, was pushing a silent mount into the side-lines.

I felt like waving my sympathy but realised that unless I wanted an earful of tarmac, I had better hang on tight and get on with it!

Through the high-speed sweeps before the Gooseneck, the Saint sped, and as I turned this very sharp, slow climbing turn, the glare of the sun was once again shining down into my face.

Now came a long engine fatiguing climb up The Mountain towards peaks that silhouetted against the perfect blue sky, where the machine swished over the tiny stone-built bridges that cross the narrow mountain streams, up through the twists and turns of this high-level raceway, and towards the Black Hut and The Veranda.

Here, I began the now familiar 4-3-2-1 count of the four bends and I wondered whether I would be brave enough to take the lot in one fast sweep.

From this point on, the road drops in a series of contorted twists to The Bungalow where the bike bucks its way across the tracks of the mountain railway.

Then came the haul up to Brandywell, left, left, and down again.

I plunged into the triple left of the 32nd Milestone, the faithful Saint, following the correct exhilarating line through the long sweep and the following drop to the bottom gear, right-angled Windy Corner.

As I accelerated away from Windy Corner, flat down behind my windscreen, I glimpsed to the left frantically waving me on, a group of enthusiasts on the roadside banking and was grateful for the encouragement given. In fact, in the remaining two laps, I looked forward to this encouragement in such an out of the way and lonely spot.

I was then at Keppel Gate, a right immediately followed by two lefts, which is entered in third, then down to second gear as the machine was picked up from the right and taken with an accompanying scrape of the streamlined fairing, kissing the road. I was reminded again of the speed at which we were travelling.

The road was now dropping steeply as I shot around the blind left-hander at Kates Cottage and Creg-Ny-Baa came into view. As I approached the sharp turn and in deference to my brakes, aware of the many peering faces studying my progress from the roadside vantage point, I shut off in good time and pulled the leaping snorting beat back down the speed scale.

From a distance, I could see Creg, a popular point for spectators. It was crowded but the patrol bike left a good impression as it dispatched its rider with chin pounding the filler cap towards Brandish and the completion of lap one.

I wondered what sort of speed would be credited to Number 23 as it shot through the radar speed check set up by the *Motor Cycle News*? I decided to turn my attention to the final testing miles ahead to the start and finish point.

The crowds were thickest in the Douglas area, and I was reluctant to perform a high-speed handstand in their view!

Hillberry has a terrifyingly bumpy right-hander where the road narrows with the progress of the curve. The full width of the road was used as the riders fought their mounts towards the close-by Cronk-Ny-Mona.

I followed the continuing left sweep up to Signpost Corner (it was about three bends together, but this series I had learnt properly).

In 26 minutes, 42.2 seconds from the drop of the flag, my 650 was beginning its second lap, and I was settled down now.

I quickly adjusted the front brake cable as the Saint swept along the Glencrutchery Road, flat out.

At Quarry Bends, on my second lap, the wise old men still sat unmoved, and I felt that the bends were becoming easier. I was enjoying myself immensely, but as each bend or straight passed under the flying tyres, subconsciously, I was noting that I would only have to pass the point once more before suppertime!

The 'bicycle' tried to get out of hand over some bumps on the right-handed kink, halfway down the Sulby Straight. Although the machine was flat out at the time and began to chop from side to side, it soon shook itself straight again. I noted to steer clear of their bad influence the next time I passed that way!

In retrospect, I was reminded of life's pathway. When you experience a sticky situation, so often you learn to adopt another, wiser approach!

My faithful, but unidentified, friends waved their encouragement as we accelerated away from Windy Corner and within 26 minutes 45.4 seconds. The middle lap had been completed without too much excitement.

As I braved Bray Hill for the third time, totally unaware of my position in the race and having seen only some of the riders who had dropped out, I began to worry lest my engine would fail, or some other ailment result and prevent me from reaching the goal.

Near the Seventh Milestone, just before Ballacraine, there were signs on the road that some rider had slid to the ground in the full-bore right-hander. It transpired that Percy Tate, a fancied 500cc class rider on the works Triumph Daytona, had cast his mount away, but that he was not too badly damaged.

I felt that I could go on for several laps more, yet all the same, I was looking forward to the finish.

As the final lap wore on, one had to be reminded that this was a time to double my concentration and not let familiarity get the better of me. Throughout the week I had consciously kept the engine within the 7,000 revs per minute range, although 7,500 would've been safe. Repayment for this care was being made in abundance, for not only did the machine function without misfire or fault, but it was also most satisfying to hear the war-cry of the motor's song as it followed, screaming in my wake, reverberating between the banks and trees on the road from Ballaugh Bridge to Ramsey.

Recounting this tale, one is repeatedly aware of my inability to properly convey the thrill of the experience. To tear at high speed beneath thick leafy branches with the sun flickering on and off in your face, to swing across the mountain route and plunge for the last time down to Creg-Ny-Baa with the warm evening air tearing at your leathers and to see the crowd lining the route, is something really great.

The Saint catapulted itself out of the dip below Governors Bridge, into the Glencrutchery Road and as I hurtled towards The Grandstand, peering through my fly-covered goggles and over the top of the equally flyspecked screen, there it was, held up for me to see; the chequered flag, sweeping down as the Saint passed under it.

The race, for me, was over.

I braked down to crawl, so far removed from my latter pace and turned onto the path, which led to the Finisher's Enclosure.

At the gate stood the figure who had become familiar to me throughout the past week, although I had not identified myself to him. It was the local Sergeant of the Constabulary, endowed with years and with the customary severe appearance. It seemed essential to demonstrate discipline and good manners in his presence.

As I rode past, I saluted and quoted the Met Police honoured expression of salutation, 'All correct Sergeant!'

The 'Saint' was parked, and my helmet removed. I was

thoroughly and joyfully recounting details of the ride to Brian 'Ginger' Phipps and other friendly well-wishers.

All of a sudden, the Skipper appeared pushing busily through the crowd, his once solemn, now twinkling eyes and a broad grin across his face approached me. He wrung my hand and pounded me on the shoulder. I'm sure that he was as thrilled as I was!

'My lad. That was great! Is this your first time here?' He asked.

I affirmed my novice state.

'That was a wonderful ride,' he continued. 'You did well. Are ya coming back?'

I said that if someone would lend me a bike, I thought I would.

'You'll be back lad, you'll be back!' said he confidently, and with a further grip of my hand, he was gone, beaming happily.

The bike was now wheeled into the field behind The Grandstand, secured with the length of rope provided, to one of the posts placed in the ground to support the racing machines, which, in their racing trim, had no centre or side stands.

I was standing, drinking, in the thrill of just finishing and picking squashed flies from my goggle lenses, as Doug Hele came into view. The Chief Development Engineer at Triumph Factory, as you recall, had been more than a little cynical and dismissive about the idea of an unknown policeman, even attempting to compete in the race on a Saint. Mr Hele had a gammy leg, which caused him to limp but he was almost running across the grass towards this off duty copper standing by his bike. He thumped me on the shoulder, grasped my hand and gave it a real 'works' shake.

'Well done. You did us a great job!' Mr Hele said.

His congratulatory greeting just about made my day. To receive words of encouragement from the man who had got the Coventry made machines going so well was almost akin to becoming a world champion!

The results of the race confirmed why Mr Hele was so 'chipper'; with John Hartle on the 'works' Triumph Bonneville, winning at 97.10mph, Lance Weil, Elite of Tooting Triumph Bonneville at 4th, Peter Butler Boyers of Bromley Triumph Bonneville at 5th, G. L. Bailey Triumph Thunderbird 'Saint' at 7th, A. McGurk Triumph Bonneville at 9th, Jan Strijbis Triumph Bonneville 10th.

It seems that thanks to some fast men dropping by the wayside, Bailey had finished seventh in the 750cc Class at an average speed of 84.6mph. The last lap had taken me 26 minutes and 40.2 seconds. So nearly five seconds had been lopped off somewhere in the last tour. It just goes to show that practice makes perfect.

On Monday morning, the boy had an engagement as a student at the Met Police Motor Driving School (MDS) at Hendon for an Advanced Car Driving Course. So, it was early to bed.

The next morning the Saint, absolutely untouched spanner-wise, save from the removal of the racing numbers, was ferried to Liverpool and carried young Bailey home to the metropolis.

What an anti-climax.

It hadn't missed a beat and had spilt no oil. All that was lost in the race was a bell-mouth from one of the carburettors. Nothing else dropped off or broke during the whole week.

It was quickly realised how fortunate I was to have been the fellow who was afforded such a coveted opportunity and it's funny how the spell of The Mountain was cast, for I was entered to ride another Triumph, this time a Daytona, in the 500 Senior Class at the Manx Grand Prix in September.

The Saint, having been so kindly loaned to me, was delivered by Triumph Engineering into the care of Jock Hitchcock, a Triumph dealer down in Folkestone, Kent.

Subsequently, the Vincent brothers saw plenty of success with the Saint, which was probably made more competitive. It changed hands several times. The last reported sighting was of the Saint living a quieter life down in the West Country! The visit to the Isle of Man later in the year was because an entry had been secured in the Manx Grand Prix.

Soon after returning to duty in London, I was privileged to receive a personal letter from Chief Superintended Harry Crowden. He congratulated me, PC Bailey, on his efforts and encouraged me that the Production TT result was equally a good result for the Metropolitan Police.

TRIUMPH NEWS from MERIDEN

Policeman quickly proves his case

Police officer Graham Bailey and police Triumph at high speed in the Isle of Man.

SOMEONE was bound to do it. Prove, that is, that the Thunderbird-based 650 c.c. Triumph police patrol Saint was capable of holding its own in the company of high performance machines. What better place than the famous Isle of Man course during T.T. week? What better opportunity than the Island's first Production T.T.?

And what rider can be more appropriate than a police patrol officer, in this case London "bobby" Graham Bailey. No-one expected Bailey to win—but his seventh place in the gruelling race is a tribute to him and his Coventry-built mount which achieved a creditable average of 84.7 m.p.h. First place went to famous T.T. rider John Hartle, mounted on a 650 c.c. Triumph Bonneville, and four Triumphs were in the first seven.

Bailey's Saint was no highly tuned one-off special. Indeed, nine months earlier, factory contracts sales manager, Neale Shilton, rode this very machine to the international police exhibition at Hannover, covering the 435 miles at a 65 m.p.h. average.

After preparing the machine for the T.T., Bailey rode it 200 miles to the Isle of Man—and he rode it home again afterwards.

SAINT PATROL MODEL

Powerful 650 c.c. vertical twin engine designed and supplied exclusively for police and official services.

Selected by over 250 international authorities as standard fleet machine.

Docile, but with 100 m.p.h.—plus performance,

Ideal for duties in all conditions.

Available with complete range of police equipment.

Neale Shilton with same machine arrives at International Police Exhibition, Hannover.

17

Just give me the facts

Sometime later, the issue black Corker Traffic Patrol motor-cycle helmet, with its distinctive and well-crafted badge, began to be replaced with a similar Corker helmet. The difference was that this new headgear was white and, from a safety point of view, would be more clearly seen. The covering fabric, as with the earlier black models, was of a material that had quite a grained finish. These new helmets, instead of the bearing former distinctive Metropolitan Police badges, were now adorned with the stencilled word 'Police' across the front.

The problem was that the fluid stencilling paint, following its application had tended to run, infiltrate and trickle along the grooves of the grained covering. To the eye, it was almost like POLICE with whiskers!

The Met was, at that time, regularly publishing a newspaper for the troops entitled *The Job*. Within its pages was a section for readers' letters.

Bailey took up his pen and with reference to the new helmet design, expressed some thoughts concerning what in *his wisdom* he considered to be a 'shoddy' job.

Hoping to raise a Constabulary smile, in his letter to *The Job*, Bailey described the lettering on the helmets *as appearing to be an example of the dying efforts of a drunken spider.*

Unfortunately, this letter had been brought to the notice of the editor of a national evening newspaper who, using his editorial skills, reprinted the story in his own words (Evening News, 26th November 1968).

It would seem that the walls of New Scotland Yard shook and Bailey was summoned to the office of his Chief Superintendent; the same guv'nor who had earlier congratulated him.

Whilst anyone will always feel good when the boss pats you on the back; the feeling is quite different when 'standing on the carpet' in his office to answer for some alleged misdemeanour.

What had not, however, been included in this reader's letter to *The Job* was that, upon examination of several of the Police issued white Corkers, your scribe had discovered that they had not been marked with what was the legal requirement.

To conform with the British Standard Institute, and thus, be legal for use on the road, the BSI 'kite' marking had to be affixed to and evident inside the helmet. Thus, the appointed *carpet time* found PC 362TD standing facing the guv'nor. Needless to say, the Chief Superintendent was not happy that this letter had appeared in the national press and asked me just what I was thinking, to have committed such an error of judgement. I did my best to explain the situation but found it necessary to attempt to enlarge upon his reasoning.

When questioned about what I was getting at, I quietly and respectfully produced a copy of 'Protective Helmets for Motorcyclists: British Standards 1869:1960 *as amended* May 1965' (PD4937 and December 1965, PD 5682). I had obtained this at my own expense when certain shortcomings in the issue helmets had been noticed.

'Sir,' I said. 'These helmets are illegal. They do not carry the required BSI markings. What would a Coroner have to say should a Traffic Patrol suffer serious or fatal head injuries in an RTA?'

The Chief Superintendent, not impressed by my *one-off* claim about defective headwear, left the office. Some minutes elapsed before he returned with a look of triumph in his eye.

The guv'nor was carrying an armful of brand-new white Corker helmets, each one still securely sealed in their factory-supplied plastic wrapping.

'So there! Gotcha sunshine! Now get out of this one,' I thought these might have been the words dancing around in my highly respected chief's mind.

To cut a long story short; each helmet was individually unwrapped and inspected by the chief. Not one of them bore the legally required marking. As they say in the trade, case closed.

Another of life's lessons: if you 'want to have a go' at someone, or about something, never put pen to paper or even open your mouth unless you are sure of the facts.

No rider who had competed in the Tourist Trophy Races in June was permitted to compete in the Manx Grand Prix event, which took place annually in late August and early September.

The Manx was termed 'The Amateur TT'. Strangely, however, in 1967 when The Diamond Jubilee Tourist Trophy races were staged (although all the other races were termed *the international TT races*), the Production event was called the 'Production Machine Race'. Thus, proddy riders were not automatically disqualified from having a *second go* around the Mountain Course in the Manx!

I seem to recall that Neale Shilton in Meriden had picked up the telephone and 'had a word' with Stan Brand of Hughes Motorcycles in Wallington, Surrey. The outcome was that

Bailey was now entered in the 1967 Senior Manx Grand Prix Race, riding Stan's Triumph Daytona Tiger 100.

This was a Production Machine with all the road-going parts removed and stripped for racing. Sergeant Len Farmer, who had been my instructor throughout the Standard Motorcycle Course at Hendon, travelled to the Isle of Man to assist with the preparation of the bike during practice, readying it for the race.

We enjoyed a pleasant time but, as always, every rider and mechanic spent so much time tinkering and sorting out problems with the machinery.

Sadly, the Triumph set off well enough at the start of the race but approaching the 13th Milestone on the first lap, cried 'enough' and came to an oil-covered standstill! It was sad but true.

I later discovered that the Triumph had been prepared for and competed in the Barcelona 500-mile Production Race in Spain earlier in the summer. Apart from replacing the single carburettor cylinder head (used in Barcelona) with a twin carb head for the Manx, not much race preparation had gone into getting it ready for the Manx.

Following our rather disappointing return home, I was quietly informed that it had been a 'kind of reliability test' for the Daytona.

Oh well, that's life, I thought.

This 'racer' was reminded that it is essential for reliability and safety that thorough preparation is completed and when possible, to do it yourself.

But hang on there, Bailey! You wouldn't even have had a second ride on the Island of Man without *their* generosity. OK, sorry. I thought to myself. I'll try to be more grateful in future.

18

Candle at both ends

This tale was originally penned within weeks of the actual TT races in 1968. Thus, with a small amount of editing, this is an account written very close to the event.

It is often said that a joke heard twice loses its humour. My tale may not be designed for laughter but having told in these pages, of a previous trip to the TT races, I am at pains to avoid repetition of details.

Although riding in my second Production Machine TT in the Isle of Man, the events of 1968 were by no means identical to those of this Pecon's first TT encounter. If he was expecting the trouble-free repetition of his 1967 Diamond Jubilee TT ride, then this lad was in for a shock.

But there I am, rushing ahead. I must slow down and start at the beginning.

The Production TT is a race held over three laps of the 37and three-quarter mile Mountain Course for Standard Sports Roadster Motorcycles during the International TT Week.

Inaugurated in 1967; this year the rules had been tightened up, limiting the amount of go-faster *goodies* fitted to each machine to the value of twenty-five percent of the total cost of the machine.

The idea was that everyone, even the ordinary club rider, was given a sporting chance. Bill Chuck, of the Essex motorcycle customising (special go-faster parts) concern, Chuck Customised Components, had ordered one of the hundred Replicas of the 1967 John Hartle race-winning Triumph Bonneville, which were to be built by Triumph Engineering.

Somehow, yours truly, had the thrill of being asked to pilot this vehicle. (How the ride was offered to Bailey may have been the result of *fifteen minutes of fame* post-67 TT news coverage, I can't recall). However, due to a policy change at Coventry, the promised 'John Hartle Replicas' did not appear. With barely two months to spare, we, The Chuck team and GB were left with the frustrating task of the building and preparation of our own Chuck Components racer. A brand-new Bonneville was grabbed from the showroom and rapidly taken apart.

John Guard, of the Chuck Brigade, prepared the engine and gearbox while I feverishly screwed and glued the bicycle parts together at home. Most of my waking hours were directed to this task and it was a pleasure to go on duty for a rest from frantic spanner work.

We had settled on the specification. As the result of an invitation from Neale Shilton to visit him at the Triumph Factory in Meriden, I was once again introduced to Doug Hele, the head man in the Competition Department.

After lunch, he took me across the yard and ushered me via a wicket gate into the *holy of holies*, the Race Shop.

Mr Hele sorted out a set of Spitfire development camshafts, stuffed them into my hand and said, 'They should make it go!'

You don't question the man who made Bonnevilles and Thruxtons perform and handle so well.

Unfortunately, my boss man at Chuck's decreed that he wanted some of his own 'really wild cams' to be used in our

Bonneville instead, with the addition of larger carbs rather than the 30mm items, race-proven by Peter A. Butler. I became aware from the start that an uphill endeavour was on the cards. It is unwise to question the manufacturers and other experts who already have a known track record. Nonetheless, Bill was the boss.

On the Wednesday before the weekend I was leaving for the Isle of Man, the now smart, yellow and black Bonneville, only just completed, was tried out for the first time at the Brands Hatch racing circuit. All went well until I found a patch of oil (or was it the clown riding the bike?) at Druids, the tightest corner of the circuit and chucked the bicycle up the road. Sitting unceremoniously on my backside, I experienced visions of my new sponsor tearing his hair!

Rex Butcher picked his way past the rider sitting on his bottom, but I'm not sure just what his thoughts were!

Ah well, back to the drawing board! One or two snags were identified during the testing and were sorted out before our departure for the Isle of Man.

The arrival at Douglas, aboard the Liverpool to Isle of Man Ferry, was quite impressive. The crossing had been a dull, misty, and boring run. I was relieved to a degree by copious cups of tea but as the ship neared its destination, the mist became a golden layer and the coastline pushed lazily out of the sea of blue beneath the dramatically sun-kissed sky. This was a forecast of the beautiful weather that prevailed for much of the two weeks stay on Mona's Isle.

I chugged my old Vincent, which had carried me faithfully from the metropolis, up the hill behind the bay to my usual digs. Here, I renewed acquaintance with some old and many new friends, all members of the Grasshopper Motorcycle Club of Chingford.

What a crowd they were! Always ready with the spanners when things got hectic and all prepared to go shopping for bits and pieces. They would even relinquish the warmth of their beds at 4 a.m. in exchange for a cold ride to the other end of the island before the morning practice, just in case I needed my sparking plug readings checked. This operation is carried out after the engine is killed from a fully open throttle run and the consequent appearance of the spark plug electrodes indicate the state of the fuel mixture, which is very critical at racing speeds.

The *Grasshoppers* were a real crowd of characters and it was only because of their humour, company, and help that I did not go potty with the frustrations, which throughout practice week, would be a constant companion.

I had only just returned from the period of 'Tom and Dick' after having had three wisdom teeth pulled out and various others extensively tuned. My bloated features produced a mini version of Robert Morley, and such an achy state is not recommended in preparation for a TT race.

Harking back to my fears of repeating details previously reported, I will not bore you with the long explanations of the circuit or my perambulations around it during practice.

Suffice to say that my first practice session saw the Bonneville lap at over 87mph, an improvement of 4mph on the previous year's best and this was with an ailing clutch.

This early morning ride was electrified by the experience of having the Italian rider, Renzo Passolini, on his four-cylinder

Benelli, World Champion Giacomo Agostini on his three-cylinder MV Augusta, and John Hartle returning to the big time on a similar machine, all overtake me at hitherto, undreamt-of speeds and disappear into the half-light of dawn like wailing earthbound projectiles.

I was tempted to get off my Coventry built touring machine and walk but on realising that I was travelling at well over the ton, thought that it might take a large chunk out of my boot allowance in one stride, and so I stayed with it. (Boot allowance: part of a policeman's perks in those days).

The day that followed was spent rectifying the clutch disorder and sorting out the various teething bothers which had manifest themselves. It must be remembered that this Triumph was brand new and thus had never been race tested.

We took the machine out for the evening session, and this time on the second lap at Quarry Bends, it seized and holed a piston (really wild cams!).

I was rescued by the official car which was a 'hairy' Imp engine Bond Three-Wheeler. This ride was almost as exciting as the actual racing. A Bond is a deceptive tool with unexpected performance and handling, albeit rather like travelling in a supercharged Oxo tin!

As the week wore on, and we were working until midnight, then rising at 4:30 a.m. to practise; tiredness and despair began to overwhelm the rider of racing number 16. As each teething problem was sorted, so a new snag would reveal itself. I was helped greatly by Vic Lane, officially caring for the famed Boyer of Bromley machines, who, having few snags of his own, willingly turned his magic touch to the Chuck Triumph.

Without all the help, which came my way, I would probably have packed up and gone home.

What was such a privilege during those racing experiences was the number of *guys and gals* who freely gave of their time (sometimes even of their money) and took such trouble to keep ordinary racers 'on track'. The racers would get the glory if all went well, but the 'unsung' were the real heroes.

Our final practice session was on the Friday evening of Practice Week. The weather was wet and misty. Rain fell steadily and the conditions were vile with a very slippery road surface. Wet weather practice on The Island is of utmost importance, as it is essential to understand where and when to be prepared for the unexpected changes in grip.

I kicked off into the murk. Still, the twin was not right. The motor was running as flat as the proverbial (Manx) kipper!

Then I arrived at the Alpine Cottage. It was normally a *flat out in the top* right-hand sweep, yet I was stooging along on my kipper, sorry, Triumph, wondering what was amiss with the motor.

I was still travelling at a fair clip when Ray Pickrell, riding the tremendously fast 750 Dunstall Norton, destined to win the race and lap at almost 100mph, hurtling past me on the bend. He was flat on the tank, cranked over, and moving.

The machine was fighting both Ray and the wet road surface. Ray was demonstrating an extreme trials-rider type body lean, to keep the bike more upright and giving the tyres more chance of gripping the tarmac.

There was very little road to spare as the monster snaked its way out of the bend, almost kissing the left-hand kerb. As he cleared the bend, Ray sat up, still moving at about 115mph, looked back at me and gestured as if to say, 'that was a bit tight, mate!'

He tucked down behind the fairing, screwed the machine away, then, almost as an afterthought, sat up again, looked back, and energetically motioned with sweeps of his left arm, in a true leadership style, for me to hang on to his rear mudguard!

He was joking, of course!

I was so bemused by this exhibition of cool skill and control that, as I followed Ray over the nearby famous jump at Ballaugh Bridge, I almost went into orbit, having reduced my speed by much less than had previously been my custom.

What was that bit in Roadcraft about concentration? Oh well, one finds new limits of achievement every day and I always wanted to be a birdman anyway!

The final outing drew to a close with the machine seeming to be irreparably sick and struggling over the mist-enshrouded mountain.

The following days were spent with my ever-willing *Grasshopper* helpers and G.A. Hopwood, feverishly seeking to cure the final problem and to titivate the bicycle for the big day, Wednesday the 12th of June.

The job I did most thoroughly was worrying. The cause of the bike's reluctance to run well turned out to be that my brand-new Bonneville had been fitted with the current model (1968) contact breaker assembly. Not too happy under sustained racing conditions, the material used to form this contact breaker cam-follower appeared to have overheated and softened, with resultant closing of the finely set gap between the contact breaker points. The consequent *late opening* meant that the ignition timing had effectively been retarded; hence, 'flat as a kipper'.

The 'Joseph Lucas' electrics boys based at North Quay in Douglas, quickly came to the rescue with much-improved bits and pieces. (Joseph Lucas manufactured and supplied most things electrical to the British motorcycle industry up into the 1970s).

Since the mid-1920s, the heel of the cam follower in the contact breaker unit (the component which dictated when to fire the ignition), had been manufactured from Tufnol, a hard-wearing proprietary brand of laminated plastic. During manufacture, the high pressure and heating applied to the Tufnol resin results in the finished product being 'cured', undergoing a chemical change and becoming a hard solid material that no longer melts with heat. To use an ancient Latin term: QED!

With the 'advances' in technology, Tufnol was being replaced by another plasticky material, which apparently did not possess the same old established solid and reliable qualities of Tufnol (for what it's worth, that is only my opinion but Production TT Race-wise, the outcome could have been rather disappointing for this *dreamer*).

The new cam-follower material looked something like white plastic, which had been 'fingered' with 'grey' greasy hands. Let's see what happens on race day.

How handsome our yellow and black racer was; just finished in time for the official pre-race Presentation on Tuesday afternoon but on the way up to the circuit for this trip, I received several tentative requests from people wishing to join the AA! I have no idea why.

Note: The Automobile Association, road assistance motorcycles were dressed in their own yellow and black livery!

Maybe I was a lookalike.

Race day arrived. The rider of number 16 was hardly in the best frame of mind for his 113 mile tour of The Island's beauty spots. What with the combination of long working hours and little sleep for the past week, feeling sorry for myself over *my poor old teeth,* I was more than a little anxious about the fact that the Bonneville had not managed three consecutive trouble-free laps, which was the race distance. Overall, things seemed black.

To add to my negative frame of mind, the entire starting list looked like a page from the 'who's who' of previous TT victors, Manx Grand Prix winners, and short circuit aces. In fact, on known performance alone it looked as though, even trying very hard, I might finish just behind the last man!

The start was to be the Le Mans dash across the road to our silent machines lined up in an echelon opposite The Grandstand. I was quite miserable as the constabulary gaze was concentrated on my unproved machine being held steady by Grasshopper Clubman, Gordon Squires. The resolve was that if I did not finish the race today there would never be a GLB return to the Isle of Man. In retrospect, I must have felt unhappy!

Above the scoreboard, the clock framed by the leaden sky ticked away the final minutes to the eleven o'clock deadline. The roads were ideally dry but the mist was promised on The Mountain; a damp swirling Manx speciality which clings to one's goggle lenses and deceptively twists the line of the road.

The Starter stood with his Union Jack raised. All was silent, but I recollect that my heart was pounding like a steam hammer.

One rider jumped the gun and had to resume his place in the line due to the tension.

Will I muff it like last year?

Will the engine start quickly?

Oh boy! Am I going to get seen off today?

The National Colours flicked down, and sudden urge and animation was injected into the tense leather-clad figures. I was running well from what I could see, keeping pace with the other sprinting riders.

Gordon had the machine braced steady, and the kick-start held out for me. Careful though, I thought.

Now swing!

She fired immediately and with a healthy roar, but all was noise and flurry now.

Into bottom gear, screw that throttle open, and the rev-counter needle rapidly climbed around the scale as my mount leapt forward amidst the jockeying melee.

Don't scratch around, start racing now boy, you can get comfortable later on.

With elation, I saw that only Ray Pickerell with the mighty Dunstall and Tony Smith on the works 654 BSA refused me a clear road ahead as the Chuck Bonneville rushed down Bray Hill.

This is too good to be true… there goes Manx Grand Prix winner, Malcolm Uphill, on one of the Works Triumphs boring past.

Now I'm fourth.

Smith's Beeza tried to tie itself in a knot at the bottom of Bray. Tony slows and I'm up to third again.

What is that though, the Uphill machine is dragging its kick-start on the road and he's braking early for Quarter Bridge or has my judgement gone to pot?

Uphill stopping; I'm second.

Apparently, Malcolm had flicked the right folding footrest down before the kick-starter had sprung up into its rest position.

There goes Ray on the Dunstall.

The mind was full of thought and counter thought as I tailed him towards Braddan Bridge, the machine stretching at full gallop.

You shouldn't be up here, Bailey boy, you're a Traffic Patrol, not one of the actual racers, I thought to myself.

'Remember what Joe Dunphy told you about the false apex on the way into Braddan, Bailey!'

I blast out of Braddan and my *Triumph of Meriden* bike got past the Dunstall. My lead, however, was short-lived, for Ray had missed a gear and soon recovered. By Union Mills, I was back in third spot as a machine passed me.

The Chuck device kept the two leaders in view for seven miles or so to Ballacraine, which included one of the fastest stretches of the course past The Highlander Public House. Radar was out today. Apparently, the 'Dusthole' machine ticked up 132.6 miles an hour while I managed an almost pedestrian 125mph by comparison.

After Ballacraine came the hairy Glen Helen section, a bogey to me and suddenly there were bikes everywhere as the slower starting aces pressed ahead. I reckon I dropped to about eighth but really lost count as the old limbs fought the bucking wayward beast through bends, twists, and cavernous gully.

Due to the practice difficulties, we had been unable to gain an accurate idea of fuel consumption, so I had filled the 5-gallon tank up to the brim. This meant that the top-weight was something terrible, making Triumph Saints back home in the Met, even with their rear-mounted steel rigged RT equipment, feel like fairy cycles by comparison.

I began to settle down to my personal race and suddenly woke to the fact that my mount was performing admirably. Although with its extra fuel load, a fine petrol vapour was being projected onto my face from the breather in the filler cap, and the beast was decidedly skittish and quite a handful.

I became involved with a BSA riding jousting partner, Bob Heath, whose machine, although with better acceleration from very low speeds, lacked the 'push' higher up the scale. His top speed was somewhat less than mine. However, he was offsetting this deficit with some prodigious and not a little adventurous feats of braking and 'ear holing' (not to be recommended over such terrain).

XOO 34F, my mount, would blast past on the fast sections and stay ahead around the twiddly bits, only to get chopped-off at some of the slower hazards.

As we climbed The Mountain on the first lap, I could see that 'the pack' was heading into the mist higher up. Ahead was Rex Butcher on the Boyer of Bromley Thruxton Bonneville. He was 100 yards or so in front and peering through my rapidly dimming lenses. I was just able to keep him in view, thus grimly following his lead through the tricky gloom.

As we swept down to Windy Corner, urgently waving arms and the yellow flag warned that all was not well. John Hartle, works Triumph, seventeen seconds in the lead, had taken a tumble in the fog and there was Rodney Gould on the third works Triumph, sitting on the bank after taking a similar toss. Hard lines, but nothing serious, I'm glad to say.

With my BSA riding opponent and I still busily engaged in our private dispute, there was little time for me to study the many blurred faces, which crowded upon us on the corners. Then they were gone as our machines accelerated away through the countryside.

I was satisfied that my bike possessed greater speed and could pass the Beeza at will. So, deciding to ride well within myself, I was happy for it to lead when its pilot wished; at least I would be able to see what he was up to!

It must be admitted that when he was behind, I was constantly worried as to just when and where the Birmingham built twin would skate by. Braking hard from my maximum speed and hooking down into second gear, I heaved the Bonnie into the left-hander of Brandish and there, as we exited, were some of my faithful friends with their signboard thrust out telling me that the Chuck entry was in eighth place.

As the first circuit was completed, I expect that to my collection of 'Grasshoppers' and to the crowd massed around the circuit, the pattern of the race was set, but out in the loneliness of my windblown seat, I was more than busily occupied keeping my concentration screwed uptight, working out where and when next to hurl my kerb clipping mount.

It was becoming apparent that even though the day was cool and overcast; with the exertions of the ride, I was beginning to feel more than a little warm under my leathers. Either I am out of condition, or I am working a lot harder than last year.

This year Bray Hill did not seem quite the formidable plunge that it was on my first visit, but what was this?

Quarter Bridge rushed towards me, and my foot was slipping on the gear pedal as I changed down through the gearbox.

Oil.

Oh, no.

Not failure. Not so soon.

Out of the bridge and the steed swept roaring towards Braddan… a quick glance down, only a smear of oil on the leather upper of my boot, but it's on the engine as well!

OK. It doesn't look too serious, I thought to myself. But you'll have to be careful changing down, Bailey boy!

The machine screamed and danced, twisting and leaping like a live thing over the indescribably bumpy roads. Now my right leg was aching as I had to jam my oil-smudged boot hard under the gear lever and lift it positively each time a lower ratio was required. A missed gear through slipping off the pedal could not be afforded and I still had that Bee buzzing around as well!

Now, worried lest oil had reached my rear tyre, I quickly puzzled how to snatch a check. The only way seemed to be to run one's hand on the tyre wall and inspect the leather glove for the presence of a lubricant.

Nope! Everything is alright there.

The second lap was completed, maybe a shade quicker this round.

There were three groups of friends around the course who were keeping an eye on me and the signals told that their actual racer, Graham, was climbing up the scoreboard.

'Old hairy' was getting on my nerves now, so I thought that it was time to try and blow him off. I was feeling really in the groove now, and the Thruxton was more comfortable to ride as much of its fuel load had been spent. There were a few more revs in hand from the engine room and the brakes had plenty of life to be lived, so into lap three we went.

The opposition was in front, so I stalked him until his motor was extended to its limit on one of the flat-out sections, and as we exploded through Crosby Village, the yellow and black machine swept easily past.

Now there are about 3 miles of flat-out going where it could establish a fair lead, and I pressed my 'trafpol podge' as flat as possible out of the air stream and prayed that she would keep going faultlessly, as on the previous laps.

Through Glen Helen across the switchback of Cronk-y-Voddy, I held the throttle open against its stop and stood wrestling on the footrests over the spine-tingling jumps.

Eleventh Milestone, Baaregarroo, Thirteenth Milestone, Kirkmichael Village, and Ballaugh Bridge.

I've not been headed yet.

Maybe that's done the trick.

Don't relax now, you have got a long way to go yet, Son.

The machine is really flying now and its contortions far surpassed the wildest antics one can ever perform on the public roads. It flies over undulations in the surface, lands and screams along for yards at a time on its rear wheel with the nose pawing the air like some captive rocket. Yet, this seems quite normal now and I thought chasing speeding motorists was dangerous!

The brakes pinion it once more to terra-firma and the landscape slows from its frantic race alongside me, swings at a crazy angle before my eyes as we sweep through the bends; then as the throttle is tugged open, the motor roars its battle cry and the twisty, diving, climbing tarmac ribbon in front of me rushes away under the wheels again.

Ramsey Hairpin, the Gooseneck, and there was still no sign of my opponent. Over The Mountain, Veranda, The Bungalow, then we began to drop from The Mountain through Brandywell, around the sweeps of the 32nd milestone, and at Keppel Gate; the bottom of the fairing tore itself along the road to the accompanying scream as the left-hand exhaust pipe wore itself out on the tarmac.

I feel my left boot edge scuffing across the road surface; I must be near the limit of lean, I thought.

Down, down, down. The horizon plunged from view as the motor cried its anguished note.

At Creg Ny Baa, hands waved with encouragement as the race neared its end.

The Beeza rider had apparently slid off at the Gooseneck; fortunately, he had injured pride only.

'You're fourth!' Read the sign.

But I can't be.

The Grasshoppers went potty and were almost falling off the bank at Brandish, then scratching around Signpost Corner, then Bedstead Corner and, roaring out of the Governors Bridge dip, I saw the Chequered Flag.

Sit up, brake hard, don't fall off now, I told myself.

The engine clatters thankfully to silence and I turn into the finisher's enclosure. Surrounded by photographers is the victor Ray Pickrell who has averaged a record speed of 98.13 miles an hour and clouted the lap record so hard that he only barely missed circulating at 100 mph on a roadster weighing nearly four hundredweight.

I recall that it was Ray who took me for an exploratory lap in his Ford Thames van last year. What a great guy and friendly man.

Second, on an ex-works 750 Norton came Billy Nelson, followed home by the works BSA, Tony Smith.

The first Triumph and first non-works machine had pushed me around at 92.59 miles an hour and, as promised by my signallers, had scored fourth place with the fastest lap of 93.68 mph.

Even now the result has not fully sunk in but I do wonder how on earth it happened.

To ride in the Isle of Man has always been beyond my wildest dreams, as a Christian whose faith made me reluctant to race on a Sunday, which is when most important racing events are held. Yet, I found myself with a machine provided on Mona's Isle for the second TT time, riding with the country's top riders, and completing the course on the leader board, collecting a coveted TT Silver Replica; the award which many strive for years to obtain.

Wake me up, someone, and tell me that I've been dreaming.

What of the future? Who knows?

Things would seem to be promising and maybe it will be possible to recount another tale in days to come.

'*In all your ways acknowledge him and he will make your paths straight*,' (Proverb 3v6).

After a couple of years, Bailey was transferred from PTU to ZTU. Incidentally, as Traffic Division evolved from Traffic Patrols based within the local Divisional areas, PTU later became TDP. ZTU became TDZ. Oh, the wonders of re-organisation.

Once more, one can only vaguely recall the details of where the offer came from but for the 1969 racing season, Vincent Davey, the head of Gus Kuhn Motorcycles in Stockwell, South London, offered me the opportunity to ride one of their new and almost revolutionary Norton Commandos in the Production Machine events of 1969.

I had met Mr Davey all those years before at Lambeth Magistrate's Court. Do you recall when that guy had been nicked by PC462L outside Kings College Hospital for stealing the Triumph motorcycle?

As you recall, the bike had originally been one of Gus Kuhn's stock and Mr Davey had been called to give evidence. During a race meeting at Crystal Palace in the summer of 1968, my Chuck Triumph Thruxton had failed during practice and Vincent Davey, who was in the Race Paddock, had kindly allowed me to ride his *spare* Norton Commando in the race.

Maybe it was the strange mixture of a Traffic Policeman and a Christian, obviously enjoying racing motorbikes and the consequent Press created *fifteen minutes of fame* but nonetheless, throughout his racing days, Bailey boy felt so privileged that such opportunities occurred. Even as I pen these thoughts, so many years later, memories of that privilege are still valued.

The 1969 season commenced at Brands Hatch. The Gus Kuhn Norton Commando had so much low engine-speed torque, thus, had great acceleration and was quick. Due to its unusual engine mounting, with rubber insulation between the engine, gearbox/rear swinging arm suspension unit and the mainframe and front forks, the handling was strangely affected. In effect, the frame was almost remote from the rest of the machine.

I can recall that accelerating hard along the bottom straight at Brands, (which was not really a straight at all) as the steering used to twitch violently and try to take control from the rider; the front wheel and forks seemingly fighting the rest of the bike. It was simply a case of accelerating/driving hard, pointing the front wheel in the planned direction required and hoping that the back-end would follow along too!

In the race, your *main man* to challenge was Dave Nixon, an outstanding competitor riding a Boyers Triumph *Thruxton*. Quite early in the race, I was lying second behind Dave and, keen to overhaul him, I entered the adverse cambered, right double apex sweep of Paddock Bend at a very competitive speed!

An additional feature of Paddock Bend is that it includes a steep downhill drop. Sadly, this Commando rider had not taken proper note of the build-up of fluid on his goggles and failed to appreciate that it had just started to rain. He ended 'on his ear' at the bottom of the hill and vaguely remembers walking back up the slope, holding firmly the right-hand clip-on bar and twist-grip in the hand which had been controlling it, not quite sure of the time of day!

One should add that the rest of the bike was buried in the bank behind him at the bottom of Paddock Hill.

Stan Shenton of Boyers saw me approaching him and recognised that maybe a lie down within the sanctity of the first-aid post would give time for the stars and bright lights flashing inside Bailey's head to fade!

First ride for Gus Kuhn. DNF-Rider did not finish! The remainder of the bike was returned later.

Duly forgiven by Vincent Davey, the Gus Kuhn boss-man, Bailey competed in a number of club events in the following weeks with some success.

A ride at Cadwell Park saw Bailey chopped off by another rider as the whole starting grid of riders fought for room on the opening lap at the Club Hairpin.

The bike was picked up off the track by its frustrated rider and ridden off in hot pursuit of the rest of the pack.

Sadly, the right side of the fairing had been torn in the tumble and was flapping wildly in the slipstream. So, three-quarters of the way around the first lap, we pulled to a halt, tore off, and skimmed the broken streamlining into the grass.

The Kuhn Commando secured its rider the fifth spot. No awards, but he gratefully received applause for effort.

The target was to ride in the Production TT, which was due to be run in early June. My green Norton Commando managed to secure five wins and four second places in Club Events during the run-up to our next attempt to challenge *the mountain* on Mona's Isle.

19

It's the spark that counts

It must again be pointed out that this tale of the 1969 Production Machine TT was written within weeks of the event. Thus, the details are fresh in my memory.

H.R.H. The Duke of Edinburgh

Fred Hanks, former TT sidecar ace and now TT Press Officer was talking to the Duke.

'This is Graham Bailey, Sir. He's a policeman from London.'

Prince Philip firmly shook my hand and with a knowing smile, looked me straight in the eye!

'Policeman, eh?'

'Yes, Sir.'

'From London?'

'Yes, Sir'.

'You've come here to get it out of your system, have you?'

'Yes, Sir,' I said, 'and it will all be gone by the bottom of Bray Hill!'

The Duke of Edinburgh, Patron of The Auto-Cycle Union, who was being introduced to the riders competing in the 1969 Production TT, laughed heartily at my less than cultured reply and moved along the line of riders. It had been my privilege to meet his Royal Highness, as a member of 'the job', as well as a competitor.

It could be said that Bailey was in the Isle of Man to *get it out of his system,* but on 11th June at 10:50 a.m. on the start-line on Glencrutchery Road, Douglas, my main concern was with having another bash at winning the TT race for road-going bikes.

For my third ride in this annual event, I was using a Norton instead of the familiar and much-proved Triumph. It wasn't that the Coventry Marque had lost any of its former glitter in my eyes, for I still reckoned that a Triumph would out-run and out-handle most other Production Machines but when one of the country's largest motorcycle dealers offers a Copper a bike for the 1969 Club Racing Season and the TT Races; he doesn't scratch his head and wonder about it!

So here I was, with one of the revolutionary new 750cc Norton Commandos, a fantastically fast machine with power on tap almost from tick-over. The form of engine and gearbox unit mounting on this machine was a break with tradition, in being remotely separated from the frame by its revolutionary Isolastic system (rubber adjusted by shims), somewhat similar to present-day car engine installations. This spares the modern-day rider the discomfort of a high-speed vibro-massage, with bits of bike fracturing and detaching themselves from time to time. The Commando was fitted with twin hydraulic disc brakes, for the bike was big, heavy and very fast! My particular bike was fitted with Colin Lyster twin disc front brakes – but more of that later maybe!

You will probably by now be familiar with the TT activities at practice time and are doubtless becoming a little used to my ramblings on the subject. Suffice to say that pretty startling lap times were put in by some extremely potent machinery. The Triumph Factory stable had three bikes running and was playing the old *Bentley Le Mans game;* timing practice runs from out in the country rather than from start line to start line. The plan was that the true performances would be kept from the opposition.

The factory entered BSAs were not slow either, but there were enough bothers in that camp to keep the mechanics busy right up to race day. Three works Norton Commandos were being ridden by Paul Smart, John Blanchard (running for my 68 guv'nor, Bill Chuck) lapping at 96 miles an hour and the remaining model was in the hands of Tom Dickie, the number one in the Gus Kuhn team of three. Mick Andrew was to ride number two on the Kuhn 'home brewed' Commando and the 'third man' would be with the *old* bicycle of the fleet. Old that is if a one-year-old, 1968 model qualified for that description.

I suppose that most years see some riders arrive at race day exhausted after too many hours spent preparing their bikes, as well as trying to become completely familiar with the 37 3/4-mile Mountain lap.

Bailey's machine demanded more than its fair share of labour and Ted Clark, based at Catford Police Station, having forsaken his Area Wireless Car, pitched in, helped by whoever was foolish enough to stick their head around the gateway of our yard!

The members of the 'Grasshopper Club' of Chingford were, as in 1968, valiant in their unpaid victory efforts for 'Graham's Flying Fuzz-mobile', as it became known. In fact, this title was clearly and professionally painted on the rear number plate by a lady member of the Grasshopper Club.

My Commando was geared to reach 130mph at 6,800rpm in top gear, although it could be safely taken to 7,500rpm in the lower ratios on occasions. There is a section on the course known as The Highlander, named after the famous roadside hostelry, which is approached after following two miles of flat-out motoring with head, elbows, knees and toecaps tucked into the 'greenhouse' (behind the fairing). The aim was to gain the greatest advantage on this, one of the fastest parts of the course. It is at this point that the motorcycle electronic speed check was sited.

Not only did my Norton feel startlingly fast past the pub during one practice lap, but the rev counter was showing 7,500rpm in top gear. Needless to say, the instrument was checked in double-quick time. It was found to be only 200rpm fast at maximum revs. So, the Norton was still moving quite respectably. However, this is where the story really begins.

Two favourites for top honours were missing this year: Ray

Pickrell, the 1968 winner, was sidelined due to a practice mishap and his Dunstall Norton had been withdrawn; John Blanchard had cast his works Norton up the road during practice and would not be starting. One or two other entrants were unable to make it but there were still twenty-six machines in the 750cc class, the largest field if I remember aright in the race's three-year history. Of these, eight were the 'works' bikes of various manufacturers with riders in the top-line category and there were a few other *aces* on faster machinery breathing heavily as the minutes ticked by to the 11 a.m. start.

The Duke of Edinburgh mounted the starter's rostrum with the Union Flag in his hand. I was number two, second in the echelon line across the road. If I could not better my 1968 fourth placing, at least no one would pass me down Bray Hill this morning!

Shades of returning to base from night-time Convoy Duty back home in The Met; on my left was number one, Mick Andrew, and on my other shoulder Tom Dickie, former Manx GP winner, poised ready to run across to his waiting 'works' Commando.

The flag dropped and the old limbs heaved me towards my regular 'holder upper', Gordon Squires, with number two. One kick, two, she's fired up!

Into bottom gear. Wind up the throttle. Mick is away too. Traffic green so far, I thought to myself. I was right behind him as we raced for the top of the frightening drop of Bray Hill. Ron Wittich, on his private Commando, squeezed past on my left shoulder.

Racer, eh?

Over the pedestrian crossing at the top of the hill, I had a comfortable racing line, and as the machine went to light over the bump caused by the cross camber, I eased back into second place. Mick was about twenty yards ahead now and the next objective was to peg him back.

We hit the dip at the bottom of Bray with the throttles wide and everything bottomed with a terrific crash. Up the incline towards Quarter Bridge, my Commando clawed skyward on its rear wheel over the hump at the end of Brunswick Road, the side road on my left known as 'Ago's Leap'. The engine revs soared and then the rear wheel tore back onto the tarmac causing the front wheel to lift again.

There is always a policeman at this junction. He is passed in a blur, but I had time to register that the Island Bobbie's never seem shocked by anything. Still, even the rider was becoming used to low-level motorcycle aerobatics on The Island.

I put my brakes on hard for the first corner at Quarter Bridge, an acute double apex right-hander approached flat-out downhill. Not the corner to take liberties with. I was flat out to the left and right of Braddan Bridge. I had just enough time to change down into third gear before hauling on the brakes for the double turn.

How my was Norton was moving, and I was closing on number one, but where were all the works bikes?

Union Mills, Glen Vine, and the gap narrowed until I saw my chance to pass as we approached Crosby Village.

Too late! Whoomp! Whoomp!

First Malcolm Uphill, and then Rodney Gould on the 'works' Triumphs rocketed past and away. The left-hand bend coming into Crosby Village can be taken with the rider flat on the tank and tucked right in. Mick raised his head for a quick look and I was through, striving hard to keep up with the two leading machines.

The *old* Commando was moving faster than it had ever gone in practice and through Crosby, was already showing 7,000rpm. Over the hill and down towards The Highlander plummeted my green painted steed.

With each drop in the road level, the front wheel became light, and the handlebars shrugged disdainfully in my hands. As I approached The Highlander, the rev-counter almost gave me heart failure, with a needle reading a steady 8,000 rpm.

This can't be true! The 'clock' must be up the spout! I'm never going that fast!

The rev-counter has been checked; the bike can't be that quick! But what if it is and I blow the motor up on the first lap?

I shut off the throttle until the grip was almost closed and shot through the speed-trap, which still recorded 130.6mph!

Sit up and change into third for the left-right swoop of Greeba Castle. As I eased the throttle, the machine began the gentle 120 miles an hour snake to which I had become accustomed in practice.

The weave lasted for only a moment until the power was re-applied to drive through the bends. This sensation did remind me that Commandos are fast, heavy, and hairy!

Greeba Castle and Seventh Milestone; how I concentrated as I flung the Fuzz-mobile from kerb to kerb, it's very heart shuddering with the effort and speed.

Is this really me riding on The Island?

Am I really in third place, on a Norton, with only two works bikes in front?

CONCENTRATE! I screamed inside.

At Ballacraine Crossroads, the course swings sharp right towards the rocky valley known as the Glen Helen Section. The smooth tarmac had gone and ahead lay the much bumpier surface for which the Mountain Course is known.

Shock waves jangle up and down your vertebrae like hammers on the xylophone and you feel your windpipe leaping about in the back of your mouth. The machine was leaping and twitching like a wild thing and I had to fight every foot of the way through Dorans Bend, Laurel Bank, the tricky left-hander at the Glen Helen Hotel, and up the winding Creg Willey's Hill. I could feel the temperature rising inside my leathers as I fought to keep on the correct racing line, aiming between the grass-covered rocky banks.

Creg Willey's opens out onto the flat-out Cronk-y-Voddy Straight and I poised on the footrests for my annual all-in wrestling match as the bars twitched left, right, then the rear wheel hopped first one way, and then the other, accompanied by tortured cries from the hard-working engine.

Suddenly, at the eleventh milestone, Paul Smart on his 'works' Commando slipped past me.

Hello, this is it.

They've all caught you. Your moment of glory is over my son!

My wrists ached as I heaved the Norton through the third gear left and right twist past Handleys Cottage, with Paul Smart now 50 yards ahead. Five gallons of fuel is a lot of weight in the tank between your knees (known as 'top hamper') to chuck about at these speeds.

Paul was still in sight as we dropped down Barregarrow Hill. I saw the uplifted and expectant faces of the crowds as we tore towards them at top speed.

Into the right-hand gutter, aim for the White House at the apex of the sharp left bend at the foot of the hill, I told myself.

The Commando dived towards it without change of speed as we arrived at the turn.

My bicycle groaned at this extreme test of its torsional strength and fought towards the right-hand banking once more.

I dashed through Kirkmichael and at the right and left at Rhencullen it is important to have the machine upright immediately upon the exit from this last bend as there is a humped brow and the machine tries to leave the ground. Arriving at this point can be tricky and the rider would prefer not to take to the banking!

The front-wheel lifted and the steering fought against the steadying influence of the hydraulic steering damper.

The jump at Ballaugh Bridge passed under my wheels. The Met Police Trials Team would've been proud of my rear wheel landing!

I zoomed out of Ballaugh Village, towards Quarry bends and into top gear.

We fairly whistled around a left-hand sweep, past the farm buildings and towards Ballacrye Road, which winds back from my left towards The Cronk. Here the road rises and drops, rather like a small hump-backed bridge.

My 750 leapt over the drop with its motor screaming, landing yet again on its rear wheel only to have the front wheel hauled heavenwards as traction was reapplied.

Ahead, the road almost disappeared from view but the front always comes down again... eventually! The momentary doubt, which accompanies the leap, with every lap, is dispelled as the front tyre slapped onto the road and we're still in business. What a stimulating place this Island Circuit is; unparalleled anywhere in the world where rider extends the machine to feats of performance perhaps never envisaged by its designer.

In 1978, many years after TT racing had become a personally treasured and happy memory, I settled behind the banking at Ballacrye to watch the riders passing this extremely fast section of the circuit; becoming aware that no one else had discovered it as such an amazing viewing point. The area, spectator-wise, was deserted! Every machine became airborne as it crossed the 'hump' and would remain airborne for many metres. It must be admitted that when a bike is off the ground, drive acceleration and therefore speed is forfeit until traction is renewed. But surely, I should keep the throttle wide open!

I watched and listened as Mike Hailwood approached from Ballaugh. As he arrived at the lift-off point, he very precisely and momentarily checked the throttle; the front wheel did not lift, his machine remained fully on the ground and Mike disappeared towards Quarry Bends, accelerating earlier and travelling quicker than any other rider; selecting the next higher gear earlier than any other machine. Hailwood was making a return to the TT, eleven years after his last ride there and having competed so successfully in Formula One Car Racing. Mike won the Formula One TT race on a Ducati and returned the next year to win the Senior TT in his last ever race! Message received, boss. There is a good way to race but there are only a few who can ride spot-on right up to the finishing flag.

Returning to my tale, I could hardly believe that only three 'works' bikes were ahead. Over the Mountain, down to 32nd

215

Milestone, Windy Corner, 33rd Milestone, Keppel Gate, Kates Cottage, and dropping over the edge of the steep hillside down to Creg-Ny-Baa. The weather was very hot and we had been warned of wet tar on this falling right-hand bend, so it seemed expedient to sit up and brake shade early. However, what's this? I thought to myself. Rushing past me on my right was a Triumph rider, really chasing something! This is where you work for your supper, Bailey! I told myself.

The Commando had the speed and I caught up and waited my chance. I passed the start/finish line with a standing start lap at a shade under 96mph.

At Crosby Village, I swept confidently past Daryl Pendlebury on his Triumph Bonneville and thought that that was the dispute settled. At the same time, I saw Rodney Gould on his 'works' Triumph coasting to a stop on the left. So, I was back in third spot with only two 'works' bikes. Uphill on his Triumph and Paul Smart on his Norton in front now!

My peace was shattered 15 miles later as I *knocked it off* for the right, then left, then right, then left, then right, and finally the third gear fight of Quarry Bends.

Pendlebury scratched past me and threw his bike into the series of turns.

Out onto the long, bumpy, Sulby Straight, I again showed my rear number plate to the Triumph. That should've done it! Yet, at the Sulby Bridge right-hander, he was through again, riding a little harder than I wanted to! He was trying hard and at the following left-hand sweep at Ginger Hall, the limit of the Bonneville grip on the road cried 'enough' and flicked into a frightening lock-to-lock battle with its jockey, thankfully won by the latter.

As my bike was faster, I settled down on his tail and waited for another chance to regain third spot; hoping to worry the Triumph now and again and keep him on his toes. After all, the race was run over three laps and barely one and a half had been completed.

No use in getting into trouble at this stage, I told myself.

Up and over the Mountain we tore. Was the motor losing its edge on the climb? No, the Kuhn engine was staying with Pendlebury, so perhaps I had just been imagining things.

I went past The Creg, Brandish and around the high-speed extremely bumpy right-hand sweep of Hillberry and up towards Signpost Corner.

Keep close to the Triumph now, I told myself, you can have him as we pass the start and finish line.

Almost two laps completed. This should be a quick one, I thought.

I shut off for the slow right-hander at Signpost. The engine gave a bang. Oh no. I went into second gear and the motor picked up. It's okay, she's running alright, I told myself. The exhaust pipe must be leaking a bit. That must be what caused the bang.

Again, the motor banged, and this time puttered onto one cylinder. A great choking sensation rushed up to my throat.

The motor must not fail, not now! I screamed inside.

I was doing so well. I had to try to get to the pits and keep the motor running!

At Governors Bridge, the motor coughed and died with a desperate roar of induction through the carburettors. Not able to accept that all was lost in so important a race, I tore off my goggles, pushed, ran and staggered with the dead monster the quarter mile or so to the pits alongside the start and finish line.

Graham Bailey at Governors Bridge 1968 (on the Chuck Triumph)

Frantic efforts by Gordon were unable to raise any life from the engine. With its years of technological advances and research, the British manufacturer's super-modern nylon contact breaker heels had melted, thus, reducing the contact breaker points gap to nothing and retarding the ignition timing, then finally killing the sparks!

My thoughts were interrupted as Malcolm Uphill on the 'works' Triumph burst across the line to win at the fantastic average speed of 99.99 mph, with a record lap of 100.26 mph on this, a fully equipped road bike!

Paul Smart slotted into second spot and my late opponent Daryl Pendlebury, made it Triumph first and third.

After so much work and effort in the weeks before the race, finishing just about makes everything worthwhile. However, with only the taste of failure to go home with, I could only hope that God willing, it would be possible to try again next year.

Half of TDP (Lewisham Traffic Garage) was going on annual leave to the Isle of Man, so I thought I'd better go too!

Sometime after the 1969 adventure, thinking back to the events at the TT, disc brakes were a relatively new development in the motorcycle racing world of the late 60s.

You will recall that my Kuhn Norton was fitted with disc front brakes as were the 'works' Norton Commandos. The Gus Kuhn disc brakes on my machine, however, were not of Norton manufacture but Colin Lyster's manufacture. Although I was not aware of the detail, the question was, were they actually listed by the Norton Factory as optional extras?

Any extras, namely special parts used, had to be listed as such by the manufacturer to qualify for their use in a Production Racing motorcycle. Although nothing was said during practice week or at any time later and this Gus Kuhn rider being completely absorbed in the preparation of racing practice with his Norton Commando, I became vaguely aware of a whisper that an objection had been raised that Lyster brakes were fitted to Bailey's Commando.

As already observed, nothing was said, and no official action was taken. Official politics were of no concern to the rider of Race Number Two. Rather, fulfilling the dream of *climbing another mountain* was foremost in my mind. Following our first practice laps and upon checking the bike over, we found that the contact-breaker points gap had closed. Shadows of the 1968 Practice Week with the Chuck Components Thruxton 'sparked' in my memory. The points were duly adjusted, ready for our next practice outing. I also recall that several days into the Practice Week, a Norton Factory technician arrived at our workshop with the news that he had been *appointed* by Vincent Davey and was taking over the preparation of our Norton from us, so we did not need to worry.

'Jim' actually visited our workshop and prepared the Commando on only one occasion! Being aware that the year before (1968), those with 'Chuck customised components' had experienced the nylon contact-breaker heel (which had replaced the tried and trusted Tufnal heel) melting on our Triumph and being so grateful that the Joseph Lucas team had provided an 'updated' contact-breaker system, I advised the 'Norton man' of our history.

My question regarding our Commando was to ask whether this matter had been dealt with and the latest points and cam-follower fitted on our Norton. Although I recall that he had a spare set of points with him on arrival at our base, he responded that 'everything was alright' with the points, that there was no problem and no need to replace those already fitted.

Perhaps it is that *this man complains too much* (with apologies to William Shakespeare). But was it that politics had taken over and that steps had been taken (or not taken) to ensure that Bailey's Gus Kuhn Norton failed to complete the race? Maybe we will never know, but it must be recorded that Mick Andrew on the other similarly equipped Gus Kuhn Commando finished in fourth position at 95.15mph. So, there you go, Bailey! Stop going on so!

Later in the summer of 1969, during a visit to the Norton

Factory in Woolwich, whilst in conversation with one of their top technicians, he was clear that my Commando had been quite competitive. He drew out his slide rule and informed me that the Commando would have been quite happy spinning over at the 8,000 revs recorded at The Highlander on the first lap. The Norton, I was told, would therefore have been travelling at 139mph.

Do you get the point of the chapter title?

The racing season following The Island was very much enjoyed as Vincent Davey of Gus Kuhn allowed me both to ride the Production bike and to compete on their rather hairy stripped-down Commando, in Unlimited (engine) Capacity races. All went well until I was at Brands Hatch riding the Production Commando. During an over-enthusiastic attempt to reach Paddock, the first bend, ahead of the field. Launching from my start line position on the right side of the third row of the grid, Officer Bailey managed to drop the front wheel onto the grass, then with great skill, pole-vaulted, using his extended right arm and ended up in an untidy heap!

Many smiles must have been exchanged in the stands as the flying copper left the field on foot with a fractured wrist and another DNF (did not finish) to his name!

Neale Shilton, 'Mr Triumph', who had left Meriden and was involved with Norton Villiers, via several friendly letters, promised to look out for a ride for the Constable by the time the new racing season got underway. I have always felt so privileged that fairly busy guys 'in the trade' often went out of their way to help this *mountain climbing dreamer.*

20

1970: a very short season

The prospect of *climbing the mountain* once more was promising as we looked forward to the 1970 racing season.

Ron Welling, a near neighbour, who was one of the top guys at Elite Motorcycles in Tooting, offered me the use of Elite's Triumph Thruxton for the season's Production Machine racing events, with the additional use of their 250cc Aer-Macchi 'real racer'. This machine would enable me also to compete in the Lightweight 250 events.

Early in the year, getting ready for the new racing season, my dear friend Rodney Ford and I loaded up the bikes and headed off to Snetterton for some pre-season practice. Although the Aer-Macchi was not fitted with a fresh set of racing tyres, it was suggested that although these would be available later, the current tyres would 'do me' for the test day.

Snetterton racing circuit, formerly RAF Snetterton Heath, historically a WW2 airfield is in Norfolk near the East coast. The countryside is low-lying; thus, the circuit is quite exposed and when the Spring winds blow, you jolly well know it!

Almost a full lap was completed and as the Aer-Macchi and its new rider swept round the continuous high-speed right-hand bend at Coram Curve, a powerful gust of easterly wind blasted through the five-bar gate width break in the right-side banking; the tyres lost traction, Bailey and Aer-Macchi parted company and that was it! Your scribe has no recall of the event as he slept for about six hours. I awoke later in Norfolk at Norwich Hospital and was diagnosed with a fractured base of the skull.

The strange thing is; following my time of rest, as I opened my eyes becoming aware that I was lying in the basic semi-prone *First Aid recovery position*, I noticed that I was bleeding onto the bed-sheet from my ear. Drawing from the first aid training I had received over my years in the Constabulary, I *self-diagnosed* my condition before being official informed! It's funny how the brain works when you least expect it!

I was totally unaware that Rodney Ford, the true friend and a genuine 'boy scout', had, without any fuss and on his own, gathered up my bits and pieces, loaded everything into his van and carried it home. Being the special guy he was, Rodney took on the responsibility of telling my mum that Graham Bailey had *done it again*. Not only that, but before he visited my mum, Rodney personally washed the blood soiled clothing so that no one else had to be made aware of just what a messy boy Bailey had been!

So, there it was, a rather short racing season, abruptly terminated by a slide up the road on my ear.

Lesson: always prepare the machine properly, and that includes the tyres!

After a restful stay in Norfolk, it was time to go back home, and following a short time of recuperation, I return to the real world, performing a short period of 'light duties' and then resuming normal shift work.

Back in 1968, Dennis, a fellow Trafpol, who was friendly with a family from Poland, now resident in England, had spoken to me about one of this family's relatives, Barbara 'Basia' Glabiszewska. Barbara was visiting England from Poland.

'I'm asking *you* to show her around the country a bit and look after her, 'cos you are the only one I can trust!' Dennis said.

Following his request, it had been my privilege to enjoy the company of Barbara who was training to be a Doctor of Medicine back home. During her stay in this country, we had taken several trips to London, down to the coast, and other places.

When Barbara returned home, we corresponded regularly, and I learned about the difficult way of life that post-war political thinking had created in her Country. Barbara had invited me on several occasions to visit her and her family in Sopot. To me, behind the 'Iron Curtain' was a scary place to even think of visiting, but in the middle of 1970, I ran out of excuses and set about organising things.

It was therefore a requirement that I officially notify 'them upstairs' of my planned visit to Poland. This resulted in an interview at New Scotland Yard. I was advised that as a serving Police Officer, there would be possible pitfalls to be aware of.

'Be careful what you say,' they said.

This advice was apparently one of the easiest precautions to avoid that simple trap or unknown pitfall.

The law of the country I was going to required that a visitor deposit a set amount of currency at their official site in London. Said office, having hold of my *sterling* would then issue me with a voucher, which would secure the equivalent exchange rate in Zloty when this traveller reached Poland. In 1970, the exchange rate was sixty Zlotych to one Pound Sterling.

On 21st August, Bailey flew to Poland, landing in Warsaw, but during the flight, it was required that an official form be completed, declaring how much Sterling I was carrying. During my visit, it was *quietly observed* that there was a higher rate of exchange, particularly popular at nearby seaports. Three times sixty was the suggested rate. Needless to say, it was obvious that should officialdom discover that a visitor's issued number of zloty had increased and the sterling in hand, as recorded in flight, had decreased; serious questions would be asked!

At the bank in the Airport Arrivals, I proffered my London issued voucher and received the allotted sum of 1077.30 Zlotych. From Warsaw Airport, it was necessary to travel by taxi to the Central Railway Station. One was quickly found. This traveller was offered the front seat; then two complete strangers climbed in behind me. They turned out to be an American couple, tourists who had 'come back home' to the land of their forebears for a look round.

Needless to say, we were soon engaged in friendly chatter speaking in our mother tongue.

The taxi driver sat quietly and drove into town, dropping the American couple off at their city centre hotel. Later, as we reached the railway station, I saw that the meter had clicked up to sixty zlotys and began to dig out the required amount.

'Have you any English money?' The driver said, in perfect English.

I was reminded of the warnings back home and was so glad that my recent fellow passengers and I had not got into politics.

At the station, a man and his son, recognising that I was a *stranger in town,* sought to assist me. Having helped me purchase a rail ticket for the trip north to Sopot; as this friendly father and son sat drinking coffee awaiting the arrival of my train, our conversation developed and I discovered that father and son were travelling to Gdansk, which in fact was the city close to but just south of Sopot.

Late in the evening, the train, pulled by an engine that looked similar to one seen in the cowboy films of my youth, steamed into the station. The platform was full of crowds of people eagerly waiting to board the train. My newfound and substantially built friend, picking up my suitcase, motioned with his elbows that I should adopt a canoe paddling stance. With a quick nod of his head indicating that I follow him, my guide then, using his elbows and my suitcase as earlier described, paddled through the surging waves of people eager to board the train, climbed up the steps into the train and motioned that I take occupation of the only available seat!

We travelled north and the father then told me that his son would travel on from Gdansk to support and help me to find the address of the family I was visiting. The father left the train at Gdansk and his son travelled with me to Sopot. We arrived in the town at 1:00 a.m. and walked through the dimly lit and deserted streets.

Upon arrival at my planned destination, Barbara's home, Chrobrego 36, we knocked on the door and waited.

There was no reply.

During our planning for the trip, Barbara had also given me the name and address of a relative in another part of town. So, in search of the location, my friend's son and I walked through the streets. We eventually found the address, which was in a

226

block of flats and knocked at the door number given, quite a few floors up. We were greeted by a rather gruff resident and an unfriendly, growling dog, and thus it was confirmed in our minds that we were on the wrong floor! Bailey and his guide had knocked on the wrong door, well after 1:00 a.m.!

We went up one further flight of stairs and arrived at the correct flat number where we were warmly welcomed in. Within what seemed a very short time, Barbara also arrived at the flat. My helpful guide left to return to Gdansk in the middle of the night, and Barbara guided me to the family home.

The Glabiszewski family warmly welcomed me into their home. It should be noted that their ground floor flat, which was occupied by the four members of the family, had recently, by the decision of the authorities, been divided into two separate units. The official reasoning was that three rooms and a kitchen would be sufficient for four, yet now there were five. I soon discovered that there was an additional *visitor* nearby my family holiday address. The experience of knowing that a plain-clothes policeman was at the end of the garden at all hours 'keeping an eye' on the Englishman, was quite scary and kept one's bodily functions regular.

By contrast, the friendliness and hospitality of my new friends and the Polish people were wonderful. They were living, to a large extent, under the control of a foreign power and certain essentials were in short supply, particularly meat. Yet, I never went without meat on my plate and was aware that, had it been necessary, I would have been given the *top brick off the chimney*.

Sopot, I discovered, was a beautiful town set on the coast of the Baltic Sea. Wandering along the beach, one could spot pieces of Amber lying in the sand and soon build up a small collection.

Happy days would be spent swimming in the sea with one of Barbara's uncles. During the war, he had briefly flown as aircrew in the Luftwaffe. Sometimes, during his early flying career, he had arrived at and flown over Southampton. As a consequence, he becomes a *guest* of our country in that city, for the rest of World War Two.

His knowledge of English was limited, except for his fluency in locally used swear words, because that was all that he had picked up as a prisoner of war in England. Yet, we got on like a house on fire.

What sticks in my memory is the time we happily splashed about in the Baltic Sea.

'When you go home, don't forget us!' Uncle Gustav said.

Although my home in the United Kingdom was barely one thousand miles distant, underlined to me was the realisation that we were greatly separated by the hand of rigid political ideologies.

One evening, during a family visit to friends in another town, we spent some of the time as the party chatted happily. Needless to say, I did not know the Polish language. Yet, with Barbara's help, I was included in the conversation.

It became clear that several of the men present were personally involved in 'running the town'. At one point, a member of the group who stood out because he was less formally dressed than his companions, giving the impression that maybe he was on his way to a music festival in the forest, became aware of my presence!

My rather informally dressed fellow guest could speak English and began to hold forth with somewhat expansive and negative views about the current political leadership in the United Kingdom. It seemed that this particular individual was looking for an argument. With my original guidance from the earlier interview back home ringing in my ears, I held my tongue. Things quietened down and the rest of the evening was a pleasant time of meeting and sharing.

The visit to Poland was nonetheless quite an adventure, but traps were there ready to be sprung. The holiday had its frightening moments when officialdom took control, or one became aware of it lurking in the shadows.

The timing of my holiday meant that I was in Poland on 1st September, the same day it had been invaded by Germany in 1939. Two days later, on 3rd September, World War Two had been declared.

One day on a trip out of town, Barbara showed me where the Germans had entered her country; a spit of land called Hel where Poland had come under the occupation of Nazi Germany.

Many years later, I discovered through Edmund Gonzik, a Polish friend who had been taken into the German Wehrmacht as a youth, that on the 1st of September 1939, the German battleship *Schleswig-Holstein* was in Gdansk (formerly Danzig), just across the bay from Hel, on a courtesy visit. Without warning, it began to shell the Polish garrison. The rest, as they say, is history.

To my mind, in 1970, Poland was still to an extent 'occupied', yet my quiet observation and experience showed so clearly that the lovely people of that land knew how to handle it!

One evening, sitting with the family, my Baltic swimming companion was clearly able to voice his views of *the hand*, which held to that rigid political ideology. With a gramophone record made by Odeon playing at full volume, a German Luftwaffe battle song with choir and military band providing the background (such records were banned in post-war Poland). His sentiments were voiced in English, using terms which he had obviously 'picked up' whilst visiting Southampton.

Uncle's observations could not have been delivered more eloquently in the middle of Camberwell Green on that Saturday night. The ladies in the room were clearly nervous about the musical choice and volume, as was your scribe because it was late August, the windows were open, and our friend at the end of the garden was on watch. The thought, however, was there. *When you get home, don't forget us!*

Before starting my return journey home, due to that 'officialdom', I was missing a required additional entry in my passport. This should have been provided as August ended and I *re-registered* my presence in Poland as we moved into a new month, September. But it was not! Simply because when we attended the office to re-register, as directed on the day before my departure for home, the officials had all got on their bikes and gone home!

One day, in the week prior to my flight back to England, an East German fellow, in his need to escape to the West, had unsuccessfully attempted to hijack a Polish aircraft. The result was that at Gdansk Airport, my place of departure on the journey to Warsaw, there to connect with the flight home, everyone was being closely checked and searched.

I moved forward in the long single-file queue (kept so by closely spaced wooden rails) and arrived at the check-in, coming face to face with two *very official* officials. One had a sawn-off haircut and wore a dark high-necked 'civvy' suit, and the other in a uniform. The three stars on each lapel indicating a man of senior rank.

I produced my Passport, still short of its required entry, handing it to the uniformed officer. Through his dark glasses, he focussed questioningly on the 'British' person, then slowly flicked through the pages of the document, three times, purposefully closing and re-opening the book each time (visions of the drowning man). The official almost reluctantly then stamped my Passport and waved me through to where everyone who had been ahead of me in the queue was being searched by officers of the blue-uniformed Militia. Yet, I was not searched!

We were all eventually waved outside and herded into a fenced-off area. Barbara and her family were waiting outside on the other side of the security fence to bid me farewell.

'Barbara, they didn't search me or arrest me!'

'Look at the colour of their passports, Graham. You don't have anywhere to escape to because you are free!' Barbara replied.

I then realised that not all the other folk who had passed through the check-in held the blue Passport with which I was blessed. They came from the wrong side of the Iron Curtain; and I was leaving my friends there!

That was *a mountain pass* that Bailey would not be able to help others across.

As the London bound aircraft took off from Warsaw Airport, gained height, passed over the River Vistula below, and raised its wheels, I finally began to breathe easily.

21

Crooks Suzuki

One day, later in the 1970 'season', I was invited to accompany Ray Knight on an outing to 'track-test' a race-winning Crooks Suzuki.

My friend Ray, the well-known motorcycle journalist and experienced racer, knew quite a bit about TT racing. For example, he was always well placed in the 500cc class of the Production Machine TT.

In the 750 class of the inaugural Production Machine TT in 1967, having suffered a non-finish, Ray had won the 500 Class of the Prod TT in 1968 at a speed of 90.09mph. Then, between 1969 and 1973, had secured second, third, fourth and seventh positions.

On our arrival at the circuit, Ray introduced me to Eddie Crooks, 'Mr Suzuki'. Eddie, who had won the Senior Manx Grand Prix in 1959 riding a Norton at a speed of 94.87mph, now ran a motorcycle business at Barrow-in-Furness, Cumbria. His company was, I believe, one of the first in the UK to be involved with Suzuki, the Japanese motorcycle manufacturers, and put that marque on the racing map. From his racing experience, Eddie also really knew The Island and it was a privilege to get to know him as a friend.

Once more I felt so fortunate and a little amazed that great characters of the motorcycle racing world helped and inspired GB as I sought to *climb my mountain*.

In 1971, Eddie entered me in the 500cc class of the four-lap Production Machine TT. I was to ride his extremely competitive T500R Crooks Suzuki. The two-stroke twin-cylinder machine, although it looked bog-standard, was fast and responsive. It handled well, but one was aware that the low-slung twin exhaust silencers would 'deck' easily if the rider was really trying. Thus, the 'angle of lean' had to be carefully judged with an additional degree of body lean, if required!

Practice went smoothly and as we prepared for the race on the 9th of June, the weather was fine and favourable for a good dry race.

The start was once more of the traditional 'Le Mans' style. All the riders were lined up opposite their individual machines on one side of the track and their machine across the road arranged in an echelon line below the scoreboard, supported by their mechanic. Crooks Suzuki motorbikes were building up a successful TT record, so Bailey had a serious job to do.

Already the excitement of the Production Machine race was in full flow because the 750cc class had been first to leave the start-line. The 500s, after the planned interval, would start next and then the 250cc class would be flagged away, following another pause. Thus, on the Glencrutchery Road, it was *all go*.

As the starting flag swept down for the 500s, every rider set off as fast as he could, running towards his machine. As I recall, not having written a tale in detail about the race immediately after the event, there was a bunch of us riding in the leading group all attacking the course. The first lap on the run through Braddan, Union Mills, and Crosby, out towards the Glen Helen section, was close fought and crowded, but as always in The Island, riders tended not to compete *wheel to wheel*.

Nine miles from the start, as we approached the crossroads at Ballacraine, the riders in our group were on the very fast straight approaching the right turn at the junction which would take them on towards the Glen Helen Section.

I was not aware of the exact identities of those who were riding in the close bunched group, simply that as we approached the critical braking point, the rear wheel of a Suzuki just ahead of me locked-up and with its smoking rear tyre skating along the surface, it was clear the rider was not going to lose enough speed to safely negotiate the turn.

I remember shouting desperately at the rider to 'go straight on', being so fearful of the likely outcome, yet happy that it *could be* alright.

The speed of his machine was too great for him to maintain and follow his chosen line. The dear man, nonetheless, attempted to negotiate the turn and I thus witnessed the rider and machine running wide and tragically, heavily impacting the front entrance of the Ballacraine Inn.

Sadly, Brian Finch passed into eternity.

To my knowledge, I had never met or even spoken to my fellow racer, Brian. *But the race must go on,* as they say. The 'but' here was that Eddie Crooks' rider did not want to go on! He was deeply shocked and saddened by what had just been witnessed. Yet, as his Suzuki flashed past the fallen rider, young Bailey was aware that a moment of lost concentration on his part could result in yet another tragedy. I was also aware that I was committed to honouring the trust, which had been placed in him by his friend from Barrow-in-Furness.

There was a job to be done and although I have no detailed recall of the race from there on to the end; the four-lap race, ridden in beautiful weather conditions, was completed and Bailey was fortunate enough to finish in fourth position at a speed of 86.42mph.

John Williams, the victor on his Honda CB450, turned in a much greater race speed at 91.04mph. Ray Knight, riding a Triumph T100T, did not finish the race as his Meriden built machine let him down after lap one. However, Ray would doubtlessly have finished ahead of the Crooks Suzuki rider because, although he only completed one lap, that lap was covered in around 22 seconds, less time than Bailey had managed!

The one thing I do recall which sadly remains vividly imprinted in my memory, however, is the tragic event of the first lap and the sadness, which must have descended upon the loved ones of Brian Finch.

For the full 1971 racing season, Eddie had in fact enabled me to compete on mainland circuits using his T500R. He even provided me with a 250cc Suzuki-outright racer for the Lightweight Class races. This machine, I believe, had earlier been ridden with much success in World Championship events by Malcolm Uphill.

It was super competitive, and I recall with some satisfaction having beaten one of those riders who would later become world-class, in a Club Race at the Kentish circuit at Lydden. The TT rules had not been changed in 1971 and therefore my trusting 'Mr Suzuki' entered GB in the Lightweight Class of the Manx Grand Prix, which would take place on The Island in early September. Not only that, but Eddie then built my 250 into a Seeley frame!

It seemed Eddie was keen to give his rider something, which would be ultra-competitive because the Seeley frame and cycle parts made for a machine that was light and would probably out-handle most other machines.

Another advantage was that the light weight allowed the machine to accelerate and decelerate more effectively, as well as travel faster and maybe secure a better finishing position.

The MGP had everything going for it, as far as *the mountain dreamer* was concerned. I recall that Practice Week went quite well as the Crooks Team, a great group of super guys, worked and prepared everything… for me!

The start of the races on The Island, for machines other than the Production Class, was different. At the drop of the starter's flag, each rider had to run, pushing his machine, which had a dead engine, jump aboard side-saddle, bump, start the engine by dropping the clutch, then get down to racing. Thus, it was necessary that the gearbox had been placed into gear and the clutch lever held in, ready to go.

Another difference on The Island was that the riders started individually at ten-second intervals. Some races were started with two riders pushing off side by side. Thus, the race was more 'against the clock' than just trying to outride the others around you, as in what was called a short circuit 'scratch' race.

My start went to plan and this wonderful and potential race-winning Seeley-Suzuki simply flew. What a joy it was to hear and feel the motor buzzing away.

By the time our *dreamer* had reached Ballacraine seven miles from the start, we had already overhauled and passed six riders. Six times ten seconds, even to my simple mathematical calculation was some kind of progress!

Ballacraine Crossroad, Ballaspur, Ballig Bridge, Doran's Bend; how she was flying. Oh boy!

As I confidently hooked the gear lever to select a lower gear on the approach to the Ninth Milestone, I realised there was no gear lever pedal there!

The dream was beginning to fade.

I came to a stop and saw that the welding between the horizontal lever pedal and the vertical linkage was fractured. A Marshal sauntered past and accidentally dropped his tools onto the pavement nearby. How careless of him! Frantic work with bits of twisted wire liberated from a passing fence and pliers from the abandoned tool kit.

I failed to jury-rig the gear change lever into a working unit and that was it. Dream over.

GB set off, taking the back roads cross-country returning to base. Bottom gear all the way!

For the whole journey, as I crossed The Island, negative thoughts about the workmanship of the Seeley craftsmen surfaced. When my team returned from the course, I clearly expressed my sentiments and disappointment about Seeley.

John, the dear man who had worked so hard preparing the bike for the race, quietly said, 'I'm so sorry, it's down to me. I welded that gear lever together. It is no one's fault but mine. I must have used a welding rod which didn't match the gear lever metal.'

What can one say to someone who has burnt the midnight oil and burnt the candle at both ends to give an off-duty copper another attempt to climb *his personal mountain* other than, 'thank you for all that you have done for me'?

As the saying goes; nothing ventured, nothing gained!

As the season drew to a close, having benefited from the privilege of being part of the Crooks Team and so aware that they could tune and prepare very competitive Suzukis, thoughts of owning and preparing a competitive machine of my own began to develop. Maybe a Crooks Suzuki 500 power unit fitted into a decent racing frame?

Perhaps, if I followed that route, it could be possible to have a competitive machine for the new season.

I had got to know Paul Dunstall of Dunstall Norton Dominator (The Dunstall Domi), the manufacturer of 'go faster' parts. He was a genuinely friendly guy and it was a privilege to visit his factory on a number of occasions and share the occasional 'brew' with him.

I learned through the press that Dunstalls was involved in the development of a special framed racer fitted with a Kawasaki engine and gearbox unit. It appeared to be a similar project to that of Colin Seeley, who had developed a Seeley frame-kit to carry AJS, Matchless, and other engine units.

At the same time that the dream about a Crooks Suzuki power unit fitted in a special frame was forming, a visit to Paul's works revealed that the Dunstall/Kawasaki frame kit project was 'on hold' and that the frame and cycle parts could be purchased by me, complete with the Kawasaki H1 three-cylinder two-stroke engine and gearbox unit!

The whole motorcycle. Wow!

Thoughts about a Crooks Suzuki power unit were now also placed *on hold*. Bailey's *mountain climbing dreams* took on a quite different dimension.

Bailey, are you up to this one? I asked myself. Remember complete preparation is the absolute goal. You've got to do it yourself now, Son.

The information came my way that certain teething troubles had hindered the Dunstall project. The engine, which was a modified H1 road-bike power unit, had been stripped of its standard road-going electrical system. Racing motorcycles (apart from Production Racing machines) are not fitted with lights, horns, and direction indicators. Thus, an electrical generating system and battery for that purpose were not required.

Earlier racers used a magneto, which was a self-generating ignition system.

Now, as things developed, many machines often had their ignition supply provided by battery power.

The lightweight battery fitted would normally be sufficient for the duration of a race; then, as required, it could be replaced with a fresh unit for the next race. To supply enough sparks for a three-cylinder two-stroke engine running at 10,000rpm had raised some difficulties.

I was told that with one ignition system, it had been found that the engine could not be made to rev at the speed required. The machine was then trialled with battery-powered ignition and it was discovered that the range of the available battery was insufficient to last the length of a race before it ran out of power.

Now, I had possession of the Dunstall Kawasaki, and I needed to get it sorted!

Although one or two basic engine items were missing, these were easily found and fitted. Ernie Bransden, the electronics wizard, when questioned about the ignition problem, which we had to overcome, was quick with his response.

'That's easy,' said Ernie. 'Fit an alternator on the end of the crankshaft. The alternator rotor has three magnets, which give *three* magnetic norths and *three* souths every 120 degrees with each revolution. That equals 360 degrees.

'So,' he continued, 'with the alternator, you will have the power for the ignition and with one of my units set up for the three cylinders mounted on the end of the rotor, using the *make and break* of the three magnets, your spark and timing will be spot on!'

Thus, with a couple of other electronic items fitted, we had a self-generating power unit with a built-in electronic ignition system. It should be pointed out that the three-cylinder engine had a 120-degree crankshaft. In other words, one piston reached the firing point every 120 degrees.

QED! A generator or rotor with three magnets that enabled a spark at 120 degrees rotation and an engine that required a spark at the exact same time.

Hugh and Eunice Evans were a great couple and both of them were very competitive racers. Hugh was also an engineer who knew quite a bit about making two-strokes fly. He took charge of the cylinders of my triple and skilfully 'tuned' the porting. Two-stroke engines of the time generally had no valve operation to control the flow of fuel and exhaust. The efficiency of the gas flow, inlet, and exhaust are dictated by the ports through which they travelled.

Hugh knew how to make them work, proper!

After a great deal of bike preparation had been carried out, the Kawasaki was ready for its first outing on a practice day at Brands Hatch. Our first test day at Brands meant that many of the people present were probably aware of the Dunstall project and undoubtedly knew that certain teething problems had been experienced. So, when the newly prepared Kawasaki ran so quickly and faultlessly, our little group was more than thrilled.

The Kwacker was such a good starter that even with the dead engine starts, which were then racing practice, it was great to be able to run only a few paces, drop the clutch, immediately leap into the saddle and be off down the track, often near the head of the field.

22

The still small voice

You will recall, I am sure, the mention I made some pages back of the young SRN and SCM nurse, sitting with Anne, her nursing friend, in a Nissen hut in the refugee camp near Lübeck in Germany, watching the final of the 1966 Football World Cup.

Remember that your scribe was at the same time sitting watching the World Cup final on his friends' television, in Bergen, Norway.

One November 'late turn' in 1972, I was on duty and posted to a motorcycle patrol. My specific duty was to patrol a temporary one-way system that had been put in place in Upper Norwood, South London. This temporary diversion was due to a burst water main and traffic, being diverted from travelling south along Beulah Hill, was turned left into Hermitage Road, then right into Eversley Road. On reaching the crossroads at the junction of Highfield Hill and Harold Road, traffic was again turned right along Harold Road to re-join Beulah Hill. My duty, therefore, was to ensure that traffic flowed smoothly around this short diversion.

It should be pointed out that it was cold, raining and the weather conditions were such that any self-respecting police motorcycle patrol officer would be looking for *a lawful reason* to escape into the warmth of a police canteen!

I, however, diligently patrolled the one-way system and then took up a stationary position at the junction of Harold Road and Beulah Hill. There I sat on my motorcycle, *professionally supervising* and watching the world go by.

After some minutes a Morris 1000 saloon car, coming from behind me along Harold Road, pulled up across the road. The driver wound down her window and called in a very cultured voice.

'Excuse me, officer! How can I drive down Harold Road?' She asked.

It must be pointed out that in those days a Morris 1000 was recognised as normal transport for a district nurse or midwife.

The police officer, who was very smartly turned out, strode purposefully and with authority across the road to the young lady.

Where have you come from?' I asked.

'I came down Highfield Hill,' replied the young lady.

'Well, you should have turned right into Harold Road and not left,' replied the very wise policeman!

'Yes, but the policeman at the junction indicated for me to turn left officer!'

'Well,' I replied, 'turn left, drive up Beulah Hill, and turn left into Upper Beulah Hill. Then turn left down Highfield Hill and when you get to the policeman again, smile at him! I guarantee that if a young lady smiles at a policeman she will get just what she wants.'

'Oh, do you think so?' Asked the young lady.

'Certainly!' I replied, smoothly.

After politely thanking me, the young lady drove off.

Not being the kind of bloke given to following young ladies, I remounted and sat on my silent machine. Something in my head said, 'follow her.'

My silent response was that such action was not the kind of action which I would take and anyway, I had no good reason to do such a thing.

'Go on, follow her!' I thought, No! And anyway, by now she would be too far away for me to catch her up. The voice again caused me to think about my actions.

Now aware that the car would be three parts around the square of roads, strangely, I started up my machine, switched on the blue light, turned the bike around and rode against the traffic, back down Harold Road. I had reached the junction with Highfield Hill as the Morris Thousand entered the junction ahead of me (turning right).

I followed and the car pulled to a standstill several hundred yards further along Harold Road and the young lady, obviously having reached her destination, left the vehicle.

I parked my bike, walked across to her and said, 'I told you that if you smiled at a policeman, you would get what you wanted!'

She smiled politely and looked at me, maybe with a sense of sympathy! We began to talk and as professionals do, I sought to define what career the young lady was following.

After some skilled thought, I said, 'Are you a teacher?'

'No,' she replied.

The thought was 50-50. If she's not a teacher, then she must be a nurse!

'Are you a nurse?' I asked.

'No,' the young lady replied.

'What do you do for a living?' I asked next.

The young lady replied, 'I am in Health Education.'

Clever Bailey then responded, 'So, you are both; a nurse and a teacher!'

The young lady responded in the affirmative.

Keen to know more, I asked, in respect of Health Education, what subjects would be covered. Apparently, among other things, there was teaching on how to give up smoking, how to avoid having babies, and how to deal with drug addiction; from which my new teacher informed me that there was no cure. My response was that oh yes there is!

The young lady looked at me questioningly, obviously wanting to know where I got that idea from. At her invitation, I said that I believed that drug addiction could be overcome by a change of heart.

Without going into great detail, I told her that I felt that *a changed heart* could be part of the cure. I told her of my love for the Lord Jesus and my trust in Him.

It did not take long to establish that Rosemary Allard, SRN SCM, had the same faith in Jesus Christ which I did.

A still small voice? As the saying goes; now read on!

23

A tale of two trophies

This story, written within weeks of the events described, has been slightly edited and thus, the tale told is as near to the events as possible.

Ah well, I'll never learn my 'A' reports, but let us sit back for a minute or two, staring into the fire and dream for a bit!

'A' reports were large sections of information contained in Police General Orders with which a candidate seeking the rank of sergeant was required to be familiar in the Metropolitan Police Promotion Examination, if success was to be achieved… and I was *in the process.*

Race Number 47, GB 1972 TT Practice at Ballaugh Bridge

Last year, 1972, during the TT week in the Isle of Man, my friend Eddie Crooks of Crooks Suzuki; for the Formula 750 Race, gave me a ride on his 500cc Suzuki. Although the machine developed a split in one of its cylinder heads, I managed, lapping at 87.55mph, to finish in 19th position and was awarded a much-valued Bronze TT Replica.

My Tartan Racing Kawasaki, however, due to ignition failure, didn't even start in the Senior TT Race. The result: being so disappointed that my own self prepared bike was a non-starter in the biggest race of the TT race week; the racing leathers, boots, and gloves had been bundled up on the spot and almost offered to any bidder, the owner determined never again to 'do The Island'.

It's funny though, what that old Island does to your body. Its thirty-seven-and three-quarter mile Mountain Course which snakes through some of the most beautiful countryside in Britain, climbs across the moorlands up towards Snaefell's rugged peak, then twists and plunges steeply back towards the sea. Just one lap is a fantastic high-speed memory test. Each year, fellows spend their last penny carefully preparing racing machinery to successfully challenge this world-renowned racing circuit.

The Isle of Man Tourist Trophy Races, founded in 1907, have their own magic history, and many tales are told in darkened rooms of the battles fought on two and three wheels in years gone by. The bug has bitten me too and having started things off with the 1967 event and missed but one year out, here I was, in the face of my 1972 feelings, all ready to go again!

This year of 1973 promised a busy two-week stay on The Island. For the Senior six-lap TT Race, my own home-brewed three-cylinder Tartan Kawasaki had been carefully nailed together. Well, almost!

In the detailed preparation of my bike, it had been discovered that the teeth on the third gear pinion had begun to flake. Ernie Hall, my tame *never say die* engineering wizard and I desperately required a replacement third gear for the Kwacker. Because this did not arrive from America until that Friday afternoon and we were leaving the next morning, Saturday the 26th of May, the rebuild would have to be completed on arrival in The Isle of Man.

It must be clearly recorded here that when Paul Dunstall, the race bike builder and specialist in 'go faster parts', having become aware of my urgent gear-box problem, almost without me realizing, had silently, set wheels in motion.

The replacement gear cluster quietly and seemingly mysteriously arrived at my front door by special delivery from the USA.

Many weeks after the TT events, having not received an invoice or message requiring that I pay Paul Dunstall for the gearbox part and carriage, I spoke to Paul and asked him where the invoice was.

Paul's reply was, 'What invoice?'

Subject closed!

But, once more, a reminder of what some folk will do to help even young dreamers like me.

I was entered in three other races. For Boyers of Bromley, the four-lap Production Sports Machine TT would find me astride their newly acquired 750cc Triumph Bonneville Twin. This event would open proceedings on Saturday the 2nd of June.

My next outing was to be the Lightweight 250cc TT and Geoff Monty, the famous Edenbridge Kent-based former racer and well-known race tuner, handed me one of his racing Suzuki two-stroke twins to contest the four-lap race on the Wednesday morning.

That afternoon, on the 6th of June, *after a quick cuppa,* the Formula 750 T.T. Race was to be run over five laps. For this much-publicised *Superbike race,* I was again with Boyers on one of their thoroughbred racing fire engines!

80bhp of tuned to the eyebrows Triumph Trident three-cylinder engine was shoe-horned into a Seeley racing frame, with disc brakes, transistorised ignition - the lot. It was geared to reach about 145mph and make The Island roads seem a great deal narrower!

Referring to the earlier thoughts concerning the gearbox parts, I was reminded that racing is expensive with many bills to pay. Well, when Ernie and I were travelling north and some way along the M6 Motorway, on the outward journey in one of the two vans which were being used to transport the machines, our Transit died on us!

We tinkered, we poked, we even pushed. To no avail!

While Ernie rested. Having climbed off the Motorway onto a side-road that crossed over the Motorway, I went for a walk and 'borrowed' a pushbike from a very helpful young native who happened to be passing by.

Following his directions, I headed for the distant civilisation to buy some new bits (the lad who had been riding his bike, aware of our difficulties, actually lent it to me. 'Onest, officer!)

The van would still not start.

Have you ever been towed on the end of a four-foot-long chain, behind a big Bedford Motorway Breakdown truck, being driven by a *racing* breakdown driver from Warrington?

After ten miles of that, Ernie and I were glad to sup the racing breakdown driver's tea, which his wife kindly prepared for us. How glad we were that this couple used to '*do the TT*' because that tow-in fee would have put an even bigger dent in the racing expenses balance sheet than it did.

The van was sorted, and we eventually made it safely to the ferry and crossed over to The Island.

There was a lot of midnight oil burned squaring up machinery. There was only time for a brief look around the course, already aired by Dave Minskip and other Police Trafpols. They had been on The Island on their BMWs in the Maudes Trophy attempt earlier in the month and it was now time for the official Practice Week to start on the evening of Monday the 28th of May.

In the past year, the circuit had been resurfaced and smoothed out in one or two places and maybe this would help one's lap times a little. I guess that every rider dreamt about lapping The Island at *the ton* (100mph) and this was certainly my hoped-for goal for the year 1973.

Our 'stroker' (two-stroke engine) was a bit thirsty and not as quick as the 'works machinery' against which I would be competing in the Senior TT.

To pit-stop more than once to refuel in the race would be a dead loss, putting us right out of the running for any decent award. Ernie had therefore played with his *engineering things* and produced a marvellous 8-gallon aluminium fuel tank. This was later called 'the Scrutineer's nightmare' because, after satisfactorily passing through the Scrutineer's tent (Scrutineers: the engineers who check for absolutely precise and complete machine preparation) and being cleared for practice, I was just about to push out onto the circuit when one of the Senior T.T. officials *put the finger on me!*

He claimed that the amount of fuel being carried was against the rules. I pointed out the other machines were running with tanks of a similar fuel capacity and that no regulation was being contravened.

My notes kept of the machine's history state:

Bandit tank fitted! Filled with 8 gallons. Removed approximately one-gallon re-chief Scrutineer's protestations*. We exchanged points of view! They were unable to name any rule, which had been broken. I produced the required sum of one pound to support an official protest. They backed off for the time being and Bailey went out, managed two laps without falling off and put in the fastest lap for the senior class that evening. Handling okay; weaved a bit at high speed on the bumpy going. (*Checking records at much later date it was discovered that the 'official' did not hold title of Chief Scrutineer)

When practising on The Island, it is always best to run with a full fuel tank so that you are used to the machine at its worst and heaviest (Joe Dunphy wisdom). It is too late to find that your bike won't handle with a full tank of fuel halfway down Bray Hill on the first lap of the race!

Reminiscing many years after my last race in the Isle of Man, the thrill of the experience of racing around the Manx TT Mountain Circuit still lifts my spirit. To realise that the privilege of racing around the most testing road racing circuit in the world had been extended to me, your scribe, and remains almost beyond belief.

We also confirmed on the first outing what the fuel consumption was and what gearing and carburettor jetting would be required. Aware that we only had one crankshaft with a limited life, mileage-wise, it was necessary to cover only one more lap and the Kawasaki would have done enough work before the Senior TT Race.

Monday evening was rounded off with a slow lap on our Lightweight Geoff Monty Suzuki, which misfired around the circuit and foretold troubles ahead for us in this class.

We hit the hay and caught a brief rest. All too soon it was 4:30 a.m. on Tuesday and our two-man crew struggled out of bed for the morning practice.

The Formula 750 Triumph Trident was going for a spin today. On a cold misty morning, it required a long tow, and to be hauled behind the van before it eventually grumbled into life. What a machine! It was big, heavy and when the taps were opened up, very hairy

I managed to be second fastest in the class over a lap and a bit, but as there was plenty of sea mist on the run out to Ramsey, it was necessary to knock it off some. As a consequence, the sparking plugs in the motor oiled up and I came back to the Pits at Douglas in the back of a furniture van!

On Tuesday evening, we did a bit of running-in on the new Production Bonneville. Triumph had increased the capacity of the Bonneville from 649cc to a little less than 750cc. I had managed two laps as the sixth fastest in the class, but I was not too happy about the twin hydraulic front disc brakes.

When I had done some miles on the twin, we returned to our digs and spent some time attempting to sort things out. The crew spent some hours bleeding the hydraulic system and we raised our concerns about the problem to our entrant Stan Shenton. Although the brakes worked reasonably well, there was still that spongy feeling as the rider squeezed the brake lever.

So, the week progressed. Plenty of work, plenty of riding, much frustration and very little sleep. We managed to stay in the running in three of our various classes but could not solve the misfire on the Suzuki.

The Kawasaki was cleaned, polished, and put away for its big day. The Bonneville was worked on, but although I had a negative feeling about the hydraulic master-cylinder, we managed to get a good solid lever movement on the front brake.

The Trident was missing third gear quite a bit on brisk upward changes, (remember the Final Ride with Inspector Whitten!?) and the machine did not fit me properly. One could not properly tuck down behind the screen as it was a bit low and the footrests, which incorporated the foot brake (left side) and gear lever (right side), were too far forward.

It's funny, when a bike is not your own, just how limited you are in altering and tailoring things to suit.

The Boyer team were up to its eyes with a total of five machines to keep up to scratch. Our personal team had to do the best we could, which took precious time.

I became fairly accustomed to riding the Trident Seeley, *sitting out in the wind*, or having to slide back and forth on the seat when either at full bore or when negotiating a bend or series of bends. The difficulty was that when riding, tucked in behind the screen, the footbrake and gear lever could not be efficiently operated. Thus, it was necessary to slide forward to *get at* the foot controls.

The essential requirements on a racing circuit, whether smoothly surfaced or rough going, is that the rider should be *locked in* by the seat configuration and have the machine tailored so that all the controls, hand or foot-operated, can be sensitively used when either flat on the tank or *acing* it around the twisty bits. The rider tends to get chucked about and lose the feel of the thing otherwise, potentially even riding the bike 'down to the road' — if you know what I mean, guv!

The scene was hotting up now as the aces, fresh from their mainland Bank Holiday race meeting battles, arrived on the island and began to *get their eyes in*.

Ernie worked till 3:00 a.m. on Saturday the 2nd of June, 'sorting' the front brake and fitting a replacement front fork oil seal, as one had blown on the Bonneville during practice .

After some frustration, when the electrics shorted out at the Weigh-in/Scrutineering, we were about ready for the start of the Production Machine TT at 4:30 p.m. and the weather prospects were not very promising.

The start was to be a Le Mans style run across the road to our machines lined up under the scoreboard. Then a hefty swing or two on the kick-start lever, into gear, and away.

I had drawn No.23, which meant that most of the fast men were nearer the front of the line. The Boyer team: Dave Nixon No.3, John Williams No.8, both on Triumph Tridents, and myself, were after the Manufacturers Agents Team Award which went to the highest placed agent's team to finish.

The flag dropped.

I hopped across the road as if someone had asked for my tea club money, kicked twice and was away in the crowd, headed towards the steep, twisting, residentially populated Bray Hill. At the bottom, the road twists, climbs, and drops towards Quarter Bridge Road and there is only one line to follow when in a hurry.

I was lying about seventh, and Dave Croxford, on one of the works Nortons, went scratching down the hill trying to pass everyone whilst he was riding on the wrong line. He managed to stay aboard and I gently picked off the odd one or two arriving at the first real corner, Quarter Bridge, only two machines behind 'The Crocket'.

This turning is a double apex right-handed downhill bend, which is blind, slow, bottom gear and tricky. Both brakes pinned me down well and around the Bonneville went!

Right boy, now *screw it* all on down to Braddan. You can get the old solo really buzzing in fourth gear on the long straight approach to the bridge, then knock it all off for the second gear left and right flick through the S bend over Braddan Bridge, I told myself.

I hit the brakes and nothing!

The front lever came up to the handlebar and was useless. A bit of overtime on the rear brake pedal and we had our correct speed, *just*, to match to the correct position and gear for the bend! (See 'Motorcycle Roadcraft', chapter two, paragraph two).

On the run out to Union Mills, I pumped the front brake lever like mad and repeated this treatment before each corner to try and find some hydraulic brake pressure. Sometimes it operated but usually, it did nothing. It truly was a matter of, 'What shall I do now, Sarge?'

Dave Nixon passed me through Crosby Village, going like a rocket. Then John Williams shot by, also in a hurry. Riders began to peg me back and I was all for chucking it in but you know what they say: 'wear the badge of courage' (a saying coined by Sir Robert Mark, the then Commissioner of the Metropolitan Police).

I passed The Highlander Pub, a *free house*, but didn't stop, deciding that if the other two in the Boyers team were going well, I had better forget the useless front brake completely, rely on the rear only and press on to at least keep the Team in one piece. We would still have a chance of claiming the Team Award if I finished the race.

The weather was a bit dull and parts of the course were wet as the odd shower of rain fell here and there around the circuit. By braking in good time on the rear stopper, I was managing to get through the twisty bits and the fairly slow revving 750cc motor (running happily at about 6,500rpm) pulled like a horse out of the corners.

I then experienced a tricky rear wheel slide going up Creg Willey's Hill towards the 11th milestone. Here, the road is still quite bumpy and with a bit of dampness around, things just let go a little!

I was pressing on up the mountain climb where it was fairly wet and Ken Huggett (1972 MGP winner) rushed by on his Triumph Trident.

Oh well, that's another place lost.

Dave Croxford 'offed-it' at the Bungalow Bridge (it had to come) and he was footing it back home when I passed.

Going down The Mountain towards Douglas (the start and finish) I caught up with Ken Huggett again. Gaining inspiration from this development, the old traffic patrol person got stuck in.

I stayed with his three-cylinder bike into the second lap and found that my Triumph rear brake worked quite effectively, as I was able to push Ken Huggett on the corners! At Ballacraine, seven miles from the start, a right-angled right turn at a crossroads junction, I somehow, with only the rear brake, managed to out-brake the Trident and nipped in front.

Now there was a bit of needle and after another 10 miles or so, my opponent, after 'closing the door' on me through Quarry Bends, began to pull away.

I aimed to pit for fuel at the end of the third lap. Ken Huggett must have stopped at the end of the second lap.

As I crossed The Mountain on lap three, the heavens opened into the biggest cloudburst ever recorded during a TT race.

The Twin went on to one cylinder. Of course, there has to be water in the works, I thought. Press on and have a look when you stop for fuel.

With cold rain pouring through the zip into my leathers, I struggled towards the pits at Douglas, rounded the hairpin at Governors Bridge, went into the very tight and slow loop which requires the rider to line up tight along the left side of the wall to negotiate the right-hander coming out onto the Glencrutchery Road, when… CRASH.

Ken Huggett was coming from behind, trying to get past me and the left side wall in a place where you don't sensibly ever attempt to overtake! But he made it, put a dent into my left boot and *did for* my rear brake pedal, as in, knocked it from its mounting point. I didn't realise that until I swept into the pits and tried to stop. That's another story. Suffice to say that already, minus an operative front brake... just imagine!

Result: Non-finisher Bailey, Second-place John Williams, Third place David Nixon. No Agents Team Award. Instead that went to the Kawasaki Agent.

Most of Sunday I had off. Monday, work! Tuesday, up on The Mountain with the Suzuki and electronic ignition wizard, Ernie Bransden.

Sparks sorted out. Our 250 Suzuki now running well. We managed to burn off (over-take) two motor coaches and a Norton Commando on the 'test run' along the Mountain Mile! Watch out in the race, you ace!

Wednesday 6th of June, 11:00 a.m. Lightweight TT. Start number 33.

When the starter's flag dropped, I ran, dropped the clutch and the engine fired up immediately but would not run cleanly. I arrived at Ballacraine, seven miles out, and the motor tightened up.

Clutch-in and stop.

Result: non-finisher. One broken crankshaft. Two starts, two DNFs, no awards.

I managed to thumb a lift back to the start and ready myself for the 2:00 p.m. start of the Formula 750 Race.

On my walk to the start, I bumped into Ken Huggett and politely asked him not to *have me over* that afternoon!

This was the ride that I was really looking forward to. The Trident Seeley had been worked on by the Boyers Team overnight. My dear friend, Vic Lane, the main 'spanner man' of the Boyer's team, had worked on the Trident. Vic had produced some modified footrest mounting plates, the footrests had been repositioned and the screen raised. This had been achieved because Vic had cut the fairing horizontally, raised the top, thus repositioning the screen and fibre-glassed the fairing back as a complete unit.

I didn't have a chance to ride it in its new trim but a quick 'sit-on' before the start showed that its rider could remain tucked in.

I was determined to finish this one and as I was given the engine speed ceiling of 8,500 rpm, I decided to keep the revs down to a safe 8,000 rpm and ride as hard as possible; being guided by any signals, which would be given at the pits, and by my helpers around the course.

The start was to be a clutch start with engines running; the riders leaving the starting line in pairs at ten-second intervals. Thus, two machines would start, then another two after a pause of ten seconds and so on. There were Works and Semi-Works Triumphs, Suzukis, Nortons, BMWs, Hondas, Kawasakis, and Yamahas beginning before my number, 54.

Dave Nixon, the number one Boyers runner, was taking up pole position in a field of 74 starters.

A racing Triumph Triple running on song, with the three exhaust pipes running into a single pipe and exiting through a reversed cone megaphone gives an engine note of almost orchestral grandeur.

It was with great relief that as the flag dropped and the clutch bit home, with my motor running on all cylinders, we left the start-line like a rocket, the rapid acceleration thrusting me against the hump at the back of the racing seat.

Race Number 44 GB 1973 Senior TT GB at 'Bottom of Bray Hill'

Bray Hill came and went in a blur as the full range of cogs in the gearbox were given a spin. There is only one sound to compare with the Trident on full power and that is the melody of its motor on the overrun with the machine undergoing full brake application, tearing the air as it is hooked down through the ratios.

The race soon became a concerto of playing tunes on the gearbox, heaving the machine from footrest to footrest (it didn't half make the old wrists and shoulders ache) gobbling up riders who had started before me and trying to keep this projectile between the banks.

My word, how the roads have narrowed since this morning, I thought.

Being tucked inside the modified fairing certainly made life more pleasant. There's plenty to do, without climbing about all over the bike at these speeds. Just before Ramsey, on the far side of the circuit, you arrive at Milntown through a series of very fast bends. You hang onto the right-hand bank round the first left-hander, knock it down a cog, heave over to kiss the left-hand apex and you're all set up for the final right-handed sweep. On the apex at Milntown Cottage you kiss the right-hand bank and leave the section, running close to and in line with the left side pavement (the kerbstone of which has thoughtfully been bevelled off to 45 degrees; just in case!).

Well, I did all that as described and must've been knocking on at around 120mph, when, whoops!

I clunked, then mounted the curb, and was now barrelling along the pavement. Being tucked in behind the screen, out of the wind for the first time on this part of the course, my trusty Strident Trident had a mile-an-hour or two more on the clock than it had been registering during the practice outings of the previous week. The old beastie didn't like it. It shook its head in reproof, ever so slowly. I then managed to get the bike off the pavement on the left side of the road where it should have been in the first place!

Unfortunately, the machine, now trying to wrest control from its rider, was now in a high-speed swoop across to the right-hand side of the road and I needed to be on the left because we were rapidly approaching the very fast right-hander at Milntown Bridge.

Milntown Bridge has a hump that causes the bike to lift off, just before the apex of a right-hander. The bike must be correctly lined up on the left of the road and not cranked over for that apex before it hits the hump. It must have its wheels firmly on the road surface before the turn. Either that or *it's tears before cocoa*!

I managed to pull the bike to the left and get it upright before we took off over the bridge. We hit the mountain climb, and here, the power of the Trident-Seeley could be felt as we whipped up through the gears, screaming defiance out across the hills.

Now, the Isle of Man is not considered to be a 'scratchers' circuit and usually, I only tended to *touchdown* with the edge of my boot at Ginger Hall, a left-hander and Keppel Gate on the mountain, another fast left-hander. Already, though, I could feel the old boot leather getting filed down on some of the other bends; and on this mountain climbing, over the little stone-bridges and through Guthrie's Memorial, everything was scraping the deck!

I was beginning to wonder how my position in the race was progressing because, although our Trident was passing quite a few riders with an interval start, thus racing against the clock; the roadside stopwatch brigade are the only informants who are of any use to you.

The climb towards Snaefell runs along the section known as the Mountain Mile, just west of and below a long ridge of the hills. This 'mile' is almost straight at certain speeds. Halfway along, the British Formula Racing Club had their signalling station. John Milligan, Competition Secretary, was going to give me the latest information. This part of the course is about the only place on the thirty-seven- and three-quarter mile lap where you can relax a little. But not today!

The Trident had its head and the road seemingly grew very narrow. The engine revolutions soared and dropped as the rear wheel leapt about on the bumpy road, losing and regaining traction. The rev. counter was showing about 8,000rpm in fourth gear, and as I poked it into top gear it was a matter of lining up the *lefty, righty wiggle* on the approach to the Mountain Box, which rushed up very quickly. There was no time to read, let alone acknowledge John's signals.

One lap down, four to go.

The Cronk-y-Voddy straight after Creg Willey's Hill is a full-on stand-up fight with the Triumph Triple using all the road! The bumps make your spine play the odd melody and the scenery comes at you in triplicate! At the end of the straight, the road sneaks to the right. It's okay, you can get through in top gear, but that left bank seems awful magnetic as the front wheel flaps about like a loose sail in a storm.

The thirteenth Milestone came and went. I belted the right-hand kerb on the way into the bend with the edge of my boot sole and knew that my racing line must be about right. I still had no clue where in the race I was placed, as even my signallers on the slow corners were telling me nothing.

After three laps, we pitted and filled up to the regulation five gallons, which was the fuel limit. I could really feel the 'top hamper' of that added petrol as I got stuck into the final two laps.

No news or instructions from Boyer's Boss, Stan Shenton at the pits, so I pressed on.

It is difficult to adequately describe the experience of racing on a *fire-eater* in the Isle of Man without the listener sitting up behind but come with me on the final lap down from Keppel Gate.

You are in second gear with your left boot scuffing the deck. The left side of the fairing is there, skating along the ground too. You screw it out of the bend and the bike drifts out to the right side of the road. You take it to 8,000rpm. Watch the surface, it's bumpy and shiny in places. Then poke it into third gear, and let it run!

The hillside drops steeply down the short straight section to Kates Cottage, a blind left-hander. In front of you is Douglas Town and beyond that the sea. No time for gazing at the view though!

You hang on to the right-side wall and then just before the Cottage, knock it off a bit and listen to that exhaust note, now screw-it on to keep the drive chains pulling and throw the machine across the camber, aiming for the left-hand bank on the apex. Your speed will take you nice and close, but just clear of it, using all the nearside camber to best advantage.

You'll come out into the drop at Creg-Ny-Ba, having used the full width of the road and with your boot kicking up the grass on the right bank. Now, give it the works, take fourth gear just before the first drop on the road. The front-wheel comes up and the seat tries to overtake you! The machine runs for some distance on his rear wheel. Who said *wheelies* were bottom gear stuff?

Take it up to 8,000rpm again and then screw it in top gear. You must be pushing 140mph. Hit the disc brakes and hook it back through the box to the bottom cog and you should be about set for the right-hander at the Creg if you keep tight to the left on the way in.

The crowd is extremely packed-in here and we can be sure that they loved the tune you play!

About two miles to go and you cross the finish line. As the chequered flag comes down, you shut off the engine room.

What a thrill it was to have managed my first finish in the week. My notebook says:

Kept revs to 8,000 rpm. No signals. No instructions re-ride or race. No info at all. Unaware of position in a race or that Dave Nixon was out (Dave had stopped on the first lap after only 17 miles). As I seem to be on the number two machine I decided to ride to finish unless told to go for it!

I recall as we checked the bike over, that during the race the fuel tank had developed a tiny split and was leaking slightly. So, that was it. The only Boyers finisher.

The Silver Replica, managing tenth place at 96.61mph with a fastest lap of 97.3mph, made me feel a bit happier and set up for Friday's Senior outing on our very own unsponsored Kawasaki.

When I say unsponsored, I mean no dealer support, because Duckhams, the oil company unit based in West Wickham, regularly helped me with the odd gallon of oil and the MPMC (Metropolitan Police Motor Club), whom I was representing, dug out some folding money from their coffers.

To add to this, a former Trafpol colleague, Jim Renwick and his dear wife Jean, now resident in Berwick-upon-Tweed where Jim was 'mine host' at The Pilot Inn, had shown financial interest in my efforts with the Kawasaki.

Jim, on leaving 'the job' had set up a driving school called The Tartan School of Motoring in Selsdon, South Croydon. After several years, Jim and his wife had moved north from Surrey to Berwick-Upon-Tweed. Jim and Jean had been paying my entry fees for race events over that period of time and in recognition, at Jim's expense because he was from north of the border, my Kawasaki racing fairing was beautifully painted with tartan markings and emblazoned with the legend *The Pilot Inn*! (For some time, however, it had been recognised as The Tartan Kawasaki). On each side of the fuel tank was skilfully painted the face of a smiling duck, simply because Kawasakis tended to be called 'Kwackers'!

The Kawasaki is really just a tuned road engine (model H1) with some racing bits fitted. The engine and gearbox unit had been mounted in a Dunstall racing frame.

Dave Simmonds, the 1969 125cc World Champion Kawasaki rider and son-in-law of Bill Boddice the famous sidecar racer, had loaned me a Kawasaki H1R Works crankshaft for the Racing Season. Once again, it was always hard to understand the privilege, that so many top-liners in the racing world helped this young dreamer.

Hugh Evans, one of the club racing gang and a skilled engineer, as already mentioned, had made some more significant modifications to the 'transfer ports' of the cylinders. For this, TT Hugh had also tuned the exhaust system of the engine, which improved its performance dramatically and gave the engine more torque. This was very useful on The Island because some of the varying twists of the TT, easily and suddenly acute bends can catch out an engine with a narrow power-band.

Joe Dunphy, 1962 Manx Grand Prix winner and TT star, now a specialist in disc brakes, had fixed me up with some special hard brake pads for my disc brakes (two front and one rear).

'They'll really work coming down the mountain when things

266

get hot! The lever might need a bit more hand pressure until the discs are working hard,' Joe had told me.

Our pride and joy was all ready to go.

Starting at number forty-four out of seventy-one riders, I got away with my starting partner, Jan Kostwinder, riding a Yamaha and was soon on full noise.

Troubles again!

At Quarter Bridge, stopping was hard work. Maybe those pads just didn't like it, although there had been no problem in practice

It took me until the slow right-turn twenty miles out at Sulby Bridge before I 'tumbled' the problem. There was no other traffic around and I could hear my motor pulling quite hard, even with the throttles shut.

A later reference to my notebook:

Throttle stuck open on one cylinder at Quarter Bridge first lap. Not able to clear problem until Mountain Mile, twenty-seven miles out. Throttle cable junction box jammed in between the front of the fuel tank and frame tube, obviously due to the bump at bottom of Bray Hill.

The first lap at 24 minutes 35.8 seconds suffered, and I lost a few places. The bike was as sweet as a nut but I kept the revs down to 9,000rpm because the Kawasaki had had a busy Club Racing season before the TT and 226.38 miles was a fair distance for our *private* runner to cover in one race.

The working life of the crankshaft was set and dictated by racing mileage, because its bearings, under competition conditions, had a limited *working life*. The bike wagged on some of the bumpy fast sections and I realised that firmer damping in the front forks was necessary on The Island, than will suffice on the Mickey Mouse short-circuits at home.

I pit-stopped after three laps for fuel and was on my way again.

The Kwacker felt good and so, after four laps, I started to *give it the works* a little bit!

I managed to cover lap five in twenty-three minutes 38.2 seconds (95mph) and the final lap at twenty-three minutes 31.2 seconds (96mph). These laps were great for spying a single machine in the distance, way out ahead and gradually to be able to peg it back. The lead machine would be lost from view around a series of bends then coming into view, with you a little closer. Lost from view again, slowly you would reel him in until suddenly you are on him. Find a spot to get past. Shoulder to shoulder for a bit and you were away, out on your own again.

It should be added that the only spot on the whole lap where a rider could even risk a glance behind was the very sharp and relatively slow Gooseneck Hairpin right turn above Ramsey, as you begin the long Mountain Climb. Otherwise, apart from any audible engine noise from behind, a rider had little idea of who was following him, poised ready to strike!

The chequered flag was out and how exciting it was to finish a real six-lap Senior TT Race on your own self-prepared race machine. Nothing had broken or dropped off and when I received my Silver Replica for another tenth place, I was over the moon!

Final result: 10th place at a race average speed of 94.04mph (2 hours, 24 minutes, and 26.2 seconds).

A few days after my happy *mountain-top* experience, I was back on duty. Posted on motorcycle duty, I had just left the Traffic Patrol Garage (TDZ) in West Croydon and was patrolling along the dual carriageway of Wellesley Road.

The driver of a passing light goods van performed a driving manoeuvre which raised *constabulary eyebrows*. Thus, it was necessary to pull him in by the Fairfield Halls and have a quiet word, to give him what was called a *verbal warning* (no pencil poised to strike, just a word of advice). Know what I mean, guv?

Having quietly endeavoured to point out to the driver the error of his ways, said driver's response was one of unfriendly disdain.

The word of guidance was quietly repeated. To which my newfound acquaintance responded, 'I don't need to listen to you. If you were Graham Bailey, it would mean something.'

I was then informed by my van-driving friend that this guy, Bailey, who was a Copper, had just recently performed like an ace in the Isle of Man TT Races.

What about that then! So, there we have it!

Even after quietly informing him that I was *he* and upon his objection to my claim, attempting to confirm my identity as Graham Bailey, (that endeavour resulting in my showing him my Metropolitan Police Warrant Card); my van driving acquaintance was sure that I was *having a laugh*. He didn't even ask for my autograph!

Oh, the shame and disappointment that my fame at performing 'like an ace in the TT' was not publicly declared that day on the streets of Croydon.

On your bike, Bailey, and get back to the real world!

24

The eye of the storm

The months of 1973, having in June allowed PC Bailey another *mountain climbing adventure* on The Island, rolled on with life back in a normal daily routine: early turn, late turn and night duty.

Talking of adventures, however, Rosemary and I were courting and enjoying just being in each other's company. One of our early shared times away from home had been to borrow my cousin Brian's caravan, tow it behind the faithful Beetle and spend a few days camped at East Creech in Dorset. Brian had strongly recommended a spot on the hilltop high above and just west of Corfe Castle.

Rosemary was becoming very precious to me, and if she was one day to be my wife, it was my responsibility to look after and protect her. That, to me for starters meant as a committed Christian, that Rosemary would not be mine until she had accepted and taken my hand in marriage.

It might sound a bit old fashioned as I check over these notes in 2020, when jumping into bed with whoever takes your fancy is normal but to me, God's word (Genesis Chapter 2, verse 24) was pretty clear and straightforward.

Rosemary and I were in tune on the matter and thus she slept in the *first-class* section of the caravan at the back where all the windows were, whilst, separated by a curtain, I slumbered at the *staff end* by the front door and toilet!

On Saturday the 7th of July 1973, Rosemary and I drove the five miles down to Kimmeridge Bay on the rocky Jurassic Coast of the English Channel. The date was easy to pinpoint because the Wimbledon Women's Tennis Final had been postponed from its traditional Friday to this particular day due to rain. Incidentally, the Final was won by Billie Jean King but she was totally unaware of 'the adventures of Kimmeridge'!

We parked up, picnicked, swam in the calm waters and then spread ourselves out in the sun on the flat rocks at the east side of the scenic bay. The weather was warm, sunny and very peaceful.

We, as with many other holidaymakers, basked in the sun. At one point, having been lying in my back snoozing with my head towards the bay, I opened my eyes, tilted my head back and looked to the West. The sky over the bay had dramatically become quite black and rain, *unannounced*, was rapidly spreading in a sheet across the water of the bay towards us.

Everyone around us scattered to escape what was so suddenly developing into a violent and very noisy thunderstorm. We gathered our bits and pieces, ran up a narrow shingle beach towards the cliffs. The rain was now so heavy that to reach the car park without a good soaking was completely out of the question.

I spotted a small shallow cave at the foot of the cliffs, which were made up out of what looked like the curving spines of pre-historic monsters, compressed between layers of rock and clay. Earlier that day I had noticed a sign further back which advised folks *not to go near the cliffs*. But surely, it's chucking it down! Just this once!?

The two of us, Rosemary and I, crouched down in our own private shelter to await the passing of what we hoped would only be a sudden yet short shower.

Kimmeridge is famed among the other natural wonders for the Kimmeridge Ledges. Expanses of flat rock spread out from the land into the sea that become more exposed at low tide.

As we waited, the rain became heavier and the heavens began to reverberate to the sounds of thunder. The view out to sea across the narrow beach rapidly diminished as a thick curtain of mist, created by the increasing rain, swept towards us. The calm sea reflected the hissing sound of heavy falling rain, which formed an advancing grey screen across the water.

The now completely darkened sky was being lit with flashes of lightning. As the storm was now right overhead, this lightning was followed simultaneously by peels of thunder. The storm reached a point when a simultaneous flash of lightning and crash of thunder was instantly followed by a shower of stones and mud falling from the cliff, immediately above where the two of us were sheltering in the cleft of the rock.

The falling rock increased until it seemed that with every fall, a large lorry was tipping its load from above!

The storm increased in its ferocity and I was becoming quite afraid, fearful that I had so foolishly brought my fiancée, the lovely Rosemary, into such a dangerous situation.

The tide was high and it was only a short distance from the water's edge.

As we watched, suddenly from our left, a group of fossil-hunters carrying the tools of their hobby rushed past us, keeping close to the water's edge out of the range of falling rocks. They were obviously heading for the car park. These fellows were soaking wet and seemed impervious to the pouring rain, yet well aware of the potential further rock falls.

I decided that after the next clap of thunder and fall of rock, it would be a good plan to run to the water's edge and then, watching the cliffs and judging a safe moment, call Rosemary to join me. Together we would then splash our way back to the car park.

I had a small portable tape-recorder close at hand, which was being put to use so I could store *know-how* to listen to and revise my knowledge before the upcoming Sergeants' Promotion Examination.

The fiendishly clever and well-prepared plan was to run as described with the recorder protecting my head. Crouching, rather like someone on the top diving board at the swimming pool, deciding whether to run and when to run, I had already pin-pointed *exactly* where to go. Then, from above, silently spinning through the air, came an enormous rock, about the size of an Austin Mini!

It arced through the air and hit the flat surface of the Kimmeridge Ledges at precisely the spot to which I had chosen to run. The rock did not bounce, but with a shuddering crash, settled solidly!

That plan was firmly shelved (ledged) and not carried through and I sincerely thanked God that he had held me back from leaving my place!

We decided that Rosemary and I would stay put. It must be emphasised that I had never before or since been so frightened by any other experience, and that includes being watched by Secret Police whilst on the trip to Poland back in August 1970.

We sincerely prayed to our Heavenly Father that we would

be kept unharmed and be able to get back to safety at the end of the storm.

After an hour, as the storm seemed to subside, Rosemary and I prepared to make our way back to the car park. As quickly as the storm was moving away, it roared back into life with renewed violence making it clear that we were sat in *the eye of the storm.*

The two of us experienced another hour of thunder and lightning. At one stage, looking east from our tiny cave in the direction from which the fossil hunters had come, I saw a complete section of the cliffs slide down onto the beach and became so aware with the continuing fall of stone, that the next cliff fall could completely cover our place of refuge.

Thoughts about the 'what ifs?' were pushed to the back of our minds as we waited for the storm to pass by. After two hours the storm abated, the rain eased and the rock falls seemed to be less frequent. Confident that it would be safe if we went to the water's edge, now, due to the outgoing tide, much further from the cliffs, the two of us to made our way through what was now a light drizzle of rain to the car park.

The car was sitting happily and unscathed. We *thankfully* loaded our bits and pieces, hopped into the Beetle and began the drive back to base. A few moments along the road, not far from the beach, we came upon a very pleasant small homely cafe. It was decided that as a genuine celebration of our safety, Rosemary and I would order and enjoy afternoon cream-tea with scones, jam and thick cream! That would really make our day and return us to reality.

We sat down in our now very comfortable surroundings, ordered a large pot of tea and fresh scones with strawberry jam and cream from our welcoming hostess. After a few moments, the dear lady who was looking after us came running over.

'I'm awfully sorry, but the cream has gone off!' She apologised.

It was on that day we realised that the *old wives' tale* 'a thunderstorm always turns cream sour', was for real!

Never mind, we were safe. It had been a unique, happy, somewhat frightening, yet memorable day.

On our short drive back to the caravan on the hill, the roads were awash with mud, stones and greenery which had been swept and torn by the storm. The caravan was safe and sound and the view south over Corfe Castle with the Isle of Wight in the distance was a very pleasant and comforting end to our little adventure.

25

Surely you deserve a medal!

With the skilled assistance of Hugh Evans and the ultra-support freely given by others during the 1972 racing season, as our newly acquired 500 was being tweaked, it was proving to be quite competitive. In fact, during the season our Kawasaki had secured three first places, seven-second places and one-fourth position for us in the various Club Racing events in which we had entered.

Following Hugh's additional winter (1972-73) tinkering with the exhaust system, the Kwacker was becoming even more competitive. It was therefore decided that in addition to competing in the 1973 TT, Bailey would have a crack at winning the British Motorcycle Racing Club 500cc Championship.

Not wanting to race on Sundays, one appreciated that Championship points could not be secured if we did not race at those events. Nonetheless, it was felt that if our Kawasaki scored enough points when running in the Saturday races, we might be able to build up a sufficient numerical advantage to secure the Bemsee 500 Championship.

The result was that, although the Kwacker achieved eight wins and one-fourth place, GB only managed to come second in the championship with eighty-seven points. Nonetheless, Dave Street, *The Champion* with one-hundred and twenty-one points, another great rider, and Ron Mellor, who gained seventy-three points and I were always upfront together and thoroughly enjoyed some close combat.

I, however, was awarded the AMC Cup for second place. So, in addition to 'being caught in a storm' with my young lady, 1973 altogether was filled with many exciting moments.

Looking back, I remember that in the early Seventies, for a time among many professional riders, the 'TT Races' had apparently lost some of its attraction and sadly received some bad press.

A six-time TT winner and Motorcycle World Champion was quoted in a national newspaper: 'Both Agostini and I agreed that the course is far too dangerous. It has got to be shortened. If they do that and become more realistic about a professional rider's start money I might consider returning.'

It must be acknowledged that as a professional rider; to spend two weeks in the Isle of Man for the TT Races could result in a loss of earnings, because during those two weeks, taking up one Practice Week, then the Race Week and not competing in other race meetings held in Europe would mean that they could not be awarded 'start money' as well as prize money, for winning races at those events. If they were unsuccessful in only one of the TT races they could be 'out of pocket' for sure.

As I was enjoying *fifteen minutes of fame*, although not involved in any 'save the TT' campaigns, my defence of the TT races was also given print space in various newspapers.

In the same newspaper referred to earlier, the report quotes me saying, 'One must always be aware of the dangers that exist. I suppose we are all afraid to a degree but if we worry all the time about the consequences of what we try to achieve, then surely we may end doing nothing.'

Referring to those professional riders who were currently criticising the TT races, I am quoted as saying: 'They have made their names here, so how was it that they suddenly find that the Isle of Man is a dangerous place?'

At the end of the 1973 racing season, The British Motor Cycle Racing Club held its Annual Dinner and Prize-Giving Ceremony to which Bailey, as an award winner, was invited. It was a privilege to be seated at the same table as one of the current Motorcycle World Champions, present with his wife. Said Champion had sought to cast a shadow over the TT Racing event, even although it had been where he had achieved much competitive success and acclaim.

I was aware that if *the subject* was raised, it would be wise to remain silent or tread very carefully.

During the meal, the wife of this racing personality looked at me and said, 'Aren't you that racing vicar?'

It was necessary to advise her that she had not quite correctly *collared* me but that, although *my clerical details* were a little different, I was able to confirm my Christian faith.

On enquiring what my TT results had been, I was able to tell her what my efforts had secured. Needless to say, although they were not quoted, my overall maximum speeds and lap times had nowhere reached those attained by a World Champion on a 'Works' machine.

'Well, you were never travelling fast enough to hurt yourself anyway!' She replied.

The inference was that only in the *Champion's League* could anyone be in any danger whilst racing in the Isle of Man.

Message: You are not up to the mark, sonny! Ah me! What a funny old world it is. But, at least I went home from the dinner carrying a big Silver Cup (AMC Trophy)... so there!

26

Just one more lap?

Hello there, 1974? Who knows!

Having just 'popped the question' and received a positive response, after that long Sergeant's Promotion Examination in January, I hoped that by March I would be taking the long walk down the aisle. Then I guess, it will be necessary to ask Rosemary's permission to *Do The Island!*

One could only hope that someone has got some quick machinery needing a jockey. There was still that one hundred mile-an-hour lap yet to be achieved!

The joyful prospect of married life also made me so aware that racing motorcycles are, to the rider, a wonderful, thrilling, yet fairly self-centred experience. Sure, all your mates must gain some pleasure from rushing about the place, sorting out your machinery, arranging the finer details and working like mad to get you to the start-line (it must be admitted, however, that it is all done by them for no personal financial gain). Surely they must gain a degree of reflected glory if the rider is successful?

I had been made aware from personal experience, that they also had to pick up the pieces and 'tell Mum' if I stuffed the bike into the bank or dropped off the edge at Coram Curve (Snetterton Norfolk, 1970). Yet, the rider has all the fun. At least that was the way I looked at it.

The 1973 racing season had drawn to a close and it was therefore decided that Bailey's racing days were at an end. That was of course until Roger Slater, an agent for the Italian manufactured Laverda motorcycles, made the offer of a ride in the 1974 Production TT.

For this London Copper, the machine was to be a 744cc Laverda SFC. The SFC has been described as 'Laverda's ultimate early 1970s factory racer'. Also 'a limited production street-legal racer'.

Oh boy! What am I to do now?

Saturday 9th March 1974 was to be Rosemary's and my big day. We were wed at the United Reformed Church in Upper Norwood, London SE19. The wedding was of course a happy and memorable event; life-changing one could almost say and in years to come, that joy and happiness was made more real and continued.

Our wedding night was going to be spent at a lovely old hotel in the centre of Crawley and then Rosemary and her new Hubby were heading off to Gatwick Airport, flying away into the bright blue yonder!

The VW Beetle had been prepared for the first stage of that honeymoon adventure, but the lads had secretly carried out a few obvious and one or two not so easy to detect, alterations to the appearance of the little red air-cooled rear-engine, beast.

As we clattered away, the peal of many tin cans firmly fixed and hidden beneath the car could be heard reverberating around the area. Sign-written *paint jobs* had been applied to the bodywork for all to see that the occupants were 'Just Married'!

We later discovered that the traditional kipper had been

placed on the engine exhausts which, when cooking, would heighten our sense of smell inside our car. Fortunately, Rosemary and I never picked up the scent because, with a rear-engine, although we *created a stink*, only those following behind would have benefitted!

A workmate, Brian Desborough, had volunteered to recover the VW from its temporary parking spot at Gatwick Airport following our departure for the Balearic Island of Majorca. Brian's wife was going to deliver him to the airport, then follow him home in their car. As he later recounted, other road users were quite intrigued and amused to see a bright red Beetle covered in 'Just Married' signage and decoration, being driven by a lonely man, very closely followed by a car carrying a lone woman driver; that lady obviously focused upon the fleeing Volkswagen!

Brian had become aware of others' interest when, whilst waiting at traffic lights, various drivers pulled alongside and closely studied the features of the *lonely* VW driver!

Spring began and the 1974 motorcycle road racing season fired into life. I was not involved, and to be quite honest, I had other new and more interesting responsibilities.

Perhaps readers will understand that Bailey's *mountain climbing* dreams were primarily heightened and had been realised by the excitement and challenge of the Isle of Man Tourist Trophy TT Mountain Circuit. Thus, the lad was quite resigned and not very bothered, to be missing-out on rides at the short-circuit events on the mainland.

With the TT dates looming in late May, early June, and the prospect of a return to The Island, young and newly married,

I proudly displayed the gold wedding ring given me by my beautiful and loving bride, Rosemary and sought permission for a *last* ride on the island.

It was the one, final opportunity to climb this particular mountain.

With her patient, certainly forbearing, yet positive response to my request, plans were set to travel north and arrangements made for our stay in Douglas.

Rosemary, who had loyally accompanied me to mainland race meetings during our courtship, was going to share another adventure. Not particularly interested in motorbikes, she was nonetheless happy to visit this unique and genuine motorcycle road racing circuit.

Moving on as they say, the plan for our journey to the Isle of Man would take us north-west to Liverpool and then, sailing with the Isle of Man Steam Packet Company, we would cross the Irish Sea to Douglas.

Rosemary was prepared to ride pillion on the Vincent as we made our northward trip.

'I'm OK with that, darling, as long as we don't go on the Motorway,' she said. 'I would not enjoy that at all!'

That was easy. North through London, along the A41, through Hendon, and join the A5 (old Watling Street). Then further up country, back onto the A41, through the Mersey Tunnel and into Liverpool. Job done!

The newly-weds, with our panniers filled with the essentials for our stay, set off and crossed London. It was a fairly pleasant day and all was going exactly to plan. As we passed over the Brent Cross Flyover and slowed down preparing to stop at the traffic lights at Hendon Central, our pilot skilfully lifted his right foot to nick the gear lever down into a lower gear, ready to go with the traffic flow. The gear lever was solid and would not move and I could not select a lower gear! We were stuck in fourth gear.

The Vincent has a two-cylinder V-twin engine of 998cc, similar in engine capacity to the famed Morris 1000 saloon car referred to earlier. How on earth are we going to manage, I thought to myself, moving a stationary motorcycle *two up* and fully loaded, from a stand-still with it jammed in top gear? We also have to cover around 200 miles in time to catch the ferry?

The Vincent 1000 is built with a very unusual clutch arrangement. It is referred to as a *centrifugal clutch* and is operated by a hand-controlled clutch lever. As the lever is released, the rotating pressure plate engages with the main central clutch body. As a result, the clutch body begins to spin. The clutch shoes, which are similar to brake shoes, pivoted at their centre point, throw out and engage with the main clutch cylinder, which looks rather like a brake drum. Drive is immediately taken up, no questions asked and the machine is then off down the road! If too much power is applied by the rider's throttle hand, life gets exciting.

Sunshine! You are stuck in top gear with a big twin-cylinder engine! Get out of that!

OK, that's the bad news. For us, the good news was that sometime before we had fitted the Vin with a much-modified multi-plate clutch using Manx Norton friction plates and thus, the clutch could be slipped until the road speed of the bike had *caught up* with the higher gear unwittingly jammed in place.

The other piece of good news was that the magneto, which

supplied the ignition for the engine, had recently been rebuilt by Fred Cooper, the famous motorcycle Sprint Racer and engineer. I believe that Fred's brother, George, was the electrics wizard! The magneto had been built to racing specification and a manual advance and retard (thumb lever operated) mechanism had been added to replace the auto advance and retard gear used as original equipment in the mag. This enabled the rider to retard the ignition so that the engine could run happily and pick up from a lower engine speed, the ignition only being manually advanced as the engine speed increased.

Although it was not an ideal situation, we were enabled to move off from stationary in top gear using a much-retarded ignition setting and by slipping the clutch. Because the Vincent 1000 was a fairly low revving engine, it could be 'plonked' along and did not require the rider to *screw its nuts off* to get moving (a colloquial expression). The pistons of an engine go up and down and are attached to the crankshaft by connecting rods. This shaft converts the 'up and down' action of the piston into a 'round and round' crankshaft rotating action, which delivers the power. For that to happen, the connecting rods join the piston to the crankshaft. The 'big end' is the part of the connecting-rod that attaches to the crankshaft and within it is the bearing that runs on the crankshaft. In *days of yore* on many engines, the big end comprised two halves held together by two threaded big end bolts, thus, attaching the rod with its bearing to the crankshaft. If too much engine speed was applied it was possible to cause bolts with their tightened nuts to fall apart! Hence the term *revving its nuts off!*

We were able to progress quite happily, but because of our *jammed in the top* gearbox, it became necessary to modify our route plan and move primarily from the A-class roads and join the M1 for our journey north.

After some distance and upon arrival at the Watford Gap Service area, it was decided that a coffee break was necessary.

Rosemary and I, having enjoyed our drink, were faced with the difficulty of starting up the Vincent engine whilst it was jammed in gear. The only answer was to leave the motorcycle on its rear stand, which kept the rear wheel off the road surface and then kick the engine into life with the kick-starter.

With the engine fired up, it was necessary, having grabbed hold of the clutch to stop the spinning rear wheel, to push the Vincent from its stand. This left Rosemary with the task of raising the rear stand, tightening the wing nut clamp and securing it into place.

We set off with assistance from the downhill slope of the car park and went on our way.

The rest of the journey, although mainly along Motorways, was fairly uneventful and the faithful Vincent, stuck in top gear, effortlessly brought us to the Princes Dock on the North bank of the River Mersey in Liverpool.

We were in good in time for the ferry to Douglas, the capital of the Isle of Man. The voyage commenced as we sailed down the Mersey out to the Irish Sea.

Once aboard the ship and underway, there was time to investigate our gearbox problem. It did not take long to realise that it was going to require more than 'gentle tinkering' to cure our transmission defect. What transpired was that the vertically positioned spindle, which supported the gear selection cam-plate, had come adrift from its position in the roof of the gearbox. This was because the gearbox casting had fractured! Thus, following our anticipated *mountain climbing* expedition to the 1974 TT, a return trip to London on the Vincent was not going to take place. Sometime in the future, Bailey had a big repair job on his hands.

Rosemary and I were welcomed by Mrs Daugherty at No.21 Bucks Hill, which since my first visit as a TT competitor in 1967, had been TT time *home from home*.

With a sick Vincent and no transport, the traditional quick ride around the Island was not possible, so it was necessary to patiently await the arrival of the Bailey race machine, the 750 Laverda SFC.

Somewhat later than we had hoped, it arrived on the ferry from the mainland and it was prepared for the first Official Practice Session, knowing very little about the bike's history and having never ridden it or even set our eyes upon the Italian flyer. Yet, the Laverda certainly looked the business.

We were told that the machine was fitted with Pirelli tyres, a type which was manufactured in a co-operation (the term used, 'a marriage') between the tyre manufacturers Dunlop and Pirelli.

It was a new experience, having to become familiar with the type of ride given by Avon and Dunlop tyres. So, at least two learning curves unravelled.

I had many months before been warned by David Dixon, a friend and motorcycle journalist who was well versed in riding racing motorcycles, that the Laverda had some unusual handling characteristics. Dave's descriptive tone had been quite negative!

Our first Official Practice, due to the delayed arrival of the bike, was an evening outing. So, with the Laverda resplendent in its manufacturer's livery, having been examined and passed by the Scrutineers, Bailey set off riding number seven down Glencrutchery Road on our first lap of practice.

The Laverda, although I had never previously sat on it, had a well thought out riding position and felt quite comfortable as we rushed down Bray Hill. Quarter Bridge, that almost off-camber right-hand turn with its hidden apex, came and went quite smoothly.

On arrival at the rapid left-right flick at Braddan Bridge, where the machine is cranked over quite steeply on both the left and right sections of the turn, I became aware that the tyres seemed to suddenly 'fall off the edge' as the bike moved from upright to full bank. This was a trifle off-putting; but one was aware of, yet had not experienced, a type of racing tyre introduced in recent years that were triangulated in profile.

I soon realised that this *fall off the edge* sensation was part of this evening's practice learning curve. The triangulated tyre profile had been developed for *'out and out'* racing machines so that at a full angle of lean when cornering, there was plenty of tyre tread on the road surface. Production Racing machines were quite a bit heavier than *real racers* and therefore, a triangulated tyre profile was not a very satisfactory set-up. This was because as a heavy bike moves from fully upright to 'full bank', there is a moment when only a small tread footprint is running on the tarmac. Fighting a sliding rear end or a shaking front wheel is a bit of a waste of time and effort for a rider in a hurry!

The evening was turning out to be quite an enjoyable re-union with my *one-man mountain* experience, having 'retired upon marriage' and been allowed, as it were, to come back for one last time!

The Laverda fitted me well, was quite a joy to ride and the first practice lap was turning into a real pleasure. We rushed north towards Ramsey, re-lived all the joys and challenges of Union Mills, Ballacraine, Ballaugh Bridge and Quarry Bends; then as we turned to climb towards The Mountain, the SFC was running and handling quite well. Everything was in good order until, nearing the end of the lap and exiting the reasonably slow right turn at Signpost Corner, the Laverda accelerated smoothly down the drop towards Bedstead Corner, a 'diving' and fairly tight left turn.

As I dropped into the turn, having approached tight against the right side of the track and began to open the taps to drive through the bend, the bike hesitated. The engine 'stuttered' and did not respond smoothly to the increasing throttle. An accelerating engine would have held the bike 'on line' to clip the apex of the bend and set us up for a fast exit. Instead, I found that we were several feet off-line, running wide and in an instant, the bike and rider were hurtling along the right side footway.

The Laverda clipped the banking, flipped and cartwheeled with its one -time pilot down the track.

After a number of, *I'm on top of, now I'm underneath the bike*, I found myself lying in the gateway of a field entrance on the left side of the road, finding it more than a little difficult to breathe and wondering where I was and why.

Looking over my shoulder towards Douglas, I saw the Laverda some distance along the road, lying on its side and looking rather second-hand.

Within what seemed moments, I was on a stretcher being run down the sunlit track towards the grounds of Government House.

My worthy helpers were a St John officer and a local Policeman. It is quite amazing that as a TT racer rides within what is, to him, his lone *bubble* of personal endeavour, there are so many volunteers 'looking out' for his welfare.

As we jogged through the trees on the grounds of this imposing building and towards first aid assistance, I looked up at the policeman who was the rearmost carrier.

'Where am I?' I enquired.

'You are in the Isle of Man,' he replied with a smile.

'What am I doing in the Isle of Man?' I asked.

'You're riding in the TT!' He replied with a friendly smile once again.

'But I've retired from racing, I've just got married!'

I was loaded into, what as I recall a green painted local greengrocer's Ford Transit van. The van was 'in service' as an unpaid ambulance. Apparently, the casualty was conveyed with a note attached: *Serious head injuries!*

Upon arrival in casualty, now fairly 'with it', GB your hero, was aware of some bodily discomfort and a fairly knocked about, rapidly swelling left hand.

The Casualty Department doctor arrived beside my trolley, saw my bruised condition and as it seemed, came from a part of the world where the importance of the Wedding Ring is not fully appreciated, said clearly to the nurse standing nearby: 'Nurse! Go and get the saw'

'What do you need a saw for?' I asked.

'We are going to cut off the ring,' replied the doctor.

'Oh no you're not,' I replied. 'That is my new Wedding Ring!'

'Oh yes, we are!'

A second nurse was within earshot and the wounded racer noted a bottle of Fairy Liquid set upon the sink unit on the other side of the Casualty Department.

'Nurse! Please will you give me the bottle of Fairy Liquid?'

The young lady moved quickly and the fluid was *professionally* passed into my possession...well before the doctor returned armed with his newly delivered surgical precision cutting instrument.

It is quite amazing how quickly and easily a wedding ring can be *Fairy-well* lubricated and with a quick slide, removed from a swollen and bruised finger!

So, that was it. Bailey's racing days were certainly at an end.

After a comfortable night of rest in Nobles Hospital, I was collected by my patient and loving wife, Rosemary. She escorted her bashed-up husband out of that truly caring establishment; former racer Bailey, who had suffered no more than a couple of cracked ribs, a headache and a swollen left hand.

John Milligan, Competition Secretary of The Bantam Racing Club and his dear wife, kindly carried the Vincent in the back of their camper, to their Norfolk home.

The Laverda? It was noted that red paint from my helmet had been firmly impressed onto the underside of the crankcase, so the confused '*on top of and underneath*' experience had been a real event.

There is the already referred to outstanding rider and racer Percy Tait. Percy had been a factory test rider with Triumph Motorcycles at Meriden and was currently a factory and works racer. He was a very competitive rider who knew how to win races!

Percy *took over my seat* on the Laverda SFC for the race. Sadly, no one came and enquired exactly what had happened to the rider at Bedstead Corner. One takes it for granted that the cause of the tumble was assumed to be as a result of the wrong move being taken by the rider and that consequently through his own mistake, he had 'offed it'!

'Down to you then, mate!'

Much later, as in weeks afterwards, information filtered down and I was told that before the TT races the Laverda had been ridden by a journalist working for a motorcycle magazine, all the way from the manufacturer's factory at Breganze in Italy, to the UK. Such a journey would have totalled approximately one thousand miles or more. Apparently, it had been planned for a story to be published of the combined Continental ride and TT race, completed on this particular Laverda SFC!

The only problem was that this rider, GB, had not been made aware of this developing project!

I was left to wonder; was Percy in the know?

As has been said; *race preparation* is all-important and it is not a good plan to ride from Italy to the United Kingdom, then enter the same motorcycle for a race on the most testing racing circuit in the world without a complete programme of race preparation having been completed. Particularly so when the rider is unaware that he is part of the project.

The thrilling prospect of riding for one last time in a TT race might well have been dimmed, had the 'newly married' been aware of the plan.

It is recorded that the machine did not complete one lap in the race, thus, the Laverda failed to complete the Marlborough Motorcycle Production Machine Race held on the 4th of June 1974 because the primary chain failed, that is, the chain that delivered the engine power to the gearbox and rear wheel.

Think back to the Laverda hesitating 'stuttering' as the power was applied to negotiate Bedstead Corner and be aware that if a primary chain is beginning to disintegrate with broken rollers becoming snagged in the drive sprockets, power delivery is, even momentarily interrupted.

At the very least, the aptly named 'Bedstead Corner' gave me a prophetic indication of where the Laverda rider would be spending the next twelve or so hours!

Nothing has ever been discussed about this event with its Practice rider and I can only *try* to piece the chain of events together!

The lesson underlined once again, however, is that full preparation is essential…Oh, and by the way, full and informative communication is also a good idea.

So, it was back to the real world and maybe *more mountains to climb.*

27

A case of 'guts for garters'

With Rosemary's encouragement and much sweat of the brow, Bailey got his head down and studied for the Promotion Examination. Success would result in promotion to the rank of a Police Sergeant.

The examination could be taken as a 'Competitor' or as a 'Qualifier'. As I understood it, to sit the examination as a qualifier, the candidate must have served as a Constable for 10 years. Qualifiers had to reach a minimum pass mark and then just ten percent of those qualifiers would be given the rank of Sergeant.

I had served as a Constable for around twenty years, sixteen of them serving as a Traffic Patrol officer and I was not too bothered about the details. I entered the examination as a Competitor and although there would be no *chequered flag* at the finish, I simply wanted to achieve success. A competitive score would be a bonus but the thought hadn't crossed my mind.

The written papers really tested my knowledge and ability to recall details. Unbelievably, having been unsuccessful in an earlier attempt, I passed and came twenty-ninth in the whole of the Met!

Apparently, for a *Competitor candidate,* achieving such a finishing position in yet another race, qualified that officer for an 'Accelerated Promotion Course' at Bramshill, the Police Staff Training College.

Er hmm! Sorry, guv, one small problem. A candidate for that course must be no more than thirty years of age! You're too old, mate. Aw, sucks I had toppled over the edge of 40 years! It's just as well that Bramshill was not another of the *one man's mountains* I had dreamed about.

After being promoted to Sergeant, Bailey was transferred from Traffic Patrol duties. 'Foot back to' was the dreaded term used by anyone attached to a specialist unit who was returned to *ordinary duties*. The new scenario to focus upon was a posting to Brixton Police Station (LD), doubling up as Number Four District headquarters and Divisional Station of L Division.

On the prescribed day, he presented himself as directed at the Divisional Office and was ushered through to the inner sanctum of the Commander's office. Bailey stood respectfully on the carpet in front of the Commander's desk, wearing his smart, newly pressed uniform jacket with three stripes on each arm, feeling honoured to have been given his new rank, PS 18L.

'Sit down, Sergeant,' said the guv'nor in his strong Southern Irish brogue.

'Golly!' I thought, 'that's a good welcome, being invited to *sit down* in the guv'nor's office!'

Having lowered my body into the comfort of the armchair in front of my new leader, I awaited the friendly development of his thoughts on me becoming a member of the L Division Team of *Peace Officers*.

'Welcome to da division, Sergeant,' he said.

Then, following a short pause, He continued with, 'All that I can say is D Department has a cheek sending you here! What use is a bloody ex-Traffic Patrol to me?'

'Hang on, Sir,' I said. 'I came twenty-ninth in the competitive examination and am a fully qualified Traffic Patrol. With respect, rather than reading between the lines, please judge me on my service and abilities.'

Sadly, from then on, it was a case of *swords drawn*.

Life at Lima Delta was sure going to be interesting; so just forget any past reflected Constabulary or TT glories settling on your head, boy!

You may well be thinking; now just what has this to do with motorcycling or racing...or even *mountain climbing*?

Several years before, whilst still based at the Traffic Unit at West Croydon (ZTU), a message arrived stating:

'Someone at CO (Commissioners Office/Scotland Yard) has suggested that you would be the right man to conduct motorcycle road tests for *The Police Review*.'

The Police Review was a regular journal published for the interest of police personnel. I hadn't a clue as to the identity of that *someone* at CO but discovered that the editor of that publication was a retired, former Metropolitan Police Inspector.

So, arrangements were made and Bailey took up the pleasant task of riding any motorcycle provided by that publication for a test.

After riding and assessing its various qualities, I was required to submit a written road test report, which would, at some stage, be published in *The Police Review*.

Apart from putting petrol in the tank, that was it. A pleasant way I felt, to spend a few off-duty hours and practise one's penmanship. It was in no way a 'soft number' to be played whilst on duty. There was no suggestion of payment and postage was paid for any writings submitted. To this *would-be* scribe, it was simply the privilege of being given the job by the editor of such a well-respected journal.

As I recall, at the most only two motorcycles came my way for test riding in the short period before the great day of promotion and transfer to Brixton.

Sometime after I arrived at Brixton, a request was received from *The Police Review* for me to road test a 750cc three-cylinder Suzuki 2-stroke motorcycle. This particular machine was assembled as a police specification demonstration machine. Fitted with a fairing, twin pannier boxes, and finished in white, it was fully equipped with blue flashing lights and a 'Police' sign mounted above the rear number plate.

To ensure that the motorcycle was not mistaken for a service police machine, everything about it, which would have given that impression, had already been thoroughly masked and covered by Suzuki GB. Of course, as it was my responsibility to road-test the Suzuki; I did just that!

Whenever the Suzuki was ridden, its rider always wore a long army surplus khaki DR (dispatch rider) heavy-duty Macintosh, my civilian and racing white crash helmet with red Florian Camathius striping and all the necessary additional motorcycling clobber. There was little chance of me being seen as an on-duty police Traffic Patrol officer.

One afternoon, having completed my duties as the Charging Sergeant (8:00 a.m. till 4:00 p.m.), I rode out of Brixton Nick at 4:00 p.m. on my Suzuki and set off south, homeward towards Croydon. The traffic state was normal for the time of day but increasing as rush-hour approached, so we just pottered along, keeping up with the flow.

At Spring Lane, alongside Ashburton Park, the heavy traffic slowed to a standstill, waiting for the traffic lights ahead to 'give us a green'. Tootling past the mouth of Estcourt Road, on my left, just before Spring Lane railway bridge, I was aware that an Area Wireless R/T Car (blue Rover) was sitting waiting to enter the main road, but it didn't ring any bells.

Turning right at the junction by Lower Addiscombe Road, the Suzuki took me towards Croydon. My worthy steed with its rider took the left turn into Shirley Road and continued to follow the fairly slow-moving line of traffic. Having been trained to always use my mirrors, I was aware that the Rover R/T Car was some distance away, several vehicles behind in the flow of traffic but I didn't give it a thought.

Now within a couple of miles of home, leaving the roundabout at the junction with Shirley Road and Addiscombe Road, I simply squirted the Suzuki into the traffic-free section of what was now a dual carriageway. I didn't exceed the speed limit *but just checking* (aware that there was a copper somewhere behind me). Of course, being a 750cc three-cylinder motorcycle, it took off smartish and reached the speed limit very quickly in bottom gear.

Bingo! That did the trick!

The R/T driver took the bait and was out from the queue of traffic as though there was no tomorrow, hooking himself onto my tail.

'I was not doin' nuffin' wrong, guv. Honest!'

The R/T crew had a different view of things. With the Suzy running at a spot-on thirty miles an hour up onto Shirley Hills, the Rover stuck to my tail through the twists and turns.

It was clear to the solo-rider upfront that the R/T Operator was using a new-fangled system of radio, talking to a computer out there somewhere, checking on the registered owner of the white Japanese motorcycle.

At the top of Gravel Hill, I doubled back at the roundabout into Coombe Lane and took the first left into Ballards Way.

Bailey was almost home.

The R/T car, which had been tracking my every move, pulled alongside and the Operator waved me to stop.

He left the car.

A brief conversation took place.

'Your bike, mate?' Asked the officer.

'No,' I replied.

'Whose is it then?' He asked.

'It belongs to Suzuki Great Britain,' I continued, 'Beddington Lane, Wallington.'

'What are you doing with it?'

'I am doing a road-test for a magazine.'

The conversation ended and the officer, seemingly satisfied with my answers, got back into the police car and it drove away.

I was well aware that he had not asked for my name, address, sought any confirmation of my identity or even required sight of my driving documents. Nor did he issue me with a HORT1 form (Home Office Road Traffic 1). This form instructed the driver to produce his driving documents at a police station within seven days.

As a Traffic Patrol trained officer, this seemed strange, so I just hit the start button and drove home.

Life by many folks is so often taken very seriously, when even a quiet smile can brighten one's day. During the evening, I took my roll of masking tape from its shelf and securely placed a few additional strips over the masking tape, which already covered the Police Sign on the back of the machine. With a thick red pen, I inscribed in clear capitals the message: 'This motorcycle is not a Fuzz-mobile. It is a Suzuki.'

'Fuzz', at that time, was a colloquial term used to describe police officers. This message could now be seen, clearly displayed on the back of my test machine. Little thought was given to the matter, but I hoped that the message would cause some observant road-user to smile!

The next morning, I was posted as Station Officer at Brixton Police Station (6:45 a.m. to 3:00 p.m.). It must be appreciated that Brixton was *the centre of the universe!* The Sergeant posted as Station Officer would always try to arrive fifteen minutes or so before his due time so that a smooth takeover from his colleague on the earlier relief could be completed; and he could get off home to bed!

Having been made aware of any work which was in hand, i.e. prisoners in the cells or activities going on around the station, he would check through the Occurrence Book (OB) and as the Station Officer, ensure that the Front Office, Charge Room, and the Brixton Police Station itself, ran smoothly.

On this particular morning, there were prisoners in the cells, officers travelling out of the Metropolitan Police District who required travel warrants, and a CID officer who wanted *a shooter with six on a clip and six up the spout Sarge.*

'We've got to spin a drum, Sarge!'

There were also enquiries by members of the public at the front desk. By 9:00 a.m. as the whole place was buzzing, a curt message arrived stating: 'Station Officer to report to the Chief Superintendent's office immediately!'

Hang on a bit, guv! I can't leave this lot, I thought. I have no Assistant Station Officer (ASO) and the place is going potty!

The fact was that PS Bailey left the Station Office with no cover to its own devices, 'cos the Chief Superintendent told him to! What's that about the *left hand* not knowing what the *right hand* is doing?

On entering the Chief Superintendent's office, standing in front of the window overlooking Brixton Road was Superintendent Terry Siggs, holding his official pocketbook, poised, with a pencil at the ready in his hand. I turned smartly to the left, came to attention *standing on the carpet* in front of the Chief Superintendent's desk, and awaited whatever excitement was to develop.

'How do you travel to work, Sergeant?' said the Chief Superintendent.

'I use a motorcycle, Sir,' I replied.

'What motorcycle did you use this morning?' He enquired.

'I am using a Suzuki motorcycle, Sir,' I said.

'Who does the Suzuki belonged to?' He asked.

'It is the property of Suzuki Great Britain, Beddington Lane, Wallington, Sir.'

'Why are you riding it, Sergeant?'

'I am conducting a motorcycle road-test for *The Police Review*, Sir.'

'What is the arrangement, Sergeant?'

I suspected that the Chief Superintendent was rubbing his thumb and forefingers together under the desk with visions of Fagin, thinking, *'you've got to pick it pocket or two, boy!'*

'I ride the motorcycle, Sir, then I complete and submit a written report to the Editor of *The Police Review*.'

'Yes, Sergeant,' he replied, 'but what is the arrangement?'

Trying to give the impression of being great at detecting and uncovering fine detail, the man behind the desk seemingly was keen to discover whether Bailey was *up to something* but appeared unable to construct a direct question.

'*The Police Review* puts petrol in the tank, pays for the postage stamp and the cost of my typewriter ribbon, and that is it, Sir.'

Aware that Superintendent Siggs was taking notes of this conversation, I quickly formed the impression that the Chief Superintendent thought that I was *on the make* and doing something that contravened the Police Discipline Code.

'Where is this motorcycle parked, Sergeant?' asked the Chief Superintendent.

'It is with the other guys' motorcycles,' I replied, 'parked in the garage under the canteen, Sir.'

'Have you permission to park that machine on police premises, Sergeant?'

'Sir,' I said, 'at the various police stations and units where I have served, sometimes there is a Roneo printed form to complete. In other places, an entry in a book 90 is used and elsewhere, no formal permission is ever required. That is *apparently* the situation at this station.'

The Chief Superintendent then decided that he wanted to inspect this machine and striding ahead of me with his rather flat-footed gait, I was ordered to walk behind with Superintendent Siggs immediately following.

We conducted ourselves in what seemed like a *close order arrest* manner, and in full uniform, descended the winding staircase towards the ground floor.

As we reached the first-floor level where the Police Canteen was situated, we were met by several of my early-turn relief officers coming up the stairs, arriving for their refreshments. What they thought, seeing the three of us in line-astern, I still do not know.

Suffice to say that they didn't know which one of us to acknowledge. Aware that the Station Officer appeared to be under arrest, without doubt they had a good chuckle as they consumed their bacon, egg, and fried slice!

On arrival at the Station Yard, the Chief Superintendent asked me to indicate the motorcycle, which occupied his dedicated constabulary law enforcement thoughts, and I pointed out the Police Specification Suzuki 750.

The rear number plate and masked sign of the motorcycle faced him and the Chief Superintendent, his complexion changing, said.

'Sergeant! What does that sign say?'

'It says, Sir,' '*This motorcycle is not a Fuzz-mobile. It is a Suzuki.*'

The Chief Superintendent blew a senior officer specification fuse and spat out, 'That word is insulting, Superintendent! Remove that sign and keep it for evidence!'

The Superintendent, who I am sure was thoroughly enjoying the pantomime, dutifully pulled this rather sticky taped sign from the number plate and placed it in his pocketbook. Whether it was ever possible to remove the masking tape from his pocketbook safely, I do not know.

'Now, Sergeant,' he continued, 'take that motorcycle and remove it from police premises.'

Suddenly, in full view of the whole relief and crowding at the canteen windows directly above us thoroughly enjoying the spectacle, the Station Officer, minus his proper uniform street headgear, dutifully pushed the dead machine out into Canterbury Crescent, parked it, and returned to normal duties, running the Front Office at Brixton Police Station.

It soon became clear that although GB had not contravened any part of the Police Discipline Code, the Chief Superintendent was going to do his utmost to pin something on him.

Superintendent Siggs was not only a good copper and leader of men, but he was also a time trial racing cyclist. As we street men were struggling to focus on the breaking dawn and wandering out onto the streets, Mr Siggs would sweep into the yard early in the morning looking fresh as a daisy, having cycled up from his home deep into the Kentish countryside.

One day, soon after the events described, the Superintendent took me to one side.

'Sergeant,' he said, 'the Manager at Suzuki is called Ormsby, you know him, don't you?'

'Yes, Sir,' I replied.

'And his lad is in the Traffic at Croydon, isn't he?' He added.

'Yes, Sir,' I said, 'I know him well. Bob is known by us as BTY (Bob the yob), He's a great guy.'

As you might recall, in 1971, I raced Suzukis for Eddie Crooks of Barrow-in-Furness. Crooks Suzukis were the fore-runners of *truly* competitive Suzuki racing motorcycles in the UK and had their own team and riders. Needless to say, Crooks Suzuki liaised with Suzuki GB. During that time, as a local copper, I had got to know the guys at Suzuki GB on Beddington Lane.

'Sergeant, I've also had a chat with the public relations people who sort out test machinery for *The Police Review*,' he paused. 'They know you as well, don't they?'

'Yes, Sir,' I replied.

'I thought that I ought to tell you, Sergeant, that the Editor of *The Police Review* was my Sergeant when I was a Police Cadet years ago at Dagenham! There's nothing in this, is there?'

'No Sir,' I replied thinking, *this gent is not only a Superintendent, but he is a friend and ally to his men.*

Sadly, it must be recalled that of all the Senior Officers observed by your scribe during his service at Brixton Police Station, it was only Superintendent Siggs who left the police station in uniform and worked on the streets.

PS 18L returned home after work, fairly happy at the day's events, but strangely, not too bothered about the 'school bully' workings of some of those 'upstairs'.

It was soon revealed, however, that the Chief Superintendent, not satisfied that now the Divisional Investigation had been completed and I was now 'in the clear', decreed that a re-investigation of his alleged misdeeds should be carried out; this time, by a CO Commissioner's Office (Scotland Yard) team.

I was made aware of a conversation between the original

investigating officer and the Chief Superintendent, where it was observed that had the Sergeant under investigation been 'P.S. *So and So*' (a *social* partner of the Chief Superintendent), thoughts of such an investigation would never have entered his head.

So, time and duties at Brixton passed by. One day, I felt so privileged when Chief Inspector Robin Oake, a dear Christian friend who was an Instructor at Bramshill Police College, invited me to accompany him to a Guest Night evening at the College.

This was quite a special event and the full evening dress was the order of the day. So, Bailey happily accepted the kind invitation to what was for him, such a unique event.

In due time, I made my way to Moss Bros and hired the appropriate evening wear. The interesting point is that several days before my evening shared with Robin, the official notification was given that I had not in any way contravened any regulation set out in the Police Discipline Code. The amazing and hilarious outcome was that on the evening of the Guest-Night down at Bramshill in Hampshire; because it is the traditional practice that guests take a stroll through the rose gardens of the estate with their host before returning for the evening meal and celebrations, PS 18L, in his smart Moss Bros outfit, strolled with Chief Inspector Oake through the gardens. Walking towards us from the opposite direction came my Chief Superintendent, accompanied by his two lady guests. Although the Chief Superintendent knew Robin quite well, both having served on the same Division, and of course, was also quite familiar with me; the two parties passed each other within eighteen inches of touching distance, almost brushing the rose-bushes and for the whole time, the man who wanted *my guts for garters* averted his gaze and kept his head down! Talk about school kids!

One final scene of this saga was revealed when my Investigating Superintendent quietly informed me of the happy outcome.

'Thank you, Sir,' I responded.

Nonetheless, it was necessary to ask this Senior, very honourable and respected Police Officer, how it could have been proved that PS 18L Bailey was the man riding the motorcycle that was stopped by police on Ballards Way?

'Well, of course, Sergeant, the R/T crew entered your details in the Stop Book -*official record of persons stopped in the street*- at Norbury,' he replied.

'Sir, they could not have done so, because the PC never asked who I was or requested me to confirm my identity. Nor were any documents inspected, or required to be produced. Thus, anything written in the Stop Book would have been a false entry, Sir.'

The matter was quietly dropped and nothing more was said. The question of who *should have* been riding the machine could have been resolved from various sources but those sources could not put a particular person on the motorcycle, which was followed and stopped at the scene, as had been claimed.

Deep consideration of the events indicated what was obvious; the Back Hall Inspector at The Yard, during the R/T car check, aware that a 'civvy' had been stopped riding a Police Motorcycle, had enquired of Suzuki GB, the owner, who the authorised user had been. QED! Something for the R/T crew to enter into The Stop Book, but that in no way identified or confirmed who the person was, stopped on Ballards Way.

Back in the 1970s, when a Constable of whatever length of service gained promotion to the rank of a Police Sergeant, that officer became a 'Probationer'. That is, he/she must serve one year in that position and at the end of that time, an Annual Qualification Report (AQR) would be submitted, and the rank held would be confirmed or otherwise!

As PS 18L was nearing the twelve months prescribed, he was called for the necessary AQR interview with his Chief Superintendent. You've got it.

We had met before on a number of occasions. The conversation went quite smoothly and it seemed clear that the lower-ranked officers (Inspectors Station Police Sergeants) responsible for supervising me had submitted favourable reports.

The interviewing officer indicated that his comments would reflect those favourable reports and gave the impression that he would add his own satisfactory observations.

Soon after the interview, a copy of the completed AQR was handed to this Probationary Skipper. Reading its full content, I was immediately conscious that I had been stabbed in the back and from a great height!

PS 18L was eventually called before the Commander of the Division who it seems had noted and would sign off the report. The Commander's remarks indicated that he took the full contents of the AQR *as read*. At which point the Sergeant, standing in front of his Commander, made clear his rejection of the content of the report at this, the end of his 'Probationary' term.

Bailey refused to accept the conclusions reached in the report because the Chief Superintendent had indicated that it showed personal satisfaction that the officer had served to the required satisfactory standard. Yet, in its final form, with the additional written comments of the Chief Superintendent, the report reached a completely negative and condemnatory conclusion.

The Commander *viewed his script* but didn't look up. He seemed to find it difficult to look his Sergeant in the eye.

'Sergeant, I have the power to take away your rank and return you to being a Constable!'

Standing there, 'on the carpet', returned me to the scenario laid out to me beforehand. The fact that *the Sergeant could easily be returned to the position of Constable*, seemed to be a case of getting 'one back on you'.

I am not too sure what God's plan was in all this; save to say that this relatively new Sergeant was never worried or frightened of the bullying from these upper echelons.

So I guess that the verse from 1 Samuel, Chapter 2, verse 30 which says: 'Those who honour me, I will honour…' rang to me and continues to ring so true.

On reflection, however, having been reminded years ago *that a text without context is a pretext;* one must read the whole of the verse, which goes on to say, '…but those who despise me will be disdained.'

I do not wish to appear to be preachy but the person being spoken to in 1 Samuel was Eli, a leader of Israel. He held a position of authority and trust; yet failed to honour that trust and was warned by God because it seemed that he despised his position.

There too was a message to me from scripture: *Be sure where you stand, son, and never compromise your loyalties!*

What were those words again?

Many years before, my mum had lovingly written them down and given them to me on the day of my Baptism.

'Trust in the Lord with all your heart and lean not on your own understanding. In all your ways, acknowledge Him and He shall direct your paths.' (Proverbs, Chapter 3, verses 5-6).

Yup! How true, Mum, even with nigh on twenty years' service in *the job*, I thought.

Life is not always a mountain-top experience, but the time at Brixton was a happy part of my service, which also added yet another fresh learning curve.

One lighter moment forms part of those times in Brixton. On one early turn, being on duty as Station Officer, a Chief Superintendent who had newly arrived at Brixton was seated in plain-clothes at the desk in the front office, checking through the entries in the Occurrence Book (OB). My duty required that I stood-by and passed to him any books or paperwork which he requested to see. This was a normal Supervisory task carried out each morning by the guv'nors to enable them to be up to date with what was going on.

As the Chief Superintendent sat quietly reading, a red-faced Superintendent stormed into the front office.

'Sergeant! Someone has left a tatty old Ford Corsair parked in my space outside! Get it moved!'

The Chief Superintendent slowly raised his head from the written page.

'Superintendent, that *tatty old Ford Corsair* is my car,' he said as he continued studying the OB.

The Superintendent, who later became a Senior Officer in the City of London Police, quietly left the office.

Quiet observations about *lack of good observational skills and space between ears* circulated within the area for some time!

The guys at LD formed a good team and were always there when you wanted them. Another character who particularly springs to mind was Station Police Sergeant (SPS) 3L R Channing.

Bob, full name Robert, was always referred to as 'RC3'. He too was a leader of men. It is recalled that whenever this ex-Trafpol with three new stripes was struggling with a new and difficult situation in the Front Office, Bob would quietly scribble a note on a small piece of paper and pass on a pearl of knowledge, i.e., 'This is the info you want. Do it this way, son.'

Bob rose to the rank of Chief Inspector but sadly passed away whilst still in service.

28

The spirit moves

It must be said that several years after my time at Brixton, now posted to Z Division, I was stationed at Addington nick (ZA).

Reporting early for Station Officer duty, as you know, was the unwritten practice; to relieve your mates on the shift who were going off duty. Early one morning PS Bailey walked into the Front Office ready to *take over* from the night duty Skipper.

'We've got one prisoner in the Detention Room brought in last night. He was nicked having done a break-in of the show-house on the new estate up by the bird sanctuary. You might be interested to know that his dad is Commander L!'

Is it un-Christian, on occasions, to smile at unusual events?

Later in the morning, the housing developer 'up by the bird sanctuary' informed the police that they were not going to prefer any charges reference the uninvited night caller. Book 12a PAS entry (Person At Station).

My time of service at Addington nick was the happiest experience and part of my continuing learning curve. Being some distance from Croydon, and even further from Norbury our Sub-Divisional Station, we worked our patch on the edge of the Met happily as quite a close-knit team.

Geoff Lewer and Dennis Giles were the R/T drivers on the relief and all together, our area was policed quite efficiently.

One night tour of duty, fairly soon after I was posted to the station, at around 2:00 a.m. as a group of us were enjoying the official 'grub break', Dennis said, 'Righto, Sarge! We want to find out what makes you tick!'

Dennis, hailed from the East End of London, had worked in the Criminal Investigation Department (CID) and clearly wanted to hone his detective abilities. Dennis, like many of his compatriots from that part of the Metropolis, spoke, using his hands to emphasise and confirm what was being said. In fact, if his hands had been tied together, Dennis would probably have been speechless!

What a great character he was.

It seemed the guys wanted to check out my beliefs. Whether any kind of 'grape-vine information' had been picked up before I arrived at Addington, it would be presumptuous to consider.

We talked and discussed. My love for the Lord Jesus was examined without any form of mickey-taking.

Among many topics, that night was the negative impact of the Ouija board, which some of the lads had recently experienced, was discussed. The opportunity was given to state that if Christ wasn't part of any 'spiritual experience', it had to be from 'the other side', as in Satan. It seemed to be taken *as read* that there was no third choice when Ouija boards were involved.

Whilst we were in mid-discussion, the Inspector, our Duty Officer, arrived from Norbury for an official visit.

After the normal constabulary exchanges, out of the blue and totally unexpectedly, Dennis said, 'Guv'nor, t'morra night we are going to have a Bible study. Can you be here with us?'

It turned out that this Inspector was a Christian. Dennis

313

obviously knew this but I was unaware, as I had never met the Inspector before.

'Sorry, guys. Tomorrow is not on for me,' the Inspector replied.

'Well, guv. What shall we study then?' Dennis replied.

The Duty Officer's suggestion was, 'Take a look at 1 Samuel, Chapter 16, and then decide whether you should *tell the truth, the whole truth and nothing but the truth.*'

(Those words comprise the Oath, which a witness is required to swear and be bound by when appearing in an English Court of Law to give evidence).

The Bible story tells of how Samuel, the boy of Eli's time, had been called by God. Following Eli's death, Samuel was recognised by the people of Israel as a prophet of God (1 Samuel, Chapter 3). Now, many years later, King Saul, who, in God's words, '*...has turned away from me and not carried out my words,*' (Ch.15 v 10), had been rejected by God.

Shades of old Eli!

God had told Samuel to go to Bethlehem and anoint one of Jesse's sons (David) to be King in place of Saul. We read that in response to God's instruction when Samuel says, '*How can I go? Saul will hear about it and kill me.*' (Chapter 16, verse 2)

To which God says, '*Take a heifer with you and say, 'I have come to sacrifice to the Lord.' Invite Jesse to the sacrifice and I will show you what to do. You are to anoint for me the one I indicate.*'

In modern parlance I suppose, because he was aware of the potential threat on his life, you could call that Samuel's 'cover story'. I'm sure that even as children, we had early in life learned the art of developing a cover story!

The next night, the relief paraded and we all went off to police our area through the night. In the small hours, once again, a number of us gathered over our sandwiches to examine the very difficult yet thrilling question, which the Inspector had set before us.

It was in no way a quiet 'micky-take' to have a bit of a laugh at this Christian Station Officer.

Having reached the time to get back in the streets, Dennis picked up the 'bat phone' (police inter-coms were so-called in the pre-mobile phone age) and spoke in official *police speak* to the Inspector who was at Norbury.

'Guv'nor,' said Dennis, 're the enquiry you gave us, we have not yet fully completed the investigation and reached a final result. But we have decided that they all lived happily *heifer* after!'

Dennis and I had many serious discussions in the following months and I introduced him to a book written by Fred Lemon titled *Breakout*. Apparently, Fred, who hailed from the East End of London, had been an *upper league* villain in his time and whilst serving a fourteen-year sentence of imprisonment in Dartmoor Prison, one night, Fred experienced God's presence in his prison cell. There and then Fred had put his faith and trust in the Lord Jesus Christ. His life had been completely changed.

Fred told me of when he first came across *that lot!* He had been made aware that a team of Christian policemen were going to conduct a Christian Witness service at his local church and he was going to attend the service and *sort 'em out!* As he walked into the building, all that he first saw was a line of boot-soles in front of him. These coppers were all kneeling down and praying!

315

Over many years Fred had come to know and become friends with many Christian police officers; members of a law enforcement authority with which he had once been completely at odds. He was a great Cockney character and whenever he prayed out loud, the listener was aware that the One to whom he was praying was standing alongside him. Dennis became very interested in Fred's book.

One day, Dennis said, 'I'd like to meet this guy!'

It so turns out that sometime later, Fred, who had become a great personal friend, was visiting us and staying with Rosemary and me overnight at our home.

The next morning, Dennis and I were required to attend Croydon Magistrates Court to take out an arrest warrant in the name of some-one who needed to be nicked. It was arranged that Dennis would pick me up on the way to Court and thus, be able to meet Fred before we left.

Dennis arrived at around 9:00 a.m. and within what seemed like moments, Dennis and Fred were in deep conversation and like genuine Cockneys, were getting on like a house on fire. At 12:30 p.m. it was realised that the morning had gone and it was time for us to separate. The two East-Enders said farewell, parting like old mates who had known each other for years.

As they shook hands and amid their farewell, Dennis said, 'Fred, I feel as though I've known you for years. Pray for me!'

With that, Fred gripped Dennis's hand more firmly, took my Constabulary colleague in a full-bodied bear hug, began talking to his friend the Lord Jesus and asked him to bless Dennis!

My colleague did not know what had hit him.

Several years later, Bailey, having left Addington nick and re-joined what was now known as the Traffic Division, was serving as a Garage Police Sergeant (GPS). I was aware that Dennis had recently been injured in a serious disturbance, a consequence of which was that his health had taken a knock.

At one stage, I visited Dennis at his home and he was rather bothered because he was due to meet the Chief Medical Officer to be examined on his current physical condition. He was most concerned because he was a Class-One Advanced Police Driver.

'The trouble is, Sarge,' he said, 'I reckon that I'm going to *lose my wheels!*' Here, he meant he was concerned that he would lose his authority to drive police vehicles. Dennis was quite distressed at the prospect.

I did not at that moment honestly know why I said it, but with great confidence, I said, 'Don't worry, Dennis. *You will not lose your wheels.*'

Following his meeting with the CMO, Dennis returned to duty, still as an Authorised Police Driver!

Many years passed by and Bailey, having retired from what was then known as the Metropolitan Police Force, heard some sad news.

Dennis had become a Police Dog-Handler and I was given to understand that one day just before the Christmas holiday, he had been with colleagues Dog Training *up at that bird sanctuary.* At the agreed time, the team of dog-handlers met up in the car park, presumably to share in a tea break. Yet, Dennis did not appear.

Following a search, Dennis was found collapsed among the trees, cuddling his police dog.

Sadly, Dennis, a friend and former colleague, passed into eternity. What can this old *dreamer of a mountain climber* say as he considers Almighty God, His unfailing love for mankind and the work of his Holy Spirit?

Could it be that when GB reaches the pearly gates, Dennis will be standing there saying, 'Hello, Sarge! What kept you?'

29

The final lap

Motorbikes were still well and truly part of the scene and my thinking. One day, a visitor at the Front Office counter at our Police Traffic Unit on Windmill Road, Croydon informed us that someone at Scotland Yard ('someone at CO' again?) had recommended that he speak with PS Bailey.

The visitor at the counter was none other than Ian Woolf, a BBC Television Producer who had been commissioned to make a series of motorcycle-orientated programmes, the title of which was: *Sorry Mate, I Didn't See You* (the title of the series mimicked the statement, which so often is made when two vehicles *unintentionally* collide).

Motorcyclists, both commuters and enthusiasts, who ride for the pleasure of powered two-wheeled transport, professional riders and others, were going to feature in this series. At the start of each programme, so it turned out, each of the riders and their field of personal experience were to be identified. It would seem that *the dreamer mountain climber's* past had caught up with him, yet again, and I was to be officially authorised (as in, by them upstairs) to be involved in that series.

The programmes were going to focus on many aspects of 'safe road use' and one programme, in which it was suggested that a police officer take part, was entitled 'Fit For The Road.'

Part of the programme would involve a police officer out patrolling in a Traffic Car. Aware that such vehicles (TAG cars) normally operated with a crew of two and, not wanting to look like some *publicity self-seeking bloke* from the Traffic Division, I requested that another traffic man could make up the crew.

One of my fellow Trafpols was Colin Howells. He was a motorcycle trials-rider. Trials riding on a motorcycle requires the competitors to ride over or through difficult terrain through marked-out areas known as 'Sections', without leaving the marked-course or putting their feet down. Such events require a great sense of balance and machine control on the part of the rider, with the essential ability to 'plan ahead'. Failure in any one of these abilities could well give the result of a *'mud in your eye'* or even *all over your trousers* outcome!

Colin, therefore, completed the Constabulary team.

We both enjoyed playing a part in this series and I recall two particular experiences; one 'on the record' in the television programme and the other appearing nowhere in BBC archives.

We were out on the streets one day filming some sequences for the 'Fit For The Road' programme. Our location was just nearby my former base, Addington nick. I was being interviewed by a young lady who was a motorcyclist and a member of the Institute of Advanced Motorists (IAM), so she was very familiar with her subject. It was a matter of a few minutes of discussion about being safely attired and clothed when riding a motorcycle.

The camera was focused on the Police Officer who was being interviewed and these various aspects were being reviewed. The whole sequence was completely unscripted and unrehearsed. The weather was warm, the sun was shining. Thus, my awareness of the present conditions focused my thoughts.

As a consequence, I emphasised that, even in good weather, it was essential that protective clothing should be worn.

To underline my point I ad-libbed, 'In the warmest of weather you should still always wear gloves, even if they are thin leather, because running along the road on your hands at thirty miles an hour makes your eyes water!'

The interviewer somehow maintained her thoroughly professional poise. It could, however, be seen that the cameraman was struggling to keep his lens steadily focussed on his subject.

Ian Woolf, standing beside the cameraman, was shaking with laughter.

Was it something I said, guv?

The Producer's view was that the speaker, although raising a smile, had as a result graphically made such a serious point. Therefore, that sequence would certainly be included in the final programme.

The other incident which has stuck with me ever since is that one day Colin and I, with the film-crew and Ian, spent the morning in an editing studio in Soho. The Editors were with Ian, checking and editing recent film sequences; involving us and the crew where their particular knowledge was required.

At lunchtime, we all retired to a nearby Italian restaurant, where we relaxed together and ordered our lunches. As the group of us sat awaiting the arrival of our meals, jokes began to be exchanged among the team. Strangely, most of the jokes were what one would call 'religious' jokes. Yet, they were quite innocuous and did not offend. After a while, Ian began to share some of *his* jokes. They were quite harmless but could maybe have upset someone of a particular religious persuasion.

In mid-flow, Ian paused and said, 'It's alright. I am *of the faith.*'

Bailey, who was sitting alongside his Producer said, 'Ian, one of my best friends was a Jew.'

His response was, 'Oh! And what did he do for a living?'

'He was a Carpenter, Ian.'

We both understood each other and *got the message*. What joy!

Your scribe also enjoyed the privilege of being included in another programme in the series called 'The Right Line'. This part of the series included a session filmed at Brands Hatch. Suzuki (GB) supplied machinery and one of their works riders, the famed Mick Grant, gave us a *close-up* demonstration of his skills.

As he led the way around the Brands lap, our *mountain climbing dreamer* on a similar Suzuki, followed him closely and matched his course and racing line, giving a running commentary via the recording device mounted on the back of his bike.

Mick's progress was also visually recorded from Bailey's machine. Throughout the afternoon, the crew also filmed us from various fixed points around the circuit.

It must be appreciated that the in-car/on motorcycle film cameras of the twenty-first century, which can transmit live-action, were a thing of the future. Thus, my Suzuki was fitted with a battery-powered Gun Camera. I understood that these devices had been used during wartime aerial combat. They only had a limited 'run-time' and so it was necessary to frequently return to base and be recharged.

The series of programmes, having been completed; *Sorry*

Mate I Didn't See You was broadcast on BBC One Television. Later, the series was repeated on BBC Two.

Time passed and one afternoon, six years into my retirement from my time served in the Metropolitan Police Force, and about ten years after the filming of the programmes, I was at home and received a telephone call.

'Mr Bailey, this is Chief Inspector *Buggins* from Croydon Police Station. Did you work at Croydon (ZD)?'

'I was at TDZ, Sir,' I replied, 'the Traffic Unit in West Croydon.'

'Do you know anything about a programme called *Sorry Mate I Didn't See You?*'

'Yes, Sir. I took part in the programme.'

'I have just received a serious *Complaint Against Police* (official term) from a member of the public,' said the Chief Inspector. 'Apparently, a remark was made in that programme about a motorcyclist running down the road on his hands, the consequence of which was that his eyes would water. The complainant says that police should take a more serious view of road use and not make jokes about it, because her young son is a motorcyclist and it is a serious matter. It is not something to be joked about!'

'Sir,' I began, 'may I suggest that you contact the BBC and get a copy of the programme. Those taking part are all identi-fied as experienced motorcyclists. Both Colin and I, apart from being Traffic Patrol Officers, have spent a great deal of time as competitors in motorcycle sport.

'Watch the programme in sequence. You will see that all of those who featured were motorcyclists and also had personal experience of the public roads. If you watch the programme and note the context from which the complaint was created, you will see that a serious point was made and *graphically* emphasised by what was said.'

End of conversation. Nothing further was ever heard.

Careful what you say, guv! Someone might write it down on a piece of paper, save it for a rainy day, and read it when the ink has run and blurred the message!

30

The end of one mountain trail

Although my days of TT competition on The Island had passed, with an almost irresistible pull every Springtime, that beautiful island in the Irish Sea and its wonderful atmosphere returned to my thoughts. I wondered whether this former TT rider could be of some service to the organisers as a Travelling Marshal.

When enquiries were made, the response was, *'Thanks all the same, but the team was fully up to strength.'*

In the early 1980s, the Auto Cycle Union considered having additional Travelling Marshals round the course, 'teaming' with a doctor standing-by. The plan was that with the doctor riding pillion on the TM's machine, medical assistance could quickly be taken to the scene of an accident. This idea saw its birth following a nasty tumble experienced by star rider, Alex George at Ginger Hall, when it was claimed that the emergency helicopter had arrived late on the scene.

Being a Police Traffic Man, 'fully tuned' in R/T procedure, trained in first aid and sadly, very familiar with personal injury and fatal road traffic accidents; Bailey felt that with his TT experience thrown in, he could perhaps be of service to his former fellow competitors.

A number of these guys were personal friends. Thus, my thoughts were that my experience could surely be of use in an emergency if the suggested 'medical taxi-rider' plan ever came into effect.

It must be acknowledged, however, that my first thought when reports of this plan were first published was, 'No Way!'

A rider taking part in any race is aiming to reach the finishing-flag as near to the front as possible. He/she is a competitor *pure and simple* and as a former racer, having experienced almost being pushed off the road by a too aggressive fellow racer more than once, I was aware that a bike 'two up' and also carrying medical kit on the TT Course, even responding to an emergency, could present an awful risk. Add to this the possibility that the passenger might not be familiar with riding pillion and the possible risk would be greatly increased.

Several years later, experience as a TM confirmed the basic thought, 'No Way!'

During one Morning Practice, I was on duty up on the Mountain Section, riding through the four continuous right-hand bends of The Verandah. On the fourth and final curve, the racing line took the rider close to, almost touching the right side apex of the road…and *you must hit that spot.*

Yes, you are ahead of me!

One of the star works-riders came from behind, rode between my machine and the right kerb and was gone! He was clearly trying to record a really fast lap in an early Morning Practice session. Travelling Marshals were *obviously visible*, dressed in fluorescent yellow over-suits and their machines marked front and rear with a large 'M' plate! (Yellow plate/black letter).

My star rider, who I had incidentally *beaten to the line* years before at Lydden Hill, travelling at racing speed, could have seen the TM as he came onto the Mountain Mile before The

Verandah, and was reeling him in, even if the Marshal was at the other end of that section.

On the Mountain Circuit there is only one safe line for a rider to take and so, to do his job properly and safely, a Travelling Marshal must take 'the right line' and ride at near race speeds.

Allan 'Kipper' Killip was at this time the Chief Travelling Marshal. Many years before, during his first TT as a TM, Allan had asked the great Bob McIntyre how best to avoid baulking competitors on the circuit.

Bob McIntyre's response was, 'Stick to the racing line.'

All racers would have expected that because if someone in front was 'ducking and weaving' to get out of the way, tragedy would be almost inevitable.

Returning to my thoughts on the matter of 'two up' medical assistance, I wrote to Ken Shierson, the boss-man at the Auto Cycle Union, offering my services. Needless to say, the plan for Travelling Marshals to convey medics and their equipment to racing incidents had wisely been shelved. Sometime later, however, Mr Shierson informed me that Bailey GL was being included as a member of the TT Travelling Marshals team, which was being increased in number. Aware that my place had been arranged by the ACU in London and not directly from those involved on 'The Island', I nonetheless felt privileged to be included in the Travelling Marshals team.

Upon arrival in Manxland for the 1981 TT, it was learned that Albert Moule, a former TT rider of many years' experience and a long time Travelling Marshal, had taken a tumble and was out of action. Albert had first competed on the Mountain

Course in the 1936 Manx Grand Prix and had continued to race in the MGP and TT until 1967 (the year of my *first* Island race).

It was a joy to meet, speak with, and be advised by this dear and very humble man.

Years before, at the start of my *mountain experience*, having been shown the correct way round the TT course by another former racer and the then Chief Travelling Marshal, Peter Crebbin, I was again reminded that TT riders are fairly 'out of the spotlight' types; humble and modest about their achievements. So, it was good to feel that maybe I would be of service to the riders who would be competing this year.

For the next two weeks, I worked for my living on an unpaid yet *happy to be here,* voluntary basis. The duties of Race Marshals were clearly laid out in written form and the *Travelling Marshal* was no different in his responsibilities as he would be on the move and thus operating from many different locations around the course.

The rule book, *Duties of officials-Marshals and Flagmen* (1981), described what was required of each specific official.

The first sentence of the duties of marshals' said: *Marshals have the power of Special Constables, are to keep the Course clear, to note any special incidents and to lend assistance in any case of an accident.*

So! There you go.

For starters, this new Travelling Marshal was immediately aware of his basic responsibilities. The time spent throughout six Isle of Man TTs and two Manx GP events had given me the experience and privilege to be involved with and serving others in such an outstanding and historic event. Needless to say, there was great pleasure in being able to ride the circuit, both very early in the morning and throughout the day.

As I have already referred to, in all that time, there was the one 'hairy moment' involving a thoughtless racer. There were also the long and seemingly regular periods of being posted up on The Mountain at Guthrie's Memorial, the only company being the Medical Officer posted at that point.

On one occasion, however, during a race, a message arrived: 'When this race is finished, the TM at Guthrie's is requested to ride against the course down to Parliament Square, Ramsey to pick up Ken Inwood and convey him back to Douglas.'

During the race in progress, Ken had broken down in Ramsey. His defective machine would be recovered when the race-day had finished but Ken needed to get back to the start at Douglas to pick up the machine prepared for the next race, which was for machines of a different capacity. So, as the race finished and the official Course Inspection Car had passed by, I had the dubious responsibility of riding the wrong-way down The Mountain to find him.

OK, so the Course Inspection Car had gone through, but what about a rider, his machine having packed up, who had managed to fix his bike and was now riding *eye-balls out* to get back to the finish… even though the Course Car had passed indicating that the race was finished?

All was well.

I found Ken, wedged him up behind and then we enjoyed a high-speed 'tour' back over The Mountain. Ken was duly dropped off, then this TM had to go like stink to get back to his post at Guthrie's before Ken's race started! On the positive side, a fast ride on a clear road around the course was the bonus!

During this first year, I was posted at what came to be the regular 'stand-by' location at Guthrie's. One morning, as the first race of the day progressed, a call was received.

'Serious accident at Keppel Gate. TM from Guthrie's to attend.'

This location is on the far side of the Mountain Section, just before the drop down to Kate's Cottage and Creg-Ny-Baa. So, Bailey had to 'join in the race' (remember what Bob McKintyre had said) to reach the accident spot quickly and safely.

Riding as a TM with the competitors concentrating on the serious business of racing for a result is quite a daunting experience for the reasons I already explained. But someone was in trouble and my presence was needed.

One of my former racing mates, Peter Davies, had come off his Laverda in a big way and was lying off the course on the hillside, very seriously injured. The rescue medical helicopter was on the scene. With the other Marshals and the helicopter Medical Crew working together, Peter was treated up there on the hillside and loaded aboard the chopper to be flown to Nobles Hospital.

That day, we all experienced one of the several downsides of TT marshalling, which nonetheless, made the job worthwhile.

One morning, en-route to my post riding along the course, the racing had not started and the roads were therefore still open to traffic. On the twisty section going towards Ballaugh, I came upon a road traffic accident (RTA) involving a motorcyclist who had clearly been on his way to find a viewing position for the race. He had come into collision with another vehicle or roadside obstacle and was lying lifeless in the road.

This young fellow, who had set off to enjoy the day, in a tragic moment passed into eternity. Kneeling beside him in the road, the best efforts of this Travelling Marshal could not save him.

The three years when I was engaged as a Travelling Marshal were, overall, happy times. Being conscious of doing something useful during the two weeks of the TT, as it were, giving a bit of a *payback* for the six memorable years of competing in the TT and MGP races between 1967 and 1974. (A serious head injury at Snetterton in 1970 prevented Bailey's involvement in the TT Races that year).

So, the long ride north on my DR400 Suzuki to Liverpool in late May 1984 to The Island for practice week, filled me with happy anticipation of once more being involved in the greatest motorcycling event; the Tourist Trophy Races.

Strangely, when I checked-in on my arrival, there was no green TM over-suit available, so, kitted out in my 'old' Travelling Marshal fluorescent over-suit which I had thought-fully brought from home *just in case*, I reported for duty early on Monday morning of the 28th May to assist in the first Practice Session of the TT.

Having been allotted a Honda VF 750F for the Travelling Marshal duties, the bike was checked over and clearly was 'ready to go' with the normal TM set-up. It was noted, however, that no two-way radio (R/T) set was fitted. I thought that this equipment presumably would have been *set up* on my Honda before the day was out.

Aware that he would be on the road without direct radio contact with race control, Bailey set out as directed. Morning practice passed, fortunately without this particular Travelling Marshal being called to any serious incidents.

It was a joy, nonetheless, to cover some miles around the Mountain Course as I visited the various fixed points to which I had been directed. The landline telephone locations were used as necessary to contact Control. The day passed and once more, in the late afternoon, I reported to Race Control, ready for the Evening Practice Session. This was going to be busier than the early morning, as more riders would be out on the course. My Honda was still without any R/T equipment.

'It will be fitted tomorrow,' they told me.

Normally, in the past, before the first Evening Practice period, all the TM's would receive their Warrant Card authorising them as and giving the authority of Special Constables. Strangely, Bailey was the only TM present who was not issued with such a warrant.

'Sorry, you will get your Warrant Card tomorrow.'

Never mind. I didn't think too much about this delay but simply considered that a slight clerical error had caused the slip-up.

The weather was warm and bright. So, aware that as the evening progressed, low sunlight would be 'in the faces' of riders on parts of the Douglas to Ramsey Section of the course, this TM brought his dark lensed goggles into service for the evening.

Posted to patrol the course and *stand-by* at The Bungalow up near the highest point on the circuit, a brisk ride brought me to the fixed point where I remained until being called back to remain on watch at The Grandstand. So, on this pleasant evening, I had already enjoyed 'doing a lap' of the Mountain Course which was one of the bonuses of these particular marshalling duties.

As the practice session built up more training mileage for the competitors, I was told to proceed to Ballacraine and there await further instructions; so I set off on what was to be Bailey's final ride as a Travelling Marshal.

The events, which occurred within minutes of my leaving The Grandstand, are best recounted by the letter, which sometime later had to be sent to the Clerk of the Course.

Written from notes, which I recorded of this particular evening, the drama, potential for tragedy and the ways of political manoeuvrings, was unfolded as its author was reminded of his part in the evening.

The sequence of events that were to take place in that hour rumbled on for weeks. Bailey, almost without any discussion, was condemned that as a Police Officer he had 'failed to stop and deal with the incident'. I was given marching orders and left the office of the Clerk of the Course at the top of The Grandstand. I returned the official Travelling Marshal's Honda to Mylchreest's Garage in Peel Road, climbed aboard my Suzuki DR400, and returned to my digs.

Strangely, a request was made for me to return my TM oversuit. You know, the one which had not been available; for use by another replacement Travelling Marshal.

Strange! He must have been waiting ready in the wings. Can't return what I haven't got, guv.

Here is the letter, unedited, save for an added note about *prayer.*

8th June 1984

Dear Jackie,

This letter is being written reluctantly following many years of happy association with the Isle of Man and the TT/MGP races. It is being written after much thought in order that the circumstances of the incident at Glen Vine on Monday the 28th of May 1984 and the developments which followed, may be put on record and the facts made clear.

On Monday the 28th of May 1984, I was on duty as a Travelling Marshal for the evening practice period, having performed duty during the practice period earlier in the day. I was equipped with a Honda VF 750F solo motorcycle. During the evening practice, I had already been posted to patrol the course and to stand-by on watch at The Bungalow. Being brought back to the Grandstand by Race Control, I remained there on watch. At about 8:00 p.m. Control dispatched to me to Ballacraine. I left the start behind Mick Grant, aware that various other works riders were on the course.

On arrival at Quarter Bridge, I was aware of a four-stroke racing machine behind me. This machine, a Ducati ridden by Alan Caldwell, passed me on the exit from Braddan Bridge, and I was behind it as we passed through Union Mills. In the dip at Union Mills, I was passed by Mick Ward, riding a Senior Yamaha. The Yamaha rider passed the Ducati on the climb to Glen Vine. The speed differential between the Yamaha and my Honda was great. The Yamaha, having passed the Ducati, was soon lost from view. It is well known that the section from Union Mills to Greeba Bridge is flat out and that the Glen Vine corner is negotiated by the fastest riders at 140/150mph. On the approach to Glen Vine, the sun was low in the sky, extremely bright and shining directly into the faces of the competitors.

I was now between seventy-five and one hundred yards behind the Ducati. As I left the dip just before the first apex of the corner known as Glen Vine, my machine was travelling at about 120mph. I saw a stationary yellow flag ahead of me on the right side of the corner and shut my throttle. The Ducati was ahead of me on the same line. A degree of instability was thus introduced into my machine. I immediately saw the body of Mick Ward lying on the left side of the track and simultaneously saw the Ducati, rider and machine, bouncing from the left side of the road to the right.

The rider, who had been in my view for most of the incident thus far, appeared to have braked whilst cranked over. This bend, which has a false first apex actually continues for some distance in the sweeping curve. The machine was bounced back into the roadway and was disintegrating. It was about one hundred yards past the first apex and was bouncing diagonally across the road.

The road was now completely blocked by the rider, although now lost from my view, the machine, various components from the machine (tank, seat, etc) and other flying debris. I now know that a concrete bus shelter was partially demolished. This debris was bouncing and moving and I knew that I was going to be thrown from my machine as there was no way through the blockage and no way of escape for me or any other following riders.

(The detail of my prayer was not included in the letter but at this point, GB very aware of what could happen in the next moments and that it was beyond his control. I prayed to our Heavenly Father, asking that as this Travelling Marshal was unable to order the events of the next few moments of his life and had a wife and two daughters at home. 'Could you sort this situation out because only your way is best?' I asked. Your scribe has never been caused to pray in a similar situation whilst travelling at such a high speed!)

By the grace of God, as I put the Honda upright to straight-line any obstacle, which was struck, a small gap opened up and I was able to manoeuvre my machine through it. Still travelling at a very high speed, no braking had been possible due to the sweep of the bend, it took some distance to regain proper control of my machine.

My immediate intention and aim were to stop.

It will be known that immediately after the scene of the incident the road surface drops steeply in two steps and any rider coming over the brows is blind-sighted to any person or vehicle on or crossing the circuit. Braking to a standstill in this situation would have been foolish and hazardous, presenting any following rider with a dangerous additional situation.

A rear observation was taken, which at the speed being travelled was at best of limited use, showing me nothing due to the gradient. Almost immediately I was passed by Brian Reid, riding a Senior Suzuki. He was travelling at a very high speed (see his comment in MCN 30/5/84, page 5). I now knew that other machines could well follow, each having been put off line at best or being out of control at worst. The circuit was clearly still open.

Police training is that in the event of high-speed multiple pile-ups (accident), it is the responsibility of emergency services to arrive at the incident from the approach side. No approach, however, is made until the following traffic has been stopped and certainly, no incident is approached from the exit side when the situation on the approach side; that is, movement and approach speed of traffic is unknown.

I had not arrived on the scene of an accident but was part of the accident, having been involved in it and been fortunate enough to escape injury and collision.

My machine, for some reason, had not been fitted with a radio set. It was due to be fitted on Tuesday the 29th of May. No contact could thus be made with race control. Communication had to be swiftly established by telephone. The precise location of the telephone at Ballacraine was known to me as Travelling Marshals are always posted to that location.

The decision, which had to be made, was based upon my judgement of the following facts:

From the speed and distance covered in the seconds immediately following the accident, I could not safely stop and on foot return to the location. It is now known that the stationary marshal was knocked down whilst standing on the footpath. I could therefore be of no practical use where I was.

By proceeding direct to Ballacraine, I would immediately be able to relay what information I had to Race Control. Having been posted to that location by Control in the first place, I was thus making myself available to cover the Ballacraine to Kirmichael section. Control had not advised me whether or not there was a Travelling Marshal already at Ballacraine waiting for my arrival and thus being released to cover the section from Kirkmichael.

Both options would have taken the same time but to try to return to the scene of the incident with riders still coming through, even if it had been possible to stop with safety, would have presented riders with an unnecessary hazard. I would not have been able to stop traffic on the approach side and was aware that the Chief

Travelling Marshal was at The Grandstand. It is always the practice to send a Marshal forward to an incident, never back against the course.

The decision made, having survived the 120mph multiple accidents, still travelling at speed, was made with safety as the prime consideration, the knowledge that no practical use could be served from the exit side and the knowledge that the Ballacraine to Kirkmichael Section would remain without cover. I proceeded to and telephoned from Ballacraine.

These factors were considered in the light of twenty-six years of police service and Traffic Patrol Duties combined with ten years of TT/MGP competitive experience and Travelling Marshal duties.

I am fully aware that the matter was prejudged in my absence before my return to Race Control at The Grandstand.

You immediately, before having the full facts, dismissed me from Travelling Marshal duties, forty-five minutes had only elapsed since the accident. The charge was made that I had failed to stop when coming upon an accident. The inference was therefore that I had neglected to perform my duties as a Travelling Marshall.

It is strange that, to date, even the press has the detail of the incident incorrectly reported, and although it was known from my testimony that I was present, no official request for a witness statement concerning the accident has been made.

When charged with a responsible position of authority, based upon qualifications and experience and acting as an arm of the overall authority, it is only to be expected that decisions made operationally and often in hazardous situations, will be supported by the overall authority. If condemnation of that decision or those decisions is made without the testimony of independent witnesses or evidence, then that overall authority is undermined by its own actions.

My record in the Isle of Man is well catalogued. 1967 to 1974. Eleven starts TT/MGP, four Silver, and one Bronze TT replicas. Club Team Award 1973. My enthusiasm for, dedication to and defence of the Tourist Trophy Races, particularly during the dark years of criticism of the races in the early 1970s, is well documented in both National and Motorcycle press. It is always wise to learn who your most trusted friends are and then not attack them.

You will know that my recruitment to the Travelling Marshal team was as a result of my offer of professional assistance, following the accident involving Alex George at Ginger Hall in 1980. On that occasion, much criticism was made of the lack of medical back-up at the scene. It is known that this was unfounded. Nonetheless, the plan was put forward that motorcyclists would be posted around the course, fully equipped with radios, emergency packs etc, standing by to convey doctors to the scene of any incident on the course.

My assistance was offered, not because the place was sought as a Travelling Marshal, nor because the retired racer wanted a few ego trips on closed roads to relive past glories, but to give a service to competitors, many of them old friends. My professional and competitive record was thought to be of use.

That such a plan of rider/doctor teams could not safely work, is well known, and thus my subsequent recruitment as a Travelling Marshal was a pleasant and honoured surprise. These duties have, at all times, been carried out with professional dedication. I would refer you to the terrifying accident involving Peter Davies at Keppel Gate in the Classic Race, June 1981. Peter suffered a broken neck and back among other injuries. I was part of the team involved in his rescue and dispatch to the hospital. He is now fully recovered.

It is well known that the ideal of having the team of Travelling

Marshals comprised of Manx riders or Manx residents has been sought for some time. In 1984, as a result of the foregoing incident, that goal was therefore achieved!

Let it be placed on record that although communication was made with both the ACU and your Chief Travelling Marshal earlier this year that I was prepared to carry out the duties which had been entrusted to me since 1981, no reply was received that these services were dispensed with.

The record will show that G Bailey was included in the duties rota, was issued with written instructions, first aid equipment and equipped with a machine. Bailey's machine was not, however, equipped with a radio set, nor did his name appear in the official programme with the rest of the team!

Strangely, a Warrant of Authority (Special Constable) was not available for him when the rest were issued on the evening of the 28th of May, the second Practice Session!

Since first performing duties as a Travelling Marshal, one has been fully aware that the presence of a non-Manx resident as a Travelling Marshal was not locally welcome. As has been said, my concern has always been for the welfare and safety of the competitors and not with local Crosby-based politics.

I am sad that a man (the recipient of this letter), whose racing achievements since the 1950s have been admired by the writer of this letter and who has been respected over many years, should use an incident such as has been recorded to seek to dishonour another, without the true facts being considered.

During the remainder of the 1984 TT period, I was made fully aware of the distorted and untrue report which was being 'tittle tattled' around the Isle of Man. It is a sad day for the Tourist Trophy Race history that such has taken place. Had someone had the common courtesy or courage to let the writer know beforehand that his presence was not wanted in the Isle of Man, by say, a letter or even a telephone call, then great personal financial outlay would have been saved. Absence from one's wife and two young daughters for two weeks would also have been avoided and an underhand sequence of events would have been unnecessary.

If condemnation of one's actions is to be made, let that be upon the testimony of those who there and in the light of this record.

I have no wish to be further involved with the running of a series of races that have for long been close to my heart. No benefit can ever come to the riders or any organisational team when one thing is said to a person's face and another comment is made behind that person's back. I will not be involved within an organisation that allows prejudice to affect its decisions and lacks the courage to base its judgements upon facts.

This letter is written based upon my personal trust in God through Jesus Christ, my open commitment to Him and the desire that truth and justice be demonstrated for the good of everyone involved in the greatest motorcycle event in the world, The Isle of Man Tourist Trophy Races.

This letter will be used as my record of the events and proceedings surrounding the 1984 TT races. It will be circulated so that future TT and MGP competitors may be sure that their safety on the circuit is being guarded by competent Marshals and race officials.

Yours sincerely,
 Graham Bailey.

Note: the flag Marshal on the apex of Glen Vine Corner cannot be easily seen by approaching riders. With low sun, as during the incident

of the 28th of May 1984, the flag is almost lost in silhouette and is
certainly lost from sight in the dip before the corner.

With approach speeds now so high as they are and engine perfor-
mance increases, a 'relay' flag must be posted on the brow outside
the campsite. The next incident at Glen Vine could be an even
greater tragedy.

Calculate riders speed of approach and rate of arrival after
leaving the start two by two, at ten-second intervals.

This letter, having been delivered to the company address of my former hero, resulting in a formal 'company' acknowledgement. And that was it!

Before the day was spent (28th May), I recall that for 'old time's sake' and to gather my thoughts, later in the evening I set off for a gentle ride into the countryside. As the Suzuki gently bore me up the hill out of Douglas towards Onchan, there on the right side of the road, on the apex of a left-hand bend, facing towards me with its front end well smashed in, was a light goods van. On the left side, lying motionless in the gutter, was a young motorcyclist who had clearly just been in collision with the damaged van. He was obviously in a very bad way, still wearing his full-face helmet and being observed by a small group of pedestrians standing across the road, doing absolutely nothing; known in the trade as *rubber-neckers.*

Under their gaze, I began to remove the young fellow's helmet, correctly conducting the operation as I had been trained.

Immediately, these highly skilled observers loudly declaring their own authority, advised me, *'Don't touch him. Leave him alone!'*

It was clear that he had suffered severe head and neck injuries. Part of my personal equipment when on TM duties had always been to carry an 'Airway' (to assist blocked airways) breathing device in a specially fitted pocket inside my leathers. Having recently been 'defrocked', Bailey was no longer so equipped. A police van pulled up and from his first aid kit, the police driver was able to provide the necessary Airway.

Efforts were made to help the young fellow and restore his breathing, but sadly, even using the Airway, the physical injury was such that air was escaping through an open wound in his neck. This young man, whose name I never knew, in the beautiful evening sunlight of the Isle of Man, (watched by a totally useless audience across the road), passed into eternity. So, at the very least, that was one accident where Bailey did not fail to stop.

This, my last Island trip which had any official involvement in the Tourist Trophy Races, was at an end and Bailey returned to his constabulary duties.

It was interesting to read the following two items published within only a few weeks of the TT event, which appeared in my regular weekly motorcycling paper:

Motor Cycle News
'WORLD'S TOP-SELLING MOTORCYCLE NEWSPAPER'
No. 1489 Wednesday, June 13th 1984

Paul Fowler's PADDOCK GOSSIP
Bailey Out EX-RACER Graham Bailey was booted out of travelling marshals' team following a practice accident at Ballagarey, near Glen vine. It was alleged that he rode past a crash without stopping.

Ton-up holidaymaker

In this article by the same writer, Paul Fowler, about TT rider Mark Johns from Cumbria, the author tells of how Mark suffered his only practice breakdown when his Suzuki seized at Glen Vine on the opening day of practice.

Mark is quoted thus:

'I went to the top of Glen Vine to watch and almost soon as I'd got there saw the Alan Caldwell crash. A marshal was holding out a yellow flag but because the sun was so low I knew that following riders wouldn't be able to see it so I ran back along the road and flagged some men down.'

It is interesting that to this day I have never met or even talked to Paul Fowler. Nor did Paul, a 'news reporter', ever attempt to confirm/clarify his report about ex-racer, Graham Bailey, by seeking any response from this witness. On the positive side, however, the view expressed by Mark Johns and included in Mr Fowler's *Ton-up Holidaymaker* article indicates that Bailey seemingly at least got something right in his closing note to the Clerk of the Course.

Confirmation of lessons in life and police training: *Reports are and must always be of established facts.*

It is amazing and so sad that often, what is claimed to be reported facts are based upon 'passed on' comments, a distortion of the truth…or have no truth at all.

Looking on the bright side under the heading, 'Better Late Than Never', it was good to read David Wright's observations in his book published in 2001: *Travelling Marshals at the Isle of Man Tourist Trophy Races and Manx Grand Prix Races.*

He reports in clear detail the circumstances of the event which culminated in 'the booting out (without) ceremony', and observes that, 'as a practising police traffic officer, he made the instant decision to get to the telephone at Ballacraine and inform race control. Graham thought that his actions were the correct ones but, unfortunately, the clerk of the course didn't agree.'

David further observes that 'Graham Bailey's dismissal was a sad business, but it is still quoted as an example to new TMs of what can happen to a mobile marshal if, deliberately or otherwise, he gets too close to the racing action.'

Sadly, viewed from the TM's seat, one is reminded that, as with the *star rider* coming from behind at The Verandah described earlier; often times the TM has no choice in the matter. Think then of the TT Travelling Marshals now diligently carrying out their duties on basically road bikes, Marshalling the Mountain Course involved with the racing speeds of the Twenty-First Century and ask yourself, what *choice* has he *to control*, or *get too close to the racing action?*

Hey, and the TMs are not awarded Silver Replicas at the end of the day!

31

TT Race Mission

Although days of *'climbing the mountain'* of my dream, to race in the Isle of Man, had been realised and more than fulfilled, Bailey's TT involvement did not cease.

Through a dear friend, a former Police Chief Inspector in London, (the welcoming host of Bramshill), who was now a Senior Officer in the Greater Manchester Police, I had been introduced to a friend of his, Pat Slinn. (This Constabulary friend, Robin Oake, was later to become the Chief Constable of *'The Isle of Man… My island!'* What a cheek).

Pat, had worked in the group design and development sector of the BSA Group and was a former Director of Sports Motor Cycles, based in Manchester. He had ridden and been awarded four Gold Medals in the International Six Days Trial (ISDT), competed in motorcycle trials all over the place. He was well known as a *spanner man* and 'tuner' of racing motorcycles.

Pat had been 'hands-on' involved in the preparation of the Ducati through which Mike Hailwood had achieved TT victory in his 1979 'come back' ride after many years driving Formula One racing cars in their World Championship events.

Pat was a Christian. He loved the Lord Jesus and was keen to tell others about his faith in and experience of God's love in his life. So, in 1981, Pat set up a Race Mission on the Island of Man; a quiet way of reaching out to riders and their friends.

With the approval of The Auto Cycle Union, the organisers of the TT races, Pat set up a mission tent in the TT Competitors' Paddock. There he quietly welcomed friends and visitors and demonstrated his Christian witness to the riders, many of whom knew and respected him for his life and skills.

It was a privilege to share with Pat in this quiet and friendly outreach for several years at TT time, initially enjoying fellowship with him whilst a TM.

After that time, travelling to the island, specifically to be part of Pat's team; with Robin who became the Chief Constable in 1986, it was a case of 'no trouble your Worship!'

(That's the police officer's response to the Magistrate when asked by him whether a drunk man appearing in his Court; during the time of his arrest had caused any difficulty).

Sorry, folks, but Coppers always have a silly sense of humour.

One day, in the mid '80s, as several of us were at Ronaldsway Airport awaiting the call to board our flight to leave the island for home (Robin was there to see us safely off his patch!), we fell into conversation with Leslie Nichol, of all things, about the Mad Sunday Open-Air Church Service. Leslie, the Sports Writer of the Daily Express. Remember, it was Leslie who had helped to 'get the ball rolling' way back in 1967 which resulted in *the constable* having his first island TT ride.

Traditionally, the day before race week, on what had become known as 'Mad Sunday', an open-air church service had been held in the churchyard of Braddan Church.

When the Manx tourist industry began to grow in the 1850s it became a custom for visitors to walk or drive from Douglas to Kirk Braddan for Divine Service on Sunday mornings. Their numbers so increased that the old church could not hold them, and in 1856 the services were held in the churchyard outside.

With improved transport links and continued growing numbers, in 1913 the services were transferred to a field to the west of the church. Sadly, the 'Mad Sunday' open-air services, which I had attended way back, had ceased to be a TT event and were now history.

As Leslie chatted to us, he said, 'Why don't you hold the open-air church service at the Grandstand in Glencrutchery Road?'

Thanks to Leslie's suggestion, that 'open air' church service was re-established and took place for many years at the TT Grandstand. It became quite a memorable annual TT event and The Salvation Army band always provided the music, with riders and other TT personalities also involved.

In your scribe's time this open-air was a witness as to the love of the Lord Jesus and celebration of His love became almost a traditional TT event.

During the open-air service on Sunday the 6th of June 1993, Nick Jefferies, the TT rider and motorcycling competitive 'all-rounder', read the Bible reading from Psalm 145

How do I know? Because Nick borrowed my Bible and then kindly signed and dated over the page he had read from!

I do not recall the message, which followed Nick's reading, but this Psalm of David includes the words: *'The Lord is right-eous in all his ways and loving to all He has made. The Lord is near to all who call on Him in truth. He fulfils the desires of those who fear Him; He hears their cry and saves them.'*

As I am putting these thoughts about the Race Mission together, the words of the song *Amazing Grace* come to mind:

The Lord has promised good to me,
His word my hope secures;
He will my shield and portion be,
As long as life endures.

My chains are gone, I've been set free,
My God my Saviour has ransomed me:
And like a flood His mercy reigns,
Unending love, amazing grace.

That was what the Race Mission's message was all about and through all the thoughts and experiences that I have sought to describe in this tale of mountain climbing, it is hoped that you, my reader, have seen that the words of Proverbs, Chapter 3, verses 5/6, have been my ongoing experience:

'Trust in the Lord with all your heart and lean not on your own understanding; In all your ways acknowledge Him and He will make your paths straight/direct your paths.'

Postscript, 12th of June 2020

Slavery

After so many years of attempting to finish this tale of *mountain climbing*; amending, adding to, and editing; now in June 2020, the world is alight with new problems. So it is necessary once more to pick up my pen.

As well as the Pandemic of Coronavirus, which has covered the globe, a new fear is rumbling across the earth. In recent days, statues of those claimed to have been involved in slave trading are being torn down and also an opportunity has been grasped to openly display hatred of those who do not precisely agree with a given point of view.

In 1743, John Newton, the man who wrote the words of the hymn which months ago were brought into my mind; *Amazing Grace*, was *press-ganged* into the Royal Navy. In 1745, John Newton was made a slave of Princess Peye of the Sherbro people, in what is now Sierra Leone. Later, in 1748, aboard a storm-bound ship, which was in danger of sinking, John Newton cried out to God for mercy and was delivered safely to shore. John Newton there began his journey to complete faith in the Lord Jesus Christ. In that same year, Newton became First-Mate on the slave ship Brownlow and later, Captain of *The Duke of Argyle* and *Africa*, also slave ships. John Newton gave up seafaring in 1754.

Apparently, John Newton was a thoroughly nasty and unlike-able person. Yet, he found and gave his life to Jesus!

In Isaiah 53 the writer describes that same Jesus:

2/ He had no beauty or majesty to attract us to him, nothing in his appearance that we should desire him. 3/ He was despised and rejected by men, a man of sorrows and familiar with suffering. Like one from whom men hide their faces he was despised, and we esteemed him not. 4/ Surely, he took up our infirmities and carried our sorrows, yet we considered him stricken by God, smitten by him and afflicted. 5/ But he was pierced for our transgressions, he was crushed for our iniquities; the punishment that brought us peace was upon him and by his wounds, we are healed.

So, one man who was not very pleasant, found faith in the Lord Jesus Christ, the man who many despised and rejected, yet Jesus loved John Newton and loves us all!

Amazing Grace how sweet the sound
that saved a wretch like me!
I once was lost but now am found,
was blind but now I see.

'Twas grace that taught my heart to fear
and Grace my fears relieved;
how precious did that grace appear
the hour I first believed

Through many dangers
toils and snares, I have already come;
'Tis grace hath brought me safe thus far
and Grace will lead me home.

The Lord has promised good to me.
His word my hope secures.
He will my shield and portion be
as long as life endures.

How sweet the name of Jesus sounds
in a believer's ear.
It soothes his sorrows heals his wounds
and drives away his fear.

When we've been there 10,000 years,
bright shining as the sun;
we've no less days to sing God's praise
than when we first begun.

What a testimony! Even if some deface, any memorial in his name.

As this is being written, it is happening to other declaimed names of history. Nonetheless, John Newton's faith in the Lord Jesus is so clear to see and his testimony can never be blotted out.

Many of those, who even unaware, were involved in Bailey's mountain climbing

Agostini Giacomo (190/277)
Allard Rosemary (245)
Andrew Mick (208/210/211)
Anning Ray SPS (76/81)
Arviddson Liv (143)
Bailey Ronald Arthur: Rab (9/17/23)
Bardot Brigit (33)
Bastone Chief Inspector (36/37)
Bell 'Dinger' (162)
Bennet A (68/75)
Blackman Victor(cover picture)
Blake Len (77)
Blanchard John (208)
Blyton Enid (78))
Boddice Bill (266)
Brand Stan (153/184
Bransden Ernie (239/258)
Brewis John (38)
Broadrib Ted (66)
Butcher Rex (188/197)
Butler Peter PAB (73/75/147/149/155/179)
Carter Charlie (79)
Caldwell Alan (334)
Camathius Florian (83/297)
Channing Bob (RC3) (311)
Charteris Leslie (132)
Chuck Bill (186)
Chatterton Len (78)
Churchill Sir Winston (133)
Clarke Peter (73))

Clark Ted (209)
Clarke 'Nobby' PS (100)
Collins John (46/57)
Cooper Fred (283)
Cooper John (168)
Crebbin Peter (136/328)
Crooks Eddie (232/236/247)
Crowden Harry Chief Superintendent (181)
Croxford Dave (255/256)
Daugherty Mrs (287)
Davey Vincent (68/203/220/221)
Davies Peter (330/339)
Desborough Brian (282)
Dickie Tom (208/1210)
Dick The 'I' (39/40)
Dixon David(287)
Drew Kenny (10/15)
Dunphy Joe (21/64/153/173/251/266)
Dunstall Paul (238/248)
Edinburgh HRH Prince Philip (206/207/210)
Erhard Chancellor (136)r
Evans Hugh/Eunice (240/266/276)
Farmer Len M F PS (111/185)
Fifield Dickie (107)
Finch Brian (234)
Ford Rodney (222)
Fowler Paul (243/344)
Gay Joe PS(35)

George Alex (325/339)
Giles Dennis (312/317)
Glabiszewska Barbara
(224/226/231)
Glaser Rudolph (89)
Godfrey Tony (168/170)
Gondzik Edmund (229)
Goodfellow Chris (95/108)
Gould Rodney (198/211)
Grant Mick (322)
Guard John (187)
Hailwoood Mike(163/215/346)
Hall Ernie (248/250/254)
Hanks Fred (206)
Harding Gilbert (92)
Harding Jim (137)
Harris 'Bomber' PS (111/129)
Hartle John (179/186/190)
Heath Bob (197)
Hele Doug (166/178/187)
Hitchcock Jock (180)
Holder John (21)
Hopwood George (73/75/131/
145/149/155/162/192)
Horne Rupert 'Daddy'(124)
Howell Colin (320)
Huggett Ken (256/257/258)
Hutchings 'The Hutch'
Sister(123)
Hutchinson 'Hutch' (45/47)
Inwood Ken (329)
Jackie (334)
Jakeman Arthur (166)
Jenkins Griff (170)
Jefferies Nick (348)
John 'Crooks'(237)
Knight Ray (114/117/173/232)

Killip Alan 'Kipper'(327)
Kostwinder Jan (267)
The Krays(65)
Lane Vic (190/258)
Lemon Fred (315)
Leston Les (21)
Lewer Geoff (312)
Lushington Superintendent (34)
Lyster (208/219)
'Mac' (98)
Makarios Archbishop (134)
Mark Sir Robert (256)
Mayne Sir Richard (109)
McConnell (19)
McGurk A (179)
McIntyre Bob (48/327)
McMorron PS (52/53)
Mellor Ronald (276)
Milligan John (262/291)
Mills Freddie (65/66)
Minskip Dave (250)
Mitchenall Doug (153)
Monty Geoff (249/252)
Morton John (144)
Moule Albert (327)
Nelson Billy (202)
Newman Max (112/131)
Newton John (351/353)
Nichol Leslie (151/347)
Nichol 'Jock' (63)
Nixon Dave
(167/209/212/214/218)
Oake Robin(306/346)
Oatway (31)
Oliver Eric(73)
Ormsby 'BTY' (304)
O'Rourke Mike (21/64)

Parnell Reg (21)
Passolini Renzo (189)
Pendlebury Daryl (216/218)
Pearcey Len (38)
Perrett Ron (32)
Perreton Reg (137)
Peye Princess (351)
Phipps Brian 'Ginger'
(164/167/169)
Pickrell Ray (191/195/201/209)
Potts Joe (48) 356
Pudney George (62)
Reid Brian (336)
Renwick Jim (265)
Richardson Brothers Charlie/
Edward (65)
Rolt Tony (21)
'Robbie' Robson (40)
Shenton (204/253/263)
Shierson Ken (327)
Shilton Neale(3021/302/304/305)
Siggs Terry (249/250/251/252)
Simmonds Dave (266)
Simpson Johnny 435L (60/61)
Slater Roger (281)
Slinn Pat (346)
Smart Paul (208/213/218)
Smith Tony (170/195/202)
Squires Gordon /Grassphopper
Club (194/210/218)
Street Dave(276)
Strijbis Jan (179)
Surtees Jack(71)
Surtees John (21/70/71/74/83
/102)
Symons David(47)
Tait Percy (152/176/292)

Tanner Geoff (116)
'The Widget' (135)
Turner Peter (75)
Uphill Malcolm (195/211/218)
Vincent Brothers (181)
Ward Mick (334)
Welling Ron (222)
Weil Lance (159/170/179)
White 'Chalky' Horace (138)
Whitten Insp (130/253)
Williams John (235/254/258)
Williams Sergeant (33)
Williams 'Taf' Ron (50)
Willoughby Roger (108))
Wise Les and Pat (124)
Wittich Ron (210)
Woods 'Timber' Inspector (80)
Woolf Ian (319)
Wright David (344)

Road racing and cross-country trials results

achieved with the great help of so many friends

Location	Date	Race	Result
WMC Barbon Hill Climb	1962	250cc & sidecar	3rd sidecar
Snetterton Bantam RC	22/04/67	Over 500cc	1st
Snetterton Bantam RC	22/04/67	Over 500cc	2nd
Isle of Man MTT	06/67	750cc Prod	7th
BMCRC Club Day	30/09/67	500cc Prod	2nd
Brands BMCRC	13/03/68	1000cc	4th
Brands BMCRC	30/03/68	1000cc	2nd
Brands BMCRC	04/05/68	1000cc	3rd
Isle of Man TT	06/68	TT Production 750cc	4th
BMCRC Brands Hatch	03/08/68	1000cc Production	1st
BMRC Thruxton	17/08/68	Production	2nd
Bantam RC Snetterton	19/10/68	Production	2nd
Bantam RC Snetterton	"	"	3rd
Cadwell Park	15/03/69	"	2nd
Cadwell Park	15/03/69	"	2nd
BMCRC Brands	03/69	Greenwich Trophy Race	2nd
BMCRC Brands	March 69	Greenwich Trophy Race	1st
IMCRC Cadwell	22/03/69	Production	1st
BFRC Snetterton	26/04/69	1000cc Production	1st
BFRC Snetterton	26/04/69	1000cc Production	1st

Location	Date	Race	Result
BFRC Snetterton	26/04/69	Allcomers	1st
BMCRC Brands Hatch	03/05/69	Production	2nd
BMCRC Brands	28/06/69	1000cc Production	1st
BMCRC Brands	13/09/69	1000cc Production	2nd
BFRC Snetterton	26/04/69	Allcomers	1st
BMCRC Brands	28/06/69	1000cc	1st
Bantam Racing Club Snetterton	18/10/69	Production	1st
Bantam Racing Club Snetterton	18/10/69	Production	3rd
Bantam Racing Club Snetterton	06/03/71	1300cc	
Lydden BFRC	26/06/71	250cc	2nd
Lydden BFRC		250cc	Club Lap Record 67.43 mph
BMCRC Brands	03/07/71	250cc	1st
BMCRC Brands	03/07/71	250cc	1st
Brands SSSRC	07/71	500cc Production	1st
BMCRC Brands	03/07/71	500cc Production	4th
BFRC	1971	500cc Production Champ	2nd
Lydden BFRC	26/06/71	500cc Production	1st
Lydden BFRC	26/07/71	250cc	1ST
Lydden BFRC	26/07/71	500cc Production	1st
Lydden BFRC	37/07/71	500cc Production	1st
Lydden BFRC	31/07/71	500cc Production	1st

Location	Date	Race	Result
Lydden BFRC	31/07/71	250cc	1st
Lydden BFRC	31/07/71	250cc	1st
Lydden BFRC	31/07/71	250cc	1st
Lydden BFRC	31/07/71	250cc	1st
Lydden BFRC	31/07/71	250cc	1st
Snetterton BFRC	06/03/71	1000cc	3rd
Brands BFRC	06/03/71	1000cc Production	1st
Snetterton BFRC	06/03/71	1300cc	2nd
Isle of Man T.T.	1971	500cc Production	4th
Isle of Man T.T.	06/72	f. 750cc	19th
Lydden BFRC	24/06/72	500cc	1st
Lydden BFRC	24/06/72	500cc	2nd
Lydden BFRC	24/06/72	500cc	1st
Cadwell BFRC	15/07/72	Allcomers	2nd
BMCRC Brands	30/09/72	1000cc	1st
BMCRC Brands	30/09/72	500cc	2nd
Bantam Racing Club Lydden	24/06/72	Allcomers	4th
Cadwell BFRC	15/07/72	500cc	2nd
BMCRC Brands	14/10/72	1000cc	2nd
Brands Hatch BMCRC	14/10/72	500cc	2nd
Isle of Man T.T.	06/73	Formula 750cc	10th
Isle of Man T.T.	06/73	Senior TT	10th
BMCRC Brands	23/09/73	1000cc	4th
BMCRC Brands	29/09/73	500cc	1st
BMCRC Brands	06/06/73	1000cc	1st
BMCRC Brands	03/03/73	500cc	1st

Location	Date	Race	Result
BMCRC Brands	16/06/73	500cc	1st
BMCRC Snetterton	03/03/73	1000cc	1st
BMCRC Snetterton	07/04/73	500cc	1st
BMCRC Snetterton	07/04/73	500cc	1st
BMCRC Brands	05/05/73	500cc	1st
BMCRC	1973	The AMC Cup	
TT Classic Parade	06/74		
Mid Wales Centre	1980	Welsh International Two Days Trial	'Bronze'
TT Lap of Honour	1996		
TT Lap of Honour	1997		